YANKEE MAGAZINE

Vinegar, Duct Tape, Milk Jugs & More

<u>1,001</u> Ingenious Ways to Use Common Household Items to Repair, Restore, Revive, or Replace Just about Everything in Your Life

By Earl Proulx
and the Editors
of YANKEE MAGAZINE

Copyright © 1999 by Yankee Publishing, Inc.
Illustrations © 1999 by Yankee Publishing, Inc.

First published 1999
First published in paperback 2004

ISBN 0–89909–379–5 hardcover
ISBN 0–89909–385–X paperback

Distributed to the book trade by St. Martin's Press

12 14 16 18 20 19 17 15 13   hardcover
    6 8 10 9 7 5   paperback

YANKEE MAGAZINE
Vinegar, Duct Tape, Milk Jugs, and More Staff

YANKEE BOOKS STAFF

Senior Editor: Kevin Ireland
Cover Designer: Christopher Rhoads
Cover Photographer: John Hamel/Rodale Images
Cover Photo Stylist: Jody Olcott

YANKEE PUBLISHING STAFF

Publishing Director: Jamie Trowbridge
Book Editor: Sharon Smith
Contributing Writers: Linda Buchanan Allen, Lori Baird, Geoffrey Bock, Gordon Bock, Tom Cavalieri, Clare Innes, Rose Kennedy, Kristen Laine, Lee Michaelides, Tina Rapp, Michelle Seaton
Editorial Consultants: Kenneth Aldrich, Harry and Marge Ambrose, Tom Asbury, Lynne Beach, Ellen Bean, Maureen Boutilier, Robin Briden, Elizabeth B. Buchanan, Russell C. Buchanan, Jackie Cahill, Cath Carine, Vito Ciavarelli, Jim Collins, Ann-Marie Cunniff, Mary Daly, Nancy Davis, Sue and Tom Donnelly, Bob and Dorothy Dous, Rick Ferris, Tori Hatch, Ed and Mildred Jensen, Christopher Laine, Ro Logrippo, Hilary Lombard, Mark Long, Dan Luce, Jim Mack, Marina Maina, Bill McCauley, Johnny Miller, Margo Nutt, Wendy Roberts, Barry Schrager, Patty Scutari, Nancy Seaton, Jim Sharvin, Laura Simoes, Lida Stinchfield, Rebecca Todd, Suze Woolf, Lauri Zack, Marc Zanatta
Book Designer: Jill Shaffer
Illustrator: Michael Gellatly
Indexer: Nanette Bendyna
Fact Checker: Tom Cavalieri
Copy Editor and Proofreader: Barbara Jatkola
Computer Keyboarder: Sheryl Fletcher
Editorial Assistant: Sue MacEwan

Contents

Contents

Contents

Earl's Top Uses for Just About Anything

'''ve never been one for a lot of fancy gadgets. Instead, I've always liked the challenge of finding a way to work with whatever I had around the house. I'd rather use a broken pane of glass than a store-bought paint scraper any day. Or a long strip of masking tape in place of a lint remover. Or an old toothbrush to clean out the gunk that builds up around the bathroom faucets. Of course, when it comes to repairs, you can't beat a roll of duct tape and a string of dental floss. Those things may not look as pretty as some of the modern gewgaws, but they get the job done just as well.

I can't bring myself to spend a lot of money on commercial cleaners either. Why should I? I can clean and polish just about anything with a bottle of vinegar and a box of baking soda—and maybe one or two other things that I already have in the kitchen.

Earl's Top Uses

So instead of collecting fancy tools and organizers and cleaners, I collect ideas for using up what I already have on hand. You know: egg cartons, coat hangers, ice cube trays, old blue jeans, the cardboard cores from used-up rolls of toilet paper. And, of course, plenty of vinegar and duct tape.

There are lots of those kinds of ideas in this book, and for the most part they're grouped according to where or when they're most likely to come in handy—in the kitchen or workshop, while you're traveling, and so on. But sometimes it's fun to go from the other direction and start thinking about all the ways you can use a particular thing besides what it was originally designed for. For those times when *that's* what you're looking for, here's a list of what I think are some of the very best out-of-the-ordinary uses for ordinary items around the house. Whether you're looking for a great use for toothpaste, old panty hose, or empty yogurt containers, you'll find all kinds of suggestions here. These are my top picks—see if you agree!

—**Earl Proulx**

Baking Soda
- Silver polish (page 18)
- Coffeepot cleaner (pages 21–22)
- Denture cleaner (page 59)
- Cleaner for leather sneakers (page 135)
- Jewelry cleaner (page 138)

- Closet freshener (page 134)
- Dishwasher deodorizer (page 22)
- Cleaner for battery terminals on a power lawn mower (page 165)
- Deodorizer for improvised ashtrays at outdoor parties (page 287)

Blue Jeans

- Patchwork quilt for a child (page 131)
- Clothespin holders (page 166)
- Carpenters' aprons (pages 147–48)
- Golf bags to transport just a few clubs (page 217)
- Storage containers for scraps of lumber (page 147)
- Covers for homemade neck pillows (page 363)

Bubble Wrap

- Toilet tank insulator (page 51)
- Frost protection for outdoor container plants (page 203)

Chopsticks

- Soil testers to determine whether plants need watering (page 177)
- Tools for maintaining a terrarium in a bottle (page 178)

Club Soda

- Cleaner for stainless steel sinks and utensils (page 19)
- Nutrition booster for plants (page 194)

Coat Hangers

- Replacement wickets for a croquet set (page 220)
- Soft-drink holders for relaxing at the beach (page 368)

Earl's Top Uses

Coffee Filters

- Containers for last-minute party favors (page 293)
- Holders for serving hot dogs (page 46)
- Porous containers to hold baking soda to deodorize a particularly smelly refrigerator (pages 23–24)

Dental Floss

- Emergency thread to repair soft-sided luggage (page 257)
- Temporary replacement for eyeglasses screw (page 256)
- Seal for a bag during microwave cooking (page 21)
- "Knife" to cut apart sweet rolls before baking (page 35)

Denture Cleaning Tablets

- China cleaners (page 18)
- Thermos bottle cleaners (page 17)
- Laundry stain removers (page 83)

Downspouts

- Containers to protect carpenters' or masons' levels (page 152)
- Planters for strawberries and other plants with shallow roots (pages 184–85)

Dryer Sheets

- Trash can deodorizers (page 28)
- Sachets (page 297)

Duct Tape

- Reinforcement for soles of moccasin-style slippers (page 136)
- Adhesive to secure improvised knee pads for jobs that involve extensive kneeling (page 191)

- Tick remover when the insect is firmly attached to the skin (page 170)
- Insulation for the handles of camping cookware (page 210)
- Emergency repair of ripped hems in skirts and pants (page 247)
- Bandage, with cotton, to cover a cut (page 259)
- Protection against blisters on feet (page 259)
- Binding for a homemade keepsake album (page 318)

**Earl's
Top Uses**

Egg Cartons

- Soundproofing in roughly finished rooms (page 353)
- Packing material for protecting fragile items in the mail (page 343)
- Oversize ice cube trays for a crowd (page 46)
- Earring organizers (page 137)
- Containers for storing and transporting golf balls (page 215)

Film Canisters

- Storage containers for hooks, lead weights, and other small pieces of fishing gear (pages 213–14)
- Organizers for pins, buttons, and other small sewing supplies (page 236)
- Travel containers for creams and lotions (pages 245–46)
- Containers for travelers' sewing kits (page 250)

Garbage Cans

- Storage containers for long-handled yard and garden tools (page 173)
- Places to preserve root vegetables over the winter (page 200)
- Containers, when thoroughly cleaned, for presenting large and unwieldy gifts (page 323)

**Earl's
Top Uses**

Garden Hoses
- Protectors for saw blades (page 153)
- Guards for the blades of ice skates in storage (page 226)
- Organizers for tangled cords and wires from office equipment (page 340)

Gutters
- Hardware organizers for the workshop (page 144)
- Planters for strawberries and other short-rooted plants (page 185)

Hair Spray
- Lipstick stain remover (page 85)
- Ink stain remover (page 86)
- Preservative for cattails in displays of dried flowers (pages 98–99)
- Preservative for greenery in Christmas decorations (pages 278–79)
- Quick killer of annoying houseflies (pages 370–71)

Ice Cream Cones
- Edible servers for egg salad, in place of bread (page 46)
- Containers for small gifts (page 322)
- Christmas tree decorations, in combination with other materials (pages 276–77)

Ice Cream Scoops
- No-mess means of filling muffin tins with batter (page 36)
- Implements for molding sand castles at the beach (page 227)

Ice Cube Trays
- Earring organizers (pages 136–37)
- Organizers for small hardware in the workshop (pages 144–45)

- Planters for seedlings (page 182)

Inner Tubes

- Clamps when regluing furniture (page 108)
- Rubber replacement grips for golf clubs (page 216)
- Weather stripping along the bases of drafty doors in winter (page 366)

**Earl's
Top Uses**

Ketchup

- Copper cleaner (page 19)
- Brass polish (page 115)

Kitchen Forks

- Props for recipe cards while cooking (page 41)
- Napkin rings, when bent into shape (page 292)
- Weeding tools for the garden (page 189)

Kitty Litter

- Part of a facial mask (page 60)
- Trash can deodorizer (page 28)
- Cleaner for car oil spills (pages 160–61)
- Filler for "sachets" to keep moisture out of stored tents and other camping equipment (pages 208–9)
- Source of traction for a vehicle stuck in snow (page 261)

Mayonnaise

- Hair conditioner (page 66)
- Remover of crayon marks from wooden furniture (page 106)
- Solvent to remove road tar on cars (page 158)
- Solvent to remove price stickers from glass (page 357)

Meat Tenderizer

- Treatment for coffee stains in clothing (pages 81–82)

**Earl's
Top Uses**

- Treatment for perspiration stains in clothing (pages 86–87)
- Relief for insect bites (page 170)

Milk Jugs

- Toilet brush holders (page 51)
- Water conservation gadget in toilets (pages 51–52)
- Clothespin holders (page 166)
- Bird feeders (page 171)
- Tool organizers for the workshop (page 144)
- Shakers, with holes punched in the bottom, for grass seed or fertilizer (pages 163–64)
- Spreaders for walkway sand in winter (page 172)
- Watering devices, with holes poked in the bottom, for the garden (page 187)
- Holders to protect growing melons from mice and chipmunks (page 198)
- Frost protection for plants (page 203)
- Basic equipment for a game of jug-ball (pages 226–27)
- Containers, when cut down to the appropriate size, to freeze large ice cubes for informal parties (pages 287–88)
- Luminaria to light up a driveway or walkway at night (page 288)
- Twine dispensers in the office mail room (pages 344–45)

Muffin Tins

- Tool organizers for the workshop (page 144)
- Holders for baking potatoes (page 37)

Panty Hose

- Window screen patches in an emergency (page 361)
- Containers for small items packed in luggage (page 249)

- Garden hammocks to keep heavy melons and squash from pulling their vines off mesh fences (pages 185–86)
- Storage containers for onions (pages 201–2)
- Scrubbers for kitchen counters (pages 24–25)
- Dust catchers for underneath the refrigerator (page 27)
- Rolling pin covers, to keep piecrusts from sticking (page 41)
- Paint strainers (page 159)
- Means of securing garbage can lids to keep out raccoons (page 167)
- Containers for soap, to allow outdoor cleanup after gardening (page 192)
- Buffers for polishing shoes (pages 247–49)
- Part of a homemade toy to entertain a pet dog (page 312)

Earl's Top Uses

Plastic Shoe Bags

- Bathroom organizers for toiletries and cosmetics (page 53)
- Holders for small toys to keep children entertained on long car trips (page 265)
- Organizers for scissors, staplers, and other office supplies (page 327)

Powdered Milk

- Makeup remover (page 62)
- Sunburn soother (page 70)
- Relief for poison ivy sufferers (page 71)
- Absorbent to protect against moisture in containers of stored seeds (page 203)

Seashells

- Scoops for laundry detergent (pages 74–75)
- Deterrents, when broken into small pieces, to slugs in the garden (page 196)
- Holders for spare change on bureaus (page 119)

**Earl's
Top Uses**

Shoelaces

- Mileage gauges to use with road maps when traveling (page 254)
- Emergency clothesline for lightweight items when traveling (page 260)

Shower Curtain Hooks

- Closet space extenders (page 133)
- Clips to hold spare gloves on the outsides of hikers' backpacks (pages 210–11)
- Organizers for costume jewelry necklaces (pages 137–38)

Socks (Cotton)

- Bath mitts (page 58)
- Painting mitts for hard-to-reach spots (page 156)
- Pouches for portable pincushions that tuck into your belt (page 238)
- Ergonomic wrist rests for computer users (pages 339–40)

Soda Bottles

- Freezer packs for picnic coolers (page 44)
- Shape preservers for tall leather boots (page 136)
- Exercise dumbbells, when filled with water (page 218)
- Watering cans for houseplants (page 334)

Sour Milk

- Silver polish (page 18)
- Shoelace whitener (page 79)

Sugar Cubes

- Temporary dice substitutes for board games (page 230)
- Party sparklers to top off ice cream (page 268)

Tea Bags

- Astringents and skin toners (page 62)
- Remedies for painful canker sores (page 70)
- Foot deodorizers (page 68)
- Treatments for puffy eyes (page 70)
- Relief for minor burns (pages 70–71)

Earl's Top Uses

Toilet Paper Cores

- Homemade napkin rings for family gatherings (pages 275–76)
- Organizers for storing rubber bands (page 331)
- Basis for homemade Christmas decoration (pages 280–81)

Toothbrushes

- Tools for removing old finish from furniture (page 110)
- Devices to release seeds from the heads of sunflowers (page 203)
- Tools to clean the blades of can openers (page 30)

Toothpaste

- Silver polish (page 18)
- Astringent for nighttime treatment of facial blemishes (page 253)

T-Shirts

- Clothespin holders (page 166)
- Cases for throw pillows (page 124)

Vanilla Extract

- Neutralizer of paint fumes inside the house (pages 156–57)
- Blackfly repellent (page 168)

Vinegar

- Streak preventer when washing fine glassware (page 18)

Earl's Top Uses

- Coffeepot cleaner (pages 21–22)
- Linoleum brightener (page 23)
- Laundry softener and freshener (pages 75–76)
- Fruit stain remover (pages 82–83)
- Trap for fruit pests (page 197)
- Refresher for cut flowers (page 200)
- Scouring powder, when combined with salt (page 48)
- Shower curtain cleaner (page 50)
- Means of clearing clogged showerhead (page 50)
- Cleaner to remove built-up shampoo residue from hair (page 65)
- Dishwasher cleaner (pages 22–23)
- Cleaner for steam irons (page 88)
- Way to clear clogged valves in steam radiators (page 115)
- Cleaner for patent leather shoes and purses (page 135)
- Solvent to remove stickers from chrome automobile bumpers (pages 159–60)
- Treatment for jellyfish stings (page 259)

Yogurt Containers

- Bathroom holders for eyeglasses (page 56)
- Molds for sand castle turrets (page 227)
- Twine dispensers, after poking a hole in each container lid (page 345)

The Kitchen

The kitchen is the heart of every home: the area where meals are prepared and some-times eaten, a place where the occasional slipup can seem to derail an entire meal, a spot where spills and stains can seem particularly daunting. That is, unless you know how to deal with all these challenges.

This chapter tells you how to handle kitchen dilemmas by focusing not on what's gone wrong or what special aids you're missing, but on the ordinary materials you already have on hand. Things such as ice cube trays and oatmeal boxes, egg cartons and dental floss, coffee filters and—well, you get the idea. You'll learn how to slice a strawberry without a knife and how to make do without a colander or flour sifter by converting common household items into kitchen tools.

In short, this chapter is jam-packed with recipes for success in the kitchen. It's just that *these* recipes call for things such as shower curtains, denture tablets, and empty yogurt containers.

The Kitchen

GENERAL ORGANIZATION AND STORAGE

Wrap Up Utensils

❏ Instead of living with drawers full of utensils scattered here and there, make inexpensive drawer dividers out of leftover boxes from aluminum foil and plastic wrap. Tear the lids off these boxes, discard them, and then cover the metal teeth with duct tape or other heavy tape. For a more decorative appearance, paper or paint over the outside of each box with craft or latex paint. These boxes make great organizers for carving knives, barbecue skewers, and silverware.

Corral Your Utensils

❏ Some people buy expensive pottery jugs to hold spatulas, wooden spoons, and other utensils. Try using an old glass pitcher instead. Or use your retired percolator or even an oatmeal box that you've gift wrapped or painted. Make sure to weight down lighter containers on the inside with some marbles or coins so that they won't tip with the weight of the soup ladles and spatulas.

Raise a Bottle to Ingenuity

❏ Who has space for a wine rack? You do if you've been saving those cylindrical boxes that oatmeal comes in. Paint them to match your kitchen cabinets and superglue them side by side, arranging them so that you have two or three across and a stack as high as you need to fill that space under the sink or between the microwave oven and the refrigerator. (If you're not comfortable that superglue will hold everything in place, bind the whole contraption together with string.) Each box will hold one bottle. Prop the front of the rack up with a couple of lids from the oatmeal boxes to make the wine a bit more accessible. This way, you can design a rack to fill the space you have rather than finding space for the large wine racks available at department stores.

Stock Up One Cup at a Time

❏ If you freeze a lot of food to be used later, old eight-ounce yogurt containers can be a godsend. Six cups of pureed pumpkin from the garden won't do you much good if you have to store it in the freezer in one big container. With these little plastic containers, you can freeze that puree in one-cup portions, the way you'll use it for pies and breads. The same goes for homemade ice cream, baby food, and all sorts of bounty from the garden. Freeze juices and other liquids in exact eight-ounce packages, too. Nothing could be more convenient.

The Kitchen

Home Freezing: Become a Cubist

❏ A home cook's best friend may be an ice cube tray. You can preserve just enough pesto (one generous tablespoon) for one serving of pasta inside a single compartment. Or drop leftover egg whites from baking projects into the compartments; one compartment will

Storage Containers You Should Never Throw Away

Sure, it seems as if that stack of plastic containers is about to topple over, but maybe that just means you haven't figured out all the things you can use them for. Maybe you need even more! Consider these possibilities.

1. Five-gallon ice cream containers. Use them to hold dry cereal, flour, and sugar to keep those foods fresh longer. Also use them to store partial bags of brown sugar, powdered sugar, coconut, and nuts.

2. Artificial whipped topping containers. Use these to solve those medium-size storage problems, such as how to freeze extra strawberries. One

of these will hold two or three servings of leftovers, depending on your appetite.

3. Glass jars. Some spaghetti sauces and other prepared foods come in glass jars. Reuse these to carry soups and sauces to potluck dinners. They also make great containers for gift foods.

4. Sixteen-ounce cottage cheese containers. One of these will hold a large serving of vegetable soup or a generous serving of a casserole.

5. Baby food jars. They'll hold everything from vinaigrette for potluck salads to metal cake decorating tips for your pastry bags.

Turning Leftover Wallpaper into Attractive Drawer Liners

I bought an extra roll of wallpaper before starting to paper the kitchen—just in case. When the project went smoothly, I had some paper left over, and rather than throw it away, I decided to put it to good use. It was, after all, easy-to-clean vinyl-covered paper. I took out some kitchen drawers and emptied them. I wiped them clean with soapy water and dried them—just as I had cleaned the walls. Then I cut the wallpaper to fit. It's easier to measure and cut a length of wallpaper to fit a drawer, I found, than it is to cut one for a wall.

I soaked the paper as I would for the walls and placed it in the drawers. (Be careful when applying the paper. You won't have as much room for error as you did on the walls.) Then I smoothed out the bubbles, starting at the center and working out to the edges, and trimmed off any excess paper with an X-Acto knife. I let all the drawers dry for a couple of hours, then wiped them with a damp cloth to remove any excess glue before putting the utensils back inside. Now my drawers match my kitchen walls, and they are easy to clean, too.

–**Mildred Jensen**
Hastings, Nebraska

hold exactly one egg white. Once either of these foods has frozen, pop a bunch of the cubes into a plastic freezer bag. Then thaw out as many as you need for a given recipe.

Make Your Own Soup Starters

❑ If you can't use up leftover mashed potatoes right away or you have only a few tablespoons left, use an ice cube tray to save them for later. Once they form hard cubes, you can pop them out of the tray and into a plastic freezer bag, then use them as needed to thicken soups and stews. You don't even need to thaw them first.

Snap, Krackle, and Reuse

❑ You don't have to go out and buy specially made plastic bags to hold sandwiches and leftovers. Just take the plastic liners from empty cereal boxes instead. And how do you seal them shut? Clothespins make the perfect clips.

Soup's On

❑ An easy way to store leftover soup is to pour it into a container that originally held prepared cake frosting. The container is waterproof and has a secure lid, so it makes a perfect cup to take to work. It's also microwave safe, so you can heat the soup—even serve it—right in the container. Just be careful to loosen the lid before you put the soup in the microwave to let the steam escape during cooking. Then wash the container and keep it for that next bowl of soup or small portion of leftovers.

Avoid That Sinking Feeling

❑ Has the space under the kitchen sink become a disaster area, with all sorts of odds and ends thrown in there and never sorted out? Get a handle on the problem and put all your old plastic milk jugs to work at the same time. Just cut off the top of each jug, clean it thoroughly, and sort out all that paraphernalia in any way that makes sense to you. The jugs are big enough to hold sponges, rubber gloves, scouring pads, dishwashing liquid, garbage bags, or virtually anything else you keep under the sink.

GLASS

Reach Inside with a Magic Solution

❑ A thermos is a wonderful way to keep coffee warm when you're on the go—until you forget to clean it out on Friday afternoon and it stays that way all weekend long. Don't fret. Simply fill the thermos with warm water and drop a denture tablet inside. When the bubbling stops, the coffee odor and stain on the glass liner will be gone.

❑ Denture tablets also work well to clean stains from vases, coffeepots, and other glass objects with hard-to-reach insides.

The Kitchen

The Kitchen

Get a Streak of Good Luck

❏ To keep your fine glassware from streaking, add 2 tablespoons vinegar or rubbing alcohol to the detergent in your dishwater. Or add 2 tablespoons ammonia for an extra shine.

SILVER

This Is Why Your Fillings Look So Good

❏ If you don't have silver polish, you can improvise with toothpaste (just make sure it's not the gel type). Dip a piece of silver in water, then squeeze about a teaspoon of toothpaste on it. Rub it with your fingers to make a foam, then rinse off the toothpaste and the tarnish. Be careful not to rub too hard, or you could scratch the silver.

Make Your Own Paste

❏ Baking soda also makes a great polish. Start with a couple of tablespoons of baking soda and add just enough water to make a paste. Spread the paste on the silver and let it sit for 10 minutes. Then rub the paste gently into the surface of the silver and finish up by rinsing with clear water. Dry each piece with a soft cloth.

A Different Twist

Make a Tempest in a Teacup

To clean especially tough stains in china cups, fill each cup with warm water and drop in a denture tablet. When the bubbling stops, the cups will be clean.

Go Sour on Tarnish

❏ You can also polish silverware with milk that's gone sour. Soak the silver in milk for 30 minutes to loosen the tarnish, then wash in soapy water. The pieces will shine like new.

Tarnish: Foiled Again

❏ Another approach to removing tarnish is called ion exchange—a process that, despite the fancy chemical name, uses nothing more sophisticated than aluminum foil. Just line a wide-mouthed one-quart glass jar or cooking pan with foil, fill it with cold water, and add 2 tablespoons salt. Drop tarnished pieces of silver into the water for 2 to 3 minutes, then remove them and rinse off the tarnish.

The Kitchen

7 Great Cleaners from the Kitchen Cupboard

Who needs fancy cleaners? You sure don't, if you happen to have a few baking basics on hand. You can battle a thoroughly messy kitchen without spending a dime. Here's all you need.

1. **Baking soda.** This is one of the most versatile cleaners and deodorizers you can find. Sprinkle it on countertops to scour them clean, or use it on a damp sponge to make a gentle scrubbing agent. You also can pour it down the drain with an equal amount of vinegar to unclog the pipes.

2. **Club soda.** Pour it on stains that crop up on cloth napkins, or use it to soak dish towels. Those bubbles also will help shine stainless steel sinks and utensils.

3. **Salt.** It works really well as a mild scouring agent, and it's a terrific odor eater, too. If your hands smell of garlic or fish, rub a little dry salt on your fingers to lift the odor right out.

Sprinkle salt on warm spills in the oven, then wipe them away when cool. Add a little vinegar to salt to clean copper.

4. **Lemon.** The mild acid in this fruit makes a great cleaner, and that fresh scent makes it a great deodorizer. Sprinkle salt on a lemon wedge and use it to scrub and shine your sink. Squeeze the wedge with your fingers to get rid of fish or onion odors on your hands. When you're done, grind the wedge in your garbage disposal to clean the blades.

5. **Flour.** Mix it with vinegar and salt to make a polish for brass.

6. **Cream of tartar.** Mix this mild acid with some boiling water, and you have a cleanser that will take some stains out of aluminum pans.

7. **Ketchup.** If you don't have vinegar, ordinary ketchup is your best bet for cleaning copper pots. Follow up by washing in ordinary dishwashing liquid and water.

The Kitchen

POTS AND PANS

Reheat Leftover Messes

❑ That spaghetti sauce sure was good, but it left quite a mess in your skillet. Clean the skillet by filling it with water, adding 2 tablespoons baking soda, and reheating the skillet on the stove. Bring the water to a simmer over medium heat and use a spatula to scrape off any cooked-on food. It should take only a few minutes. Turn

The Inside Story

Save Our Saucepans

Edwin Cox was having trouble selling his new aluminum pans door-to-door.

The women he approached complained that they didn't need new pans; they needed a way to clean the pans they already had. They were tired of standing at the sink, scrubbing away at baked-on food stains.

Cox decided that if he could solve this homemaker's problem, people would be more likely to listen to his sales pitch. He took a piece of steel wool and soaked it in dishwashing liquid. When it was saturated, he let it dry out on the kitchen counter.

His wife tried it and loved it. So he made up a bunch of the special scrubbers and went out on the road again. He found that women would patiently listen to his sales pitch if he first presented each of them with one of the scrubbers. Although they didn't buy any more pans, they wanted desperately to buy the scrubbers.

It didn't take Cox long to get the message. Soon he was out of the frying pan business and into making and selling scrubbers. When he asked his wife what he should call this new product, she suggested Save Our Saucepans—or S.O.S., for short. And that *almost* turned out to be the new product's name. S.O.S., of course, is the official Morse code distress signal, and therefore not available to be trademarked. Dropping the final period created a unique designation, and so S.O.S became the official product name.

off the heat and let the pan sit on the stove until the water has cooled. Then wash the food away without any fuss.

Wipe Out

❑ Detergent won't get rid of hard water stains on stainless steel pots and pans. But here's an approach that will. Just pour a little rubbing alcohol on a sponge and wipe those ugly marks away.

Clean before Using

❑ Copper pans need to be cleaned *before* every use—not just after. While hanging around the kitchen, the metal in these pots builds up toxins. Clean copper by squeezing a lemon wedge over the pot and sprinkling with a tablespoon of salt. Use what's left of the lemon wedge to scrub the inside of the pot. (If the juice turns green, that means the pot sorely needed cleaning.) Wash the pot thoroughly with dishwashing liquid and water before whipping up that batch of meringue.

APPLIANCES

Microwaves: Don't Let Grease Be the Word

❑ To keep your microwave clean, sprinkle a little cornstarch or baking soda on greasy spots. Let it sit for a few minutes until the grease is absorbed, then wipe it up.

Skip the Heavy Metal

❑ It's tempting to seal a bag for microwave cooking by using a twist tie from a loaf of bread. But metal will throw sparks in the oven and could actually damage it. Use dental floss instead.

Hard Water Makes Weak Coffee

❑ It's not the coffee grounds that clog up your electric drip coffeepot or percolator; it's the hard water. To clean the pot, fill it with water, add ¼ cup vinegar or baking soda, and run it through the usual cycle. At the end of

You Can Dispose of This Problem

I'm not one to spend a lot of time in the kitchen, and I sure don't want to waste time fixing things if there's an easier way. So I like this idea. When a fork or spoon gets down inside a garbage disposal, I recommend you attach a blob of putty to the end of your kitchen plunger's handle and use that to pick up the lost silverware. It's safe, it works, and if a little of the putty falls off, you can just rinse it down the drain.

the cycle, fill the pot with clean water and run it through again. Now the pot will make a fresh cup of coffee.

Dishwashers: Apply a Soda Solution

❏ If you have to clean a particularly greasy batch of dishes, don't use extra detergent. Too many suds can actually clog up the dishwasher, making it less able to clean your dishes. Instead, sprinkle ½ cup baking soda on the bottom of the dishwasher before you run it. The soda will cut the grease in the first wash cycle, allowing your detergent to work more efficiently.

❏ Baking soda is also a great tool for deodorizing your dishwasher. When that's your goal, add 1 cup soda to the dishwasher when it's empty. Run the machine through the rinse cycle, then shut it off. Once it has dried, it should smell fresh.

Splish, Splash, Give Your Dishwasher a Bath

❏ Is the inside of your dishwasher starting to look disgusting? You can clean it without a lot of scrubbing if you have a bottle of vinegar in the cabinet. Pour 3 cups vinegar into a bowl and place the bowl right side up on the bottom rack of the dishwasher. Don't place any other dishes in the machine, but run it through the wash and rinse cycles, shutting it off before the drying cycle begins. The normal action of the dishwasher will splash the vinegar all over the inside of the appliance, cleaning as it goes.

Get Widespread Coverage for the Fridge

❑ You know that a box of baking soda is a good deodorizer for the refrigerator. But when perishables go bad—*really* bad—and the fridge smells as if something died in there, you need to spread out that baking soda rather than leaving it in the box. If possible, empty the fridge first and turn it to its lowest setting. Then sprinkle the soda on a cookie sheet and set that in the fridge overnight.

❑ Alternatively, take five or six coffee filters and fill each one with ½ cup baking soda. Tie the filters closed with string or leave them open at the top, then set each one on a shelf of the fridge. (Be especially sure to get them in the corners.) The filters will allow the baking soda to

If Only They Could Bottle All That Power . . .

Actually, somebody *did* bottle the best cleaner and deodorizer you could possibly want. It's called vinegar. This mild acid will clean and shine nearly everything in the house. Mix 1 cup vinegar and 5 cups water to clean windows or eyeglasses. Use it full strength to kill stale food odors in kitchen containers. Dilute it with water and boil it on the stove to get rid of unpleasant cooking smells. Moisten a paper towel with vinegar and lay it over faucets to remove mineral deposits. Dampen a cloth with it and wipe down oven walls to prevent grease buildup. (It's great for wiping off greasy stovetops, too.) Add ¼ cup vinegar to 1 gallon warm water to clean and shine linoleum or no-wax vinyl floors. And that's just how you can use it in the kitchen!

absorb odors faster. To *keep* things smelling fresh, leave the filters in place for up to a month.

Wipe Out Refrigerator Odors

❏ When refrigerator smells get too awful to ignore, empty the fridge and wipe down the walls with vanilla extract on a clean rag. Then wipe again with a dry rag. You may have to do a bit of scrubbing, but you *will* get rid of the stench.

COUNTERTOPS

Make a Counter Move

❏ You can extend limited counter space with an open drawer and a spare cutting board. (In a pinch, a cookie sheet works well, too.) First, open the top drawer below a convenient section of your counter and take out all the measuring cups and utensils you will need. Then, leaving the drawer open, lay the cutting board across it. Shut the drawer until the board fits tightly under the lip of the counter. Now you have added work space ready to go.

Cut Stains with Lemon

❏ Butcher-block counters seem to collect tomato and berry stains, but cleaning them with harsh detergents will damage them. The best way to bleach out stains is with a little lemon juice. Squeeze a lemon wedge over the stain, then sprinkle with salt. Scrub lightly with the lemon wedge until the stain comes out.

Run for the Panty Hose

❏ Your countertop has a stain that needs scrubbing, but you don't want to scratch the counter. It's time to grab one of those old pairs of panty hose you've been holding on to. Just cut off one or both of the legs, knot them several times to increase their bulk, and scrub away to your heart's content.

SINKS

Scrub without a Scratch

❏ Once a spill has dried into a stainless steel sink, it's tempting to use a pot scrubber made of steel wool to scrub it out. Unfortunately, that will leave an unsightly patch of scratches. Try this instead. Pour boiling water on the spill to loosen the food, then sprinkle baking soda on the area and let it sit for a minute or two. Scrub lightly with a soft sponge to get rid of any remaining stain and preserve the sink. Finally, rinse with hot water.

Look on the Bright Side

❏ Sometimes stainless steel sinks yellow a bit, or they collect stains from coffee, tea, and other foods. To brighten things up, pour a few tablespoons of ammonia on a sponge and wipe out the sink. Then rinse both sponge and sink with hot water.

SPONGES AND SCRUBBERS

Sponge Up Freshness

❏ Kitchen sponges tend to soak up odors like a—well, you know. Even though you conscientiously rinse them out, they can start to smell pretty ripe after only a few uses, especially if they stay wet all the time. You can keep your sponge fresh by storing it on a porous sponge stand. Take a plastic berry basket and cut down the sides so that the basket is only one to two inches deep. Turn it over, and your sponge has a resting place that will allow air to circulate around it after every use.

Wash before You Wipe

❏ A sponge will smell fresh longer if you wash it regularly. Use a clothespin to clip the sponge to a rung on the top rack of your dishwasher before you run the next

The Kitchen

load. Once the dishes are dry, the sponge will be clean and ready to go again.

Refresh That Sponge

❏ Another way to keep a kitchen sponge fresh is to sprinkle a couple of teaspoons of baking soda on it after every use. Rinse it out under warm water before you use it again.

Resist Rust in Steel Wool Soap Pads

❏ Don't you hate it when a steel wool soap pad starts to rust in the soap dish soon after you use it once? Next time, try this trick. Place a piece of scrunched-up aluminum foil in the dish. After you finish scrubbing, place the soap pad on top of the foil. Amazingly, the soap pad won't rust.

FLOORS

Get Rid of Those Burnt Sienna Blues

❏ If your exuberant coloring book artist has left crayon marks on your linoleum floor, fear not. You can remove the marks without scratching the floor if you warm the wax first. Use a hair dryer to do this, or pour very hot water on the crayon marks. Then mop up the softened wax.

Get That Floor Clean Enough to Eat Off

❏ Looking for a way to cut through a lot of built-up grime on a linoleum or tile floor? Haul out the automatic dishwasher detergent. That's right. Detergent made for dishwashers contains trisodium phosphate (TSP), which is a terrific cleaner. Add about 2 tablespoons detergent to 2 gallons warm water and scrub away. Be sure to rinse thoroughly.

Mop on Wood

❏ Sometimes soapy water isn't enough to get a dirty wood floor clean. To get up the dirt *and* the odor, add

Cleaning Can Be Hazardous to Your Health

If you don't want your obituary to read "Died While Cleaning House," keep these cautions in mind as you scrub.

1. Check the label of any cleanser you use. If it contains the word *caustic,* the substance can burn your skin. Be sure to wear rubber gloves when handling such substances.

2. When using harsh cleaners, make sure your work area is well-ventilated and avoid gas or flames of any kind.

3. Be sure to store that indispensable supply of vinegar in glass containers only. When vinegar comes in contact with lead or copper, it can create a deadly poison.

4. Never mix chlorine bleach with toilet bowl cleaners or ammonia. When combined, these chemicals can create chlorine gas—a potentially lethal substance.

5. Once you are through using cleaners, be sure to seal the containers tight and store them in a well-ventilated space. Make sure the space you choose is well out of reach of children.

¼ cup vinegar to 1 gallon warm water, then mop the floor with the mixture.

Round Up the Dust Bunnies

❏ Cleaning up all the dust bunnies that collect under and behind your refrigerator can be a challenge. You can meet that challenge with an ordinary coat hanger and some old nylons or scraps of cloth. Bend the coat hanger so that it makes a loop. Then tie several scraps of cloth or old nylons to the loop and swirl the whole thing around under the refrigerator. The dust bunnies will be history.

❏ Alternatively, poke a yardstick partway down one leg of an old pair of panty hose, leaving the foot and the bottom of the leg free. Reach under the fridge with the yardstick, and the panty hose will snag all sorts of dusty treasures.

The Kitchen

I Told You
I Didn't Like Mashed Peas!

❏ Your toddler is just learning to eat solid foods but has already become a master at throwing them. Use an old shower curtain as a drop cloth under the high chair during those messy meals. This makes most of those inevitable spills much easier to clean up, and any remnants will rinse away quickly in the bathtub.

TRASH CANS

That's a Litter Better

❏ If last night's fish is putting up a stink but the garbage collector doesn't come until tomorrow, tame the odor by pouring a couple of cups of clean kitty litter into the garbage can. Or toss in the grounds from this morning's coffee. This will absorb the odor for a little while, until the problem can be carried away.

Deodorize the Trash Can
with a Dryer Sheet

❏ Keep trash can odor to a minimum by tossing a dryer sheet in the bottom of the can before adding the liner. When you lift out the trash, the perfume in the sheet will cover any odors left behind. In fact, it will freshen the whole kitchen. Change the sheet once every couple of months or when the perfume has faded.

PESTS

Put the Squeeze on Ants

❏ Keep ants out of your kitchen by squeezing a little lemon juice on the windowsills and doorways.

❏ Once the ants have found their way into the kitchen, you can get rid of them by mixing a poison of equal parts borax and confectioners' sugar. Add enough water to make a syrup. Pour a little of this syrup in a few old jar lids and place them in cupboards where you've seen ants. You can also place them in the corners of the room or behind appliances—but *only* if you don't have

Pass It On

8 Items from Your Trash That Any Kindergarten Teacher Would Love to Have

Sure, kindergartens can always use extra crayons, tissue paper and construction paper, art supplies, and scraps of textured fabric. But they can use certain discards from your kitchen, too. Here are a few that a kindergarten teacher near you is hoping you've saved.

1. Plastic tops from milk bottles, water bottles, and soda bottles may look like recyclables to you. To a kid, they are great game pieces and counters for those first math lessons. Oversize buttons work well, too.

2. Egg cartons are really dragons and alligators in disguise. A little bit of work with scissors and glue, and they become classroom mascots.

3. Baby food jars have a thousand and one uses. They hold paint, glue, seeds, or buttons. No kindergarten teacher can have too many of these little helpers.

4. Coffee cans store puzzle pieces and small toys. They hold water for painting projects, as well as orphaned crayons. They also become mailboxes for the kids.

5. Cereal boxes, the bigger the better, hold construction paper. Cut diagonally, they also store coloring books very neatly.

6. Aprons and oxford shirts become painting smocks to keep kids from decorating their clothes while they make their masterpieces.

7. Oatmeal boxes hold found objects, art materials, scraps of paper, and flash cards. They also make great castle towers and dollhouses.

8. Plastic ice cream containers of all sizes make perfect homes for stray toys and their parts. The bigger they are, the more space gets tidied up as they're filled.

pets or small children who might be tempted to eat the toxic mixture.

Is Your Kitchen Bugged?

❑ Keep creepy crawlers out of your sugar and flour by popping a few bay leaves in the canisters where you keep those foods. The bay leaves will deter the insects without affecting the taste of your baked goods.

The Kitchen

TOOLS

Can Openers: End Their Life of Grime

❏ That hand-operated can opener doesn't seem to be as sharp as it once was? Maybe it needs a good cleaning. After opening dozens of cans of tuna, tomato sauce, and dog food, a can opener can pick up a layer of black grime that is as dangerous as it is ugly. Clean it with an old toothbrush that's been dampened and sprinkled with baking soda or borax. If the grime seems especially stubborn, loosen it by pouring boiling water over the blade. And be sure to turn the wheel while you work so that you can scrub the whole blade.

❏ An electric can opener will respond to the same treatment. Just be sure to check the manufacturer's instructions and unplug the opener before breaking out the toothbrush and boiling water.

Get a Firm Grip . . .
On the Countertop

❏ Meat grinders and pasta machines seldom attach firmly to kitchen counters. If the vise doesn't close tightly on your counter, steady it by folding up a piece of old sandpaper and placing the sandpaper between the vise and the work space. It will fill the extra space and add a little bite to the vise. If you are working on a Formica tabletop or a nice table that might get scratched, use a terry cloth towel instead.

Use a Flour Strainer

❏ If you don't have a flour sifter, use a fine metal strainer instead. Hold it over a sheet of waxed paper and pour the flour in the top. Simply shake the strainer gently until the flour runs through. You may have to tap it against the side of the bowl or the heel of your hand. Keep a spoon handy to crush lumps along the way.

For Grease Spatters,
There's No Place Like a Dome

❏ A spatter guard keeps the grease off the walls while you fry hamburgers or fish sticks. If you don't have one,

Pretty Foods Mean a Lot

Cutout cookies have always been associated with special days, probably because they are so time-consuming to make. The very first cookie cutters were carved from wood. Instead of cutters, they were more like molds. Cookies could be baked right inside them, like dense, shallow cakes. Dutch New Year's cookie (or *koekje*) molds were most often shaped like eagles, stars, or other patriotic symbols to celebrate the new year. In fact, some were carved with the faces of American presidents.

To both carvers and cooks, however, it was obvious that the edges of the wooden molds weren't thin enough to cut the cookie dough cleanly. Soon wooden cookie molds came with copper or tin along the edges to sharpen the outline of the cookies. Before long, cookie cutters came in metal only. At the turn of the nineteenth century, tinsmiths were besieged with requests for cookie cutters, usually in simple shapes such as birds, people, animals, and stars. Unlike today's cutters, each one had a top to it and a handle that made it look like an ink stamp.

Shaped sugar cookies and gingerbread cookies became more popular over the years. By the 1860s, a couple of companies were mass-producing them. By the end of the nineteenth century, cookie cutters in all shapes had become so ubiquitous that flour companies were giving them away. Today they're a staple at kitchen stores everywhere, and inventive craftspeople have found uses for them that go well beyond the traditional (and much-loved) Christmas cookie. We even know some folks (admittedly, they have a perfectionist streak) who use cookie cutters to cut the eyes in their Halloween jack-o'-lanterns.

improvise by turning your metal colander upside down over the skillet. It will guard your kitchen and stovetop, but won't make the food soggy by trapping too much steam in the pan. You may need to spike your dishwater with a few teaspoons of ammonia to cut the grease on the colander afterward.

Much Ado about Margarine

Necessity may not be the mother of all invention, but it was certainly the mother of margarine. In the late 1860s, a sudden population spurt had caused a scarcity of butter in France. Napoleon III decided to turn the problem into a contest. He offered a prize to whoever could find a suitable substitute for butter.

Hippolyte Mege-Mouriès won the contest by softening beef fat and then adding salt and milk acids. He called the product oleo margarine. It didn't taste like butter. In fact, it tasted like salted lard, which is pretty much what it was. The product didn't exactly change the way people cooked, but it was a sign of things to come.

Margarine jumped the Atlantic in 1871 when Henry Bradley of Binghamton, New York, obtained a patent on the same basic process that had been developed in France. He used vegetable oils, which were cheaper than animal fats. This product still wasn't much of a threat to real butter, except in cost, but folks were toying with ways to make the new product taste better.

In a few years, manufacturers had sprung up throughout New York. Margarine began to taste more like the real thing. Local dairymen could see the hoofprints on the wall. What if demand for margarine cut into butter sales? What if unscrupulous dairy farmers mixed cheaper butter substitutes with their product to stretch it? What if margarine manufacturers marketed their product as butter?

In 1877, New York legislators answered these questions with the first law "to protect dairymen and prevent deception in sales of butter." It gave butter a legal definition. It also regulated and taxed the manufacture of butter substitutes. By 1886, these same principles had become incorporated into federal law, and since then butter and margarine have enjoyed an uneasy truce.

And Then You Can Cook the Tester

❏ To test a cake without a cake tester or toothpick, use an uncooked strand of spaghetti. It's long enough to test deep cakes and thin enough to leave no scars on the cake itself.

Now You Can Start That Spaghetti

The Kitchen

❏ One of the nice things about having a summer camp is its rusticity. Every little thing doesn't have to look as if it came from an expensive housewares store, and that goes for kitchen equipment, too. Don't bother running out to the five-and-dime when you need a colander to rinse off your vegetables. Rather, put that empty milk jug to use. Cut the top off the jug and then, with an awl or other sharp instrument, poke holes in the bottom. You have an instant vegetable, berry, or pasta drainer. Just place the food inside and rinse. The water will flow out of the holes.

Try a Cool Way to Make Refrigerator Cookies

❏ Here's a handy way to store the dough for refrigerator cookies (the kind that need to cool in the fridge before baking). Next time you open a can of frozen juice concentrate, hold on to the cut-off end. Thoroughly wash the can and end, then fill the can with cookie dough and replace the end. The container will keep the refrigerated dough fresh and perfectly shaped until you're ready to slice and bake it.

COLLECTING RECIPES

Create a Recipe Album

❏ Instead of stuffing loose recipe cards into boxes or drawers, organize them in an old photo album. Most index cards are the size of photos, so they'll fit perfectly in the ready-made sleeves. Rather than flipping through endless cards, you can easily turn the pages of the album to find the recipe you need.

❏ Some cooks love to clip recipes from magazines and newspapers even more than they love to cook. If you have a pile of clippings stuffed into a kitchen drawer, move these to an old photo album as well. The best albums to use in this case are the ones with the peel-up plastic coating on each page. Peel up the plastic and arrange your recipes on the page by course or main in-

The Kitchen

gredient, whichever you prefer. A loose-leaf album will work best because it allows you to take the pages out one at a time and gives you room to insert new recipes as you find them. And the protective covering will keep spills off the recipes themselves.

SHORTCUTS

Cheese: Try a Grater Way to Clean Up

❏ Sometimes cleaning a cheese grater is more time-consuming than shredding the cheese because of the cheesy coating that quickly accumulates on the sharp ridges. You can shorten the cleanup by spraying the grater with nonstick cooking spray before each use. Then use an old toothbrush to scrub the tiny spaces after you're done.

Make a Bagful of Good Taste

❏ Forget about marinating meats in a big plastic bin or a shallow baking pan. Plastic containers tend to leak, and baking pans inevitably leave some meat exposed to the air rather than the flavors in the marinade. To get the best results, use a resealable plastic bag, especially if you are marinating steak tips or chicken tenders. Put the meat and the marinade inside the bag, seal it, place the whole thing in another container if you're concerned about a possible leak, and put it in the fridge. The meat will be easier to check on and turn. It also will marinate more evenly.

Peel-and-Bake Piecrust

❏ The easiest way to keep a rolling pin and work area clean while rolling out piecrust dough is to keep the dough between two sheets of plastic. Thin plastic bags from the produce section of the supermarket are perfect for this. (Make sure you've rinsed them if they held produce.) Put the dough in the bag and roll it out. Once the crust is the right size, just peel off the plastic (you may need to cut the bag apart to do this easily), and the crust will be ready to set into the pie plate.

Baskets Are Berry, Berry Good

You love fresh berries, so those little green baskets they come in stack up during the summer. They may not seem very useful, but they are.

1. Use one as a colander to strain canned beans. The weave is just fine enough to hold the beans, while letting the water run through.

2. Put them on the top rack of the dishwasher to hold cookie cutters, decorator tips, or baby bottle nipples so that they won't fall down into the washer.

3. Use them to hold hard-boiled eggs in the fridge so that they won't get mixed up with raw eggs.

Make Short Work of Strawberry Shortcake

❏ Making fruit salad, mushroom bisque, or strawberry shortcake for a big crowd? Grab the egg slicer that's been sitting at the bottom of a kitchen drawer. It will slice soft vegetables and fruits perfectly, which will keep your prep work to a minimum.

Grease the Baking Pans, Not Your Hands

❏ Looking for a way to keep your hands clean while greasing cookie sheets or baking pans? Here's another use for those cereal box liners. Stick your hand inside a liner, dip it in the shortening or butter, and rub it over the cookie sheet or pan. When you're through, remove the liner from your hand by turning it inside out. Then just toss it in the trash.

Cut Sweet Rolls without a Knife

❏ If you make sweet rolls from scratch, you'll need to cut them into individual rolls. If you use a knife, that's likely to flatten them a bit, so they won't be nice and round. Avoid this by using dental floss to cut individual rolls. It will make a nice, clean cut without smashing the rolls.

Milk in a Can: How Sweet It Is

In the days before refrigeration, milk had a pretty short shelf life. This bothered inventor Gail Borden, who decided that if there was a way to preserve meats and fruits, there should be a way to do the same for dairy products.

As Borden studied how the Shakers preserved fruit by drying it, he decided to experiment with that concept. He developed a vacuum method to concentrate milk by removing most of the water. He added sugar as a preservative and sealed the resulting liquid in tin cans. He obtained his first patent in 1856—just in time to supply the Union army with cans of his new product, called sweetened condensed milk. Since Civil War soldiers often had little access to fresh milk or dairy products, it was a hit in the field.

Better yet, its success didn't end with the war, because it soon became clear that condensed milk could serve an even more important postwar function—as baby formula. During ocean voyages, ships would sometimes bring cows on board to provide extra milk for babies or small children making the trip without their mothers or wet nurses. The problem was that if the cows got sick, the children went hungry. Although parents today would shudder at the thought of feeding babies such a sugary syrup as condensed milk, in those days the product was a miracle.

By the end of the 1930s, people had refrigerators and more nutritious baby formulas. Condensed milk was on its way out of style. Then World War II broke out, and home cooks again turned to condensed milk—this time as a sweetener while sugar was in short supply. It worked perfectly as a sugar substitute in pies and cookies and has been a baker's staple ever since.

Here's the Scoop

❏ Does your favorite muffin recipe have a cakelike batter that makes an awful mess when you put it in the baking tins? Grab an ice cream scoop or soup ladle and use it to scoop the batter into the tins. The job will go far faster and be much less messy.

Hamburgers and Plastic Go Hand in Glove

The Kitchen

❏ When you're ready to make a batch of hamburger patties for the freezer, here's a way to manage the job without dirtying your hands. Just grab a few of those plastic bags that you originally used to bring fruits and vegetables home from the grocery store. Cover each hand with a bag, using the bags as makeshift gloves to form patties.

❏ Alternatively, spoon the amount of hamburger you want for one patty into a bag. Form the patty from the outside so that your hands stay dry. Then crop the bag with household scissors, leaving one-half inch on each side of the patty. Fold the plastic around the patty so that it has its own tidy container. When you are ready to start the barbecue, take the patty out of the freezer and peel off the plastic.

Freeze Burgers in the Round

❏ Once those hamburger patties are shaped, what's the best way to stack them in the freezer? If you're smart, you're probably already stretching that hamburger with oatmeal. Once you've used up the oatmeal, save the cylindrical container it came in. Use the lid of the container as a guide to form each patty. Wrap the burgers in foil or plastic, then slide them into the cardboard canister. They will keep neatly in the freezer until you need them. At that point, you can just open the lid and slide out the number of burgers you need.

Just Don't Plan Blueberry Muffins for the Same Meal

❏ The worst part about baking potatoes is removing them from the oven without burning yourself. Avoid this problem by placing the potatoes in muffin tins. You can easily grab a whole tin with a pot holder.

Needed Fast: Ripe Tomatoes

❏ You have dozens of green tomatoes stashed away, but you need a few ripe ones now. What to do? You can

The Kitchen

ripen green tomatoes quickly by placing them in a brown paper bag with an apple or a banana. Put the bag in a warm spot, and in a day or two the tomatoes should be ripe. Apples and bananas emit ethylene gas, a chemical that encourages ripening.

Peelings, Nothing More Than Peelings

❏ One of the worst parts of cleaning up after a day of cooking is picking up the assortment of peelings, vegetable cores, greens, and other tidbits and carrying the whole soggy mess to the trash can. One way to clean up food scraps as you go is to use the plastic grocery bag in which you carried home the ingredients. Hang one handle over the knob on a kitchen drawer, then toss the scraps into the bag as you work. Tie the two ends together and throw the whole bag away. Or add the contents to your compost pile. Not only does this technique make cleanup easier, but it also seals in the odors that build up between trash days.

SITUATION SAVERS

Soak Up Sogginess

❏ Oops. The rice you've been boiling for dinner is ready 20 minutes before the guests are due. You know that if you take the lid off to let the steam out, the rice will be cold by the time you sit down to eat. But if you leave the lid on, the steam will condense and leak water on the rice, making it soggy. Compromise by using a couple of old cotton T-shirts (clean, of course) to keep the rice dry. Remove the pan from the burner, lift the lid, lay the shirts across the top of the pan, and replace the lid. The shirts will soak up the steam, and the lid will keep the rice warm.

Get Steamed Up over Stale Bread

❏ No need to throw out stale bread. If you have a spatter guard or vegetable steamer, you can easily revive it on your stovetop. Boil water in a saucepan, set the spatter guard or steamer over the water, and set the bread on top for about a minute, or until it is moist enough to eat. Be sure to check it every 30 seconds or so, or you'll end up with a soggy mess.

Brighten the Brown Sugar

❏ Once a bag of brown sugar is opened, the sugar seems to harden overnight. Keep brown sugar soft by putting a few marshmallows, an apple slice, or a lemon peel in the bag before closing it. Any of these will add enough moisture to the sugar to keep it soft.

The Inside Story

A Rare Bit of Stew

A very long time ago, a Welsh chieftain suffered the same fate that most home cooks fear in the midst of a big party. He ran out of meat dishes. His solution was to summon his cook and ask him to devise something from whatever he had left over from the other dishes. The cook went into the kitchen, stirred up a spicy cheese sauce, and poured it over some stale bread. It was pretty good, he thought, and so did everyone else. When the banquet guests asked him what it was, he told him it was rabbit. It was a bald lie, but no one complained. And so the cook was able to salvage his boss's party.

Although this is a great story, it may or may not be true. It was the story often told in early American dining rooms by wily homemakers who had themselves run out of meat for the table and wanted to remind their families that it happens to the best of us. By then, the dish had become Welsh rabbit—a Cheddar cheese sauce tempered with beer and spices, then served over toast points. Over the years, it became Welsh rarebit, mostly because persnickety cookbook writers don't like to call something rabbit if there isn't any rabbit in it. It's too bad in a way. Clever cooks have long known that honesty is not always the best policy.

The Kitchen

Kill the Oil Slicks

❏ To skim the oil off the top of a pan of soup, use a raw cabbage or lettuce leaf. The oil will stick to the leaf, leaving the broth behind.

De-Salt the Soup

❏ If you've put too much salt in a soup, add some raw potatoes. If you are making a stew that could use some potatoes anyway, dice them fairly finely. They will absorb some salt and stretch the soup as well. If potatoes are not appropriate for the recipe, cut them into large pieces, let them cook through as the soup cooks, then remove them just before serving. They will have soaked up some of the salt without otherwise altering the taste of the soup.

COOKING CONVENIENCES

Make a Wraparound

❏ If you have an unexpected helping hand in the kitchen and need an extra apron, use an old work shirt instead. With the sleeves tied around your assistant's waist like apron strings, he'll be ready to roll . . . the cookies.

Prevent Eggs from Cracking Up

❏ To keep eggs from cracking and leaking when you boil them, add a tablespoon of vinegar to the water before you heat it.

Recipe Cards: Bag 'Em

❏ If you've saved clear plastic bags from the supermarket produce section, or even the clear bags that the newspaper comes in on rainy days, you can make a convenient recipe card holder for a budding chef. Cut a pair of horizontal slits in the top of the bag—one on each side—so that it has handles. Slip the card inside and hang the bag on the handle of a kitchen cabinet. It will stay in plain view and can be consulted front and back at every stage of the cooking process. What's

Nylons Are a Pie's Best Friend

My father is a baker. I grew up working in his shop, learning how to do just about everything—except roll out a good piecrust. It's so frustrating to have the dough break up because there isn't enough moisture. But that's fairly easy to fix with a bit more water. The bigger problem is having a moist crust stick like glue to the rolling pin.

My mom had the answer (having made more than a few pies herself). She covered my rolling pin with panty hose. No kidding. She cut the toe off a clean knee-high stocking and then slipped the rest of the stocking over the pin. The nylon held enough flour to keep even a very moist crust from sticking to the pin. Finally, piecrusts became easy—even fun.

I make pies and pastries of all kinds now, and I don't need to use the nylon anymore. But I keep one handy, just in case.

–Nancy Seaton
Hastings, Nebraska

more, the card will be protected from spills, spatters, and sticky fingers.

Fork Over Those Recipes

❏ Another way to keep recipes visible near the scene of the culinary crime is to prop them up using a fork and a drinking glass or empty can. Put the fork in the glass so that the tines point to the ceiling. Weave the recipe card through the tines, where it will stay while you work.

Wrap Your Bands around This

❏ When you're making a recipe from a cookbook, you need a way to keep the cookbook open that leaves your hands free for more important things. That's easy if you have a couple of spare hair bands. You need the kind of bands that consist of elastic covered with fabric. Make sure they're clean, then wrap one around each side of the opened cookbook. The bands will hold the pages in place just as they hold your hair.

The Kitchen

Iron Out Some Counter Space

❏ Even if you have a big kitchen, you may not have enough counter space. Several racks of cooling cookies or a few covered dishes waiting to be served can take up a lot of room. In these cases, don't be afraid to break out the ironing board and cover it with a clean table-cloth or towel for protection. The ironing board can be placed anywhere in the kitchen to give you enough space for one more batch.

How Not to Throw Rice

❏ Everybody loves rice, and yet everybody hates pouring it out of a box or bag and into those little mea-suring cups because the grains scatter everywhere. Pre-vent the mess by storing your rice in a large plastic soda bottle or plastic milk carton. Be sure to wash the con-tainer thoroughly and let it dry completely. Then use a funnel to pour the rice into the container. The cap will keep the rice fresh and also will keep little critters out. Now you can pour exact amounts of rice as surely as you pour soda.

SUBSTITUTIONS

Make Your Own Brown Sugar

❏ If you don't have brown sugar, use white sugar. For every cup of white sugar, add a tablespoon of molasses to the recipe, stirring the molasses in with the other wet ingredients. Re-duce the amount of other moisture in the recipe by one tablespoon.

Let Your Piecrust Go Undercover

❏ The recipe says to cover the rim of your piecrust with little strips of alu-minum foil to protect it during the last few minutes of baking. The trouble is that it takes 20 minutes to cut out the foil and arrange it lightly around the pie. Then it falls off when you close the oven door. Try this instead. Take one of those old disposable aluminum pie tins you've been saving and cut out the bottom. That leaves you with just the sides and rim, which you can turn upside down and set on top of the pie to provide an instant cover for the edges of the crust.

A ring around the piecrust will keep it from burning.

Junk Mail Does Have Its Uses

❏ You've spilled some salt or cinnamon in a neat pile on the counter. How can you get it back into the jar without a conventional funnel? Easily, if you have a clean business envelope (say, the reply envelope from a direct mail piece). Just brush the spice into the open envelope, snip a small corner off one end with scissors, and you have an instant funnel.

SIMPLE PICNICS AND BACKYARD BARBECUES

It's a Perfect Fit

❏ Want an attractive cotton cloth to cover the picnic table without spending any dough? Try a twin-size fitted sheet in a colorful print. The elastic edges will grip your tabletop nicely on a windy day, and when the cookout is over, you can toss all those mustard and ketchup stains right in the wash.

For the Squirty (Half)-Dozen

❏ Tired of making multiple trips from kitchen to backyard for a simple barbecue? Save those cardboard six-pack holders from soda or beer bottles. Stash all the condiments, salt, pepper, napkins, and even silverware in the compartments, and they're ready to go when you need them.

The Kitchen

Keep Your Cool

❑ If you have a cooler but the freezer packs that should keep it cold have disappeared, make some of your own with old plastic soda bottles. Fill them with water the day before your picnic (leaving room at the top so the water can expand as it turns to ice) and freeze them overnight. The next day, pack them in the cooler around your food. They will cool the freezer, and even when the ice melts, they won't leak. By the time you finish eating, they will have thawed enough to give you something to sip on the way home.

Give That Soda an Insulated Life

❑ Soda sorta warm? Beer been cooler? Don't run to the convenience store for an insulating can or bottle holder. That old closed-cell foam sleeping pad you used to take camping may be ready for the scrap heap. If so, you can use it to make insulating sleeves for cans or bottles of water, beer, or soda. Cut the pad into pieces big enough to wrap around the containers, then secure the ends with duct tape. That's what we call recycling.

Add a Protective Coating

❑ You'd like to take a bottle of wine on a romantic picnic, but how to keep it cold? How to keep it from breaking? Solve both problems with that old down jacket that is on its way to the trash. Cut off one sleeve and transform it into a portable wine cooler. Use an old wine bottle to determine the appropriate length, or just cut the sleeve so that it's 11 inches long. That will accommodate a typical bottle, covering the wine while letting the top peek out. Leave the elastic cuff alone, but sew the other end closed. Just slip the chilled bottle into the sleeve, and it will stay cool and safe until you're ready to enjoy the contents.

Bring Fresh Fish à la Carton

❑ If you'll be taking that fish you caught last week on a long drive to a barbecue or picnic, freeze it so that it is ready to travel. After you've filleted the fish, put the fil-

Go West, Young Man—And Bring Lunch

When the pioneers traveled across the country, they couldn't be too picky about what they ate. Food tended to spoil during the long trips in hot weather. Pioneer women knew that they had two choices: eat what they had or not eat. So when they cracked eggs and found they'd gone a little south, they didn't blink. Instead, they fried them up with whatever might hide the taste—onions, peppers, bits of salted meat, and whatever seasonings they had on hand—then plunked the whole thing between a couple of slices of bread.

Legend has it that these humble beginnings were the origin of the western sandwich, a spicy egg mixture served on bread. The western is still served in some parts of the country as a quick lunch—and the best thing about it is that it tastes good even if the eggs are fresh.

lets in an empty milk carton and fill the carton with water. Freeze the carton. Then put the block of ice in your cooler, and you're ready to go.

❏ Fish fillets will also stay fresh longer in the freezer if they're packed this way—and they'll resist freezer burn, too.

Take the Edge off Knives

❏ Bringing a loaf of fresh bread or a whole turkey breast on a picnic will impress your friends and relatives. Now all you have to worry about is the prospect of impaling yourself on the sharp knife you'll need to cut it. Make a sheath for your knife with the leftover cardboard core from a roll of paper towels. Smash it under a heavy dictionary to make a nice flat sleeve. Measure it against your knife, then cut it so it's one-half inch longer than the blade. Staple one end shut or tape it with duct tape, and you have a tailor-made cover for your knife.

Simple Picnics and Backyard Barbecues

The Kitchen

PARTY FOOD
Improvise an Egg-cellent Ice Maker
❑ Thirty people will be stopping by for drinks tonight, and you have only two ice cube trays to get you through. It's lucky you also have a supply of Styrofoam egg cartons, because they make great ice cube trays. Cut off the tops and fill the bottoms with water. Place the cartons in the freezer, and you'll have ice enough for everyone.

Wrap 'Em Up and Send 'Em Out
❑ The hot dogs are on the grill, but you've run out of paper plates to hold them. Use coffee filters instead. They are part holder, part napkin—and all convenience.

We All Scream for Egg Salad
❑ You have egg salad for 10, but only enough bread for 5 sandwiches. Instead of making sandwiches at all, serve the egg salad in flat-bottomed ice cream cones. Sprinkle a little paprika on top for an unexpected treat that kids will love.

The Bathroom

Considering that it's usually the smallest room in the house, a lot sure goes on in the bathroom—and that's just counting the stuff we're not too embarrassed to talk about!

It's the room where we make ourselves beautiful, perform minor feats of first-aid, and get clean. It's also, in many homes, a place for keeping and organizing personal care and cleaning items. Big jobs for such a little room. So why on earth would you want to add more items to the room—especially all that stuff you were going to throw away?

Because you can use many of those items to keep yourself *and* the bathroom clean. (Think vinegar and baking soda.) Or to save and organize space. (Think old window boxes and plastic shoe bags.) Or even to cope with minor scrapes, burns, itches, and irritations. (Think tea and cornstarch.)

Then *keep* thinking—and keep reading—and you'll find lots more bright and beautiful ideas!

The Bathroom

GENERAL CLEANING
Rise to the Occasion
❏ Who needs expensive household cleaners? Head for the kitchen and pull out the baking soda instead. Add 1 cup baking soda to 1 gallon hot water. Sponge this mixture on any bathroom surface—sink, toilet, floor—then rinse it off with fresh water. Baking soda cleans, freshens, and gets rid of odors, too.

Oomph—Ahh
❏ Sometimes you need a little extra oomph to clean a dirty surface. No problem. Sprinkle 2 tablespoons salt in a bowl and add 2 teaspoons vinegar (or enough to form a paste). Use the mixture as a scouring powder, applying it with a sponge. It's gentle and effective and produces no unpleasant (or hazardous) fumes.

❏ Alternatively, sprinkle baking soda full strength on a damp sponge or on the surface you want to clean, then scrub. It will work as a gentle scouring and deodorizing powder.

SINKS, TUBS, AND SHOWERS
Scrub Those Tiny Cavities
❏ Worn-out toothbrushes won't do your teeth much good, but don't throw them out. They're terrific for scrubbing hard-to-reach areas around the fixtures in your bathroom. (Just make sure your family knows which brushes are for cleaning fixtures and which are for cleaning teeth!)

Picky, Picky
❏ Perhaps you're one of those people who walks right by the toothpick dispenser when you leave a diner, never giving it a second thought. Well, here's a reason to grab a couple. Toothpicks work really well for scraping away the soap scum that builds up under the faucet fixtures in the bathroom. And it sure doesn't fit

Baking Soda:
Elbowing Out the Competition

In the years immediately following the Civil War, the baking soda business was no place for weaklings. Brooklyn businessman James Church knew this when he closed his spice business in 1867 to go into soda sales, even though it was a viciously competitive market in which dozens of nearly identical companies selling an identical product fought for the same small customer base.

Church did what everybody did to get into the baking soda business. He bought a few barrels of soda, scooped it into paper bags, and set off to make his fortune in door-to-door sales. Church knew that, like every other struggling entrepreneur, he needed sales gimmicks to succeed. So he hired the most flamboyant salesman alive —a seven-foot four-inch giant whose booming voice and beaming charm turned heads wherever he went. Church also included recipes in his bags of soda—recipes for cakes and breads that, of course, all required his Church & Company brand of baking soda.

These ideas worked—to a point. Then Church realized that he needed a new name. His original name, Church & Company, didn't do anything to enhance the appeal of the product. His old spice business had a great name: Vulcan Spice Mill. It also had a terrific sign that featured a muscular arm holding the kind of hammer used by blacksmiths of the time. In fact, Church had kept the sign from his old storefront for good luck. On a whim, he gave his new product the logo of the old spice mill but changed the name to Arm & Hammer. It quickly muscled out all the competitors, and today it is the best-known brand name associated with baking soda.

the frugal mentality to go out and actually *buy* a tool for that purpose!

Break the Mold (and Mildew)

❏ Vinegar will clean tile or Formica shower walls and inhibit the growth of mold and mildew there. Just wipe

Sinks, Tubs, and Showers

down the walls with a sponge dampened with water and vinegar. It's just as effective and much less expensive than store-bought cleaners.

Withdraw Deposits

❏ If your showerhead seems to be sputtering, a buildup of mineral deposits may be clogging the holes. Don't buy a new showerhead if you have some vinegar in the kitchen. Place the showerhead in a pot and add enough vinegar to cover it well. Heat the vinegar to just below boiling, then turn off the heat and let the showerhead soak for about eight hours. As it sits, the acid in the vinegar will eat away the deposits. Rinse the showerhead, and it's ready to use.

TOILETS

Pucker Up and Clean

❏ Lemon juice is a good toilet bowl cleaner, but for the best results, you'll need to mix it with some borax. Mix 1/3 cup borax and 1/4 cup lemon juice until they form a thick paste. (The powder will absorb the juice fairly quickly, so if you wait very long before applying the paste, you may have to add a little more juice.) Flush the toilet to wet the sides of the bowl, then don a pair of rubber gloves and use a sponge to smear the paste around the bowl, above the water line. Let it sit for about 2 hours, scrub with a toilet brush, and flush.

Hold That Scrubber

❏ Need a container to store your toilet brush? Cut off the top and handle of a clean plastic milk jug and pop the brush in there.

Tanks: They Needed That

❏ Does the tank on your toilet drip condensation in warm, humid weather? That happens because the water entering the tank after every flush keeps the tank colder than the surrounding air. One way to break the condensation cycle is to insulate the tank. Try lining it with thin plastic insulation—bubble wrap or thin Styrofoam sheets left over from shipping packages. First shut off the supply valve and drain the tank with a flush, then wash and dry the inside walls for good adhesion. Cut pieces of packing material to the appropriate size and glue them to the walls with silicone sealant, making sure they won't interfere with the operation of the toilet mechanism. You don't need to cover every square inch—just the major, flat surfaces.

Flush with Less

❏ These days, municipalities are charging more than ever for water, and many folks want to conserve this resource anyway. You can reduce the water consumption of old-style flush toilets by displacing some of the

A Different Twist

Something's in the Air

Looking to freshen things up a bit when it comes to bathroom odors? When it's time to take down the Christmas tree, don't complain about all those dried-up needles that are about to cascade onto the floor. Instead, spread an old sheet on top of the rug and give the tree a good shake over it. Then scoop up the needles, put them in a decorative bowl, and place them on a shelf or on the floor in your bathroom. Long after the holidays, the needles will emit the fresh smell of the forest. Stir them up every couple of months to revive the scent, and your homemade air freshener will last six to seven months.

The Bathroom

water in the tank. Take a one-quart plastic milk container—washed, filled with water, and securely capped—and place it in the tank. (Usually, there's room under or to one side of the float arm.) The container will save its own volume of water every time you flush.

This Tie Will Bind

❏ When the flush lever in your toilet fails because the chain connecting the arm to the ball cock valve has broken, you can often make a temporary repair with electrical wire ties. These nylon straps are quick to use (just slide the pointed end in the ratcheted clasp), they won't rust or rot, and they're flexible enough to double for chain or metal linkage until you get to the hardware store for the real thing.

SPACE SAVERS AND STORAGE

Hang a Six-Pack of Towels

❏ There never seem to be enough racks in the bathroom to hold your family's facecloths, let alone all the bath and hand towels. Then, when your sister and her family come for the week, it gets even worse—there's a towel on every doorknob in the house. Next time you're expecting company, try this idea for adding more towel-hanging space. Save two or three of the plastic holders from six-packs of soda or beer. Before your guests arrive, suspend each holder from an existing towel rack or hook. (Hang it by one of its six rings.) To hang a towel, just pull a corner through one of the rings so that it stays. Now each rack holds six times as many towels as it did before.

Turn the (Changing) Tables

❏ The baby is long gone, but the changing table lingers on. Most folks get rid of these tables once the kids are out of diapers, but if you're smart, you'll hold on to yours. Its multilevel construction makes it a perfect bathroom organizer. Use it to store towels and facecloths, toiletries, or anything else that won't fit in your existing closet space.

And You Don't Even Have to Water It

❏ Here's a way to use an old window box and give your bathroom an attractive decorative touch. First, clean or paint the window box if it needs it. Next, spray the box with wood or metal sealant to protect it from getting mildewed (if it's wood) or rusted (if it's metal). Place the window box on the back of the toilet or anchor it on the inside of the bathroom window. Use it to store toiletries such as bubble bath, or roll up facecloths and hand towels and stand them up inside the box for ready access.

The Bathroom

Put Toothpaste in the Corner Pocket

❏ The more folks in the family, the harder it is to keep everyone's toiletries and cosmetics separated in the bathroom. Solve that problem by cleaning a spare plastic shoe bag with multiple pockets and hanging it on the back of the bathroom door. Assign specific pockets to individual family members, or designate them for certain types of items, and you'll always be able to find what you need.

---

10 Long-Term Uses for Fast-Food Containers

Yum: hot and sour soup from the local Chinese restaurant. Yuck: another odd container (with a lid) to stack in an overflowing kitchen cupboard. Before you relegate these containers to the recycling bin, consider using them to organize the bathroom. Here are just a few of the things they'll keep contained.

1. Bath powder
2. Cotton swabs
3. Loose Band-Aids
4. Loose bobby pins, barrettes, and hair ribbons
5. Cleaning sponges
6. Makeup
7. Combs and brushes (Use the tall, one-quart containers.)
8. Extra toothbrushes
9. Rubber cleaning gloves
10. Spare shower caps

The Bathroom

Play Hide-and-Sink

❏ Perhaps you have a pedestal sink in your bathroom. You'd like to use the space beneath it for storage, but having your cleaning and plumbing supplies in plain sight wouldn't really add to the decor, and you don't have the room (or the budget) for a vanity. Try this. Take an old fabric tablecloth and cut it wide enough that it fits around the sink with a few inches to spare and long enough that it reaches the floor. Cut the cloth into two pieces, each wide enough to go a little more than halfway around the sink. Attach some dots of Velcro (perhaps salvaged from an old jacket) to the sink and along the top edge of your new curtain. Hang the curtain so that one side overlaps the other in the middle. Place an additional bit of Velcro at the top corner of the overlap to keep it closed. Now you have a place to hide some of those bathroom necessities such as spare toilet paper or the plunger.

Shelve It

❏ Those of us with pedestal sinks were definitely in the back of the line when they gave out bathroom space. Here's an ingenious way to give yourself a temporary shelf when you need it. Measure the opening of your sink, then haul out that old plastic cutting board you squirreled away in the kitchen. (Plastic is better than wood in the bathroom because moisture causes wood to warp.) Try to find one that fits over the space to form a shelf. Ideally, it should be long enough to lay across the sink but narrow enough that it doesn't interfere with water running from the tap. Tuck the cutting board into a hidden spot, and when you need an extra shelf on which to place your makeup, shaving equipment, contact lenses, or cleaning supplies, pull it out.

Use Your Magnet-ism

❏ Here's a great way to organize all the metal items in your bathroom, such as nail clippers, razors, and manicure scissors. Go to the kitchen and see if you can put your hands on a spare rack that's designed to hold knives in place with a strong magnet. Mount the rack

You Bet Your Brass

Years ago, the business I work for started a renovation project on a building it owned. That business was pretty old—I bet it went back a hundred years—and there were all kinds of beautiful fixtures throughout the building. My favorites were two tubular door handles, each about 18 inches long, made of solid brass. They were absolutely gorgeous, and when I found out they were getting tossed along with a lot of other stuff, I immediately snatched them and took them home.

I polished them, and they looked great, but I really had no idea what to do with them. That is, until a friend saw them leaning up against the wall. "Wow," he said, "those look like expensive towel racks." Bingo—I had my answer. Of course, those solid brass towel racks are the most elegant things in my bathroom, so now *I* have to renovate.

–Tom Donnelly
Flushing, New York

behind the bathroom cabinet or closet door, attach all those metallic odds and ends to it, and you have useful, out-of-the-way storage space.

Place Mats Here

❏ Why waste money buying shelf paper for your linen closet when there are so many perfectly suitable substitutes around? Clean up those old plastic place mats that have been relegated to the back of your kitchen drawers and use them to protect your linens and your shelves. The best part is that you can wipe plastic-coated place mats clean and use them over and over again.

Try a Little Shelf Help

❏ Old fabric tablecloths or sheets can be substituted for shelf paper in the linen closet. If you prefer a more finished and durable edge, cut the fabric a little larger than the shelf and hem the edges. That way, you'll be able to wash the fabric and use it over and over. If you don't have the patience to sit and sew (and don't care that the fabric won't last through more than a single washing),

Space Savers and Storage

The Bathroom

trim the fabric to fit with a pair of pinking shears, which will keep the edges from fraying in the short term. You may want to use a few thumbtacks to secure the fabric to the shelf.

Steady a Wig Stand for a Song

❏ A store-bought wig stand made of plastic or Styrofoam can be a bit unsteady, particularly for older or palsied hands to contend with. Here's your chance to do something with one of those scratchy LPs you've long ago abandoned in favor of compact discs. Glue the LP to the bottom of the wig stand to give the stand some stability.

Keep an Eye on Eyeglasses

❏ If you constantly misplace your eyeglasses when you wash up in the morning or after you take them off to go to bed at night, here's a way to keep those glasses where you can find them: Simply mount a special container for them next to the sink where you brush your teeth. One good option: Mount a couple of cup hooks next to the bathroom mirror, then hang a small plastic handbag or child's pocketbook by its strap from the hooks. Make it a habit to drop your glasses there each time you take them off, and you'll never have trouble locating them again.

❏ Alternatively, take a large yogurt container, cover it with scrap fabric or leftover wallpaper from the last time you redecorated the bathroom, and mount the container on the wall. Then just pop your glasses in the container before stepping in the shower.

BATH TIME

Make a Pillow from (and for) Peanuts

❏ Here's a way to pamper yourself in the bath and re-cycle some of those packing peanuts from mail-order packages at the same time. Get a large plastic freezer bag and pour in at least three cups of peanuts. Then squeeze out some (but not all) of the air. Presto! You have an instant bath pillow. Just prop it under your neck when you lie in the tub.

❏ If you want to make the pillow a little more comfy, sew it up in a towel. Put snaps on one end so that you can change the bag and the peanuts occasionally.

Take the Citrus Plunge

❏ Here's a way to treat yourself to an aromatherapy bath using what you might otherwise have (gasp!) thrown in the garbage. After using at least three or four lemons or limes for cooking, trim off the skins with a vegetable peeler. Then cut the foot section from an old pair of panty hose and place the peel inside. Knot the top and float the whole thing in your bathwater. The aroma will refresh and relax you, and the oil will mois-turize your skin.

Got Milk?

❏ Everybody knows milk is great for teeth and bones, but did you know it's good for your skin, too? And you don't even have to swallow it. The lactic acid in milk acts as a very mild, but effective, exfoliant—meaning that it removes dead skin and leaves you as silky smooth as a baby. Just pull out the powdered milk from the back of the kitchen cupboard and add it to your bath. Any type of milk—low fat, nonfat, or whole—is fine. But don't sprinkle the dry milk into the tub. It won't dissolve well, and you'll end up with a tubful of little floating clumps of milk. Instead, while the water is run-ning, find a jar with a tight-fitting lid. Following the di-rections on the package of powdered milk, combine in the jar enough milk powder and water to make 1 cup

The Bathroom

reconstituted milk. Replace the jar lid and shake the jar like crazy until the milk dissolves. Then pour the milk into your bathwater, sit back, and soak.

Sock It to Me

❏ Don't toss out your old mismatched socks, especially the white cotton ones. Once laundered, a sock makes a terrific bath mitt. Most white athletic socks are more nubbly on the inside, so if you turn the sock inside out before slipping it over your hand, it'll be more effective in exfoliating dead skin.

Earl's Favorites

Don't Can the Can

I can't stand to throw out something just because it's old, no matter how inexpensive it is to replace. If it's reusable, I find a way to reuse it. Not long ago, I received a letter from a reader that perfectly illustrates my philosophy.

It seems he was remodeling his bathroom. It looked fine, but his wife was complaining about the accessories they had, especially a little trash can. It was brown and plastic, and they thought it was pretty ugly. But it was usable, and neither one of them could see throwing it out just because it didn't match. So they figured out how to save it.

These were pretty frugal folks, and the wife had already sewn a new shower curtain from some fabric she loved. In fact, she liked it so much, she'd made some matching curtains. Luckily, there was enough fabric left over to cover the trash can. They measured and cut the fabric to fit the can. The wife hemmed the edges and put a Velcro strip on the top edge so that she could remove the fabric and wash it. They both loved it, and the best part was they saved a perfectly serviceable trash can.

In my book, saving something old is always a darned good investment.

Bath Time

Rub-a-Dub-Dub,
Bring Your Socks to the Tub

❏ If you're looking for a way to get rid of all those soap slivers, drop a few into an old cotton sock and tie a ribbon or string around the end. Now you have a body scrubber with an almost endless supply of scrubbing bubbles.

The Bathroom

TOILETRIES AND COSMETICS

Get Dentures Clean and White Overnight

❏ When you need an inexpensive way to brighten up dentures, just head for the kitchen and grab the baking soda. Brush a thin layer of baking soda on the teeth with—what else?—a clean toothbrush. Then set them to soak in a cup of water with another teaspoon of baking soda stirred in. Leave them overnight, and they'll be sparkling clean in the morning.

Shake Things Up

❏ Baking soda is a great cleaner for real teeth, too. It's a mild abrasive that not only cleans and whitens your teeth but also freshens your breath. But keeping a box of soda in the bathroom isn't a great idea, because the box can get damp and start to fall apart. Instead, dig through the kitchen cabinets and find an old saltshaker or pepper shaker—the plastic kind with a removable lid is best. Put a few grains of rice in the bottom to absorb moisture, then fill the container with baking soda. The shaker will be small enough to fit neatly into most bathrooms, and it's the handiest way to use the soda. Just sprinkle some into your wet hand and scoop it up with your brush.

Be the Masked Woman

❏ Day spas—those fancy-schmancy salons where ladies of leisure get permed, powdered, and pampered—are all the rage, but the prices they charge are

The Bathroom

outrageous. Why spend the dough when you can pamper yourself for pennies in the privacy of your own home? To make a skin-freshening mask, process 1 banana with 1 tablespoon honey in a blender. Apply the mixture to your face, let sit for 15 to 20 minutes, and rinse. The honey will soften your skin, while the banana will firm it up.

Wait for the Tone

❏ Although it's generally used as an antiseptic, witch hazel also makes a terrific skin toner. Just splash it on after you wash your face. It has a wonderful, clean scent.

❏ In the summer, keep the bottle of witch hazel in the refrigerator. On a hot, humid day, the cold liquid is wonderfully refreshing when splashed on the skin.

Raid the Kitty to Pamper Your Face

❏ Sure, those cosmetics companies want you to think the clay they use in their masks is better because it's European or comes from the foothills of the Himalayas after a three-day spring rain. But clay is pretty much clay, and that includes the clay that your kitty "goes" in. That's right, you can make a perfectly good clay facial mask, one that detoxifies your skin, with kitty litter. Use all-natural clay litter, not any sort of clumping or scented litter, which might harm your skin. Place 3 tablespoons litter in a bowl and add about the same amount of water. Crunch the mixture up with a pestle. When it is good and soupy, pat it on your face and let it dry. (Don't worry if small bits fall off. It's the liquid you're interested in.)

Or Try a Fine Technique

❏ If you prefer a clay mask that's powder-based, place 2 tablespoons kitty litter in an old coffee grinder and let 'er rip. In about 10 seconds, the litter will become a fine powder. Add 1 to 2 tablespoons water, mix until it is the consistency of wet mud, and spread it on your face. Just don't get near your cat.

Toothbrushes

Old ones serve as fingernail brushes when we travel, brush dried dirt off our suede shoes, and keep our eyebrows looking neat and trim. New ones even clean our teeth. Try doing all that with a twig.

Toothbrushes didn't arrive on the scene—at least in Europe—until the late fifteenth century. Before then, when people bothered to clean their mouths at all, they used sticks or small sponges. When brushes (made from the hair of horses, badgers, or hogs) finally did appear, they weren't very effective. The bristles were often too soft. They dried slowly, allowing bacteria to form between uses. And they had a disturbing tendency to come loose from the handle and lodge in the teeth.

The first nylon-bristle toothbrush hit the market in the late 1930s. Thanks to the discovery of nylon by DuPont, Americans were treated to a toothbrush that dried completely between uses and was resistant to bacterial growth. And unlike natural bristles, the fibers in these brushes retained their stiffness even when wet. Perhaps a little too much so: Some people complained that these new bristles were *too* stiff.

The toothbrush we know and love first came to be in the late 1950s, with nylon gentle enough for gums but stiff enough to clean teeth. And fingernails. And suede . . .

Use a Magic Wand

❏ Since your eyes are among the most sensitive parts of your body, it's best to toss out eye makeup that's more than six months old; it can become a haven for bacteria. But when you do, salvage the mascara wand and wash it well with soap and water. These brushes are perfect for neatening and brushing your eyebrows, and they're a lot easier on the wallet than store-bought eyebrow brushes.

Beauty Aids You'll Never Find in the Cosmetics Aisle

1. Tea bags. The tannin in tea is an effective astringent. Wipe a damp tea bag over your face to tone your skin.
2. Oatmeal-honey mix. Grind 2 tablespoons dry oats (it doesn't matter whether they're rolled, quick, or instant) in your blender, then add 2 table-spoons honey to make a facial wash. Massage it in, then rinse it off. Oatmeal acts as a slough-ing agent, scrubbing away dead skin.
3. Eggs. They make a wonderful facial mask for dry and oily skin. Break an egg, separate the yolk and white, and beat each gently. Spread the yolk on dry skin (it will moisturize) and the white on oily areas (it will tighten).
4. Salt, especially sea salt. Keep a small plastic container in your shower and sprinkle a wee bit into your wet hands. A mild abrasive, salt is a terrific body and facial scrub.

Milk This One for All It's Worth

❏ Out of makeup remover? Fear not. If you have some powdered milk, you can use that instead. Place 3 table-spoons powdered milk in a jar with about ⅓ cup warm water, screw on the lid, and shake well. The mixture should be the consistency of heavy cream; add more water or milk powder if necessary. To use it, wipe it on with a facecloth, then wipe it off and rinse with water.

SKIN CARE

Wear Kid Gloves

❏ You can buy miracle skin softeners that cost $30 an ounce—or you can use things you already have in your bathroom. One of those products is petroleum jelly. At night before you go to bed, slather the jelly on your hands, then put on an old pair of cotton gloves. (Make sure you take care of tasks such as setting the alarm clock, brushing your teeth, and removing contact lenses before you load up on the jelly.) The jelly will form an airtight layer on your hands, protecting them from the drying air and preventing moisture loss. (Every night, you lose about a pint of fluid in sweat and probably don't even notice.) Next morning, you'll see a real difference.

"E" Is for Excellent Skin

❏ Check the ingredients in some of the lotions at your local pharmacy. Chances are that many of them contain at least some vitamin E oil, which promotes healing and softens skin. Give you an idea? Next time vitamin E capsules are on sale at your local health food store, pick some up. Prick a capsule with a pin, squeeze out what you need, and rub it into your skin. If you don't empty the capsule, the hole will heal itself, and you can use the remaining oil another time.

Take a Shortcut

❏ Solid vegetable shortening such as Crisco makes your piecrust crisp and flaky, but it has the opposite effect on your skin. When your hands are feeling dry and scaly, rub in a little shortening. It's natural, has virtually no odor, and best of all costs a fraction of what you'd pay for fancy lotions. In fact, some hospitals use it to keep skin soft and moist.

Don't Be Down at the Heel

❏ Try vegetable shortening on rough and scaly feet, too. Rubbed in just before you go to bed at night, the stuff does wonders for your feet. Just protect the sheets by wearing an old pair of socks.

Go Ahead, Rub It In

❏ But wait! There's more. Massage shortening into your cuticles to soften them and make them easier to push back.

Sprinkle Away Skin Problems

❏ Prickly heat. Minor scrapes. Contact dermatitis. When you have a minor skin irritation, the temptation may be to ignore it or to bring out the big guns such as antibiotic cream. Don't do either. To ease the irritation, grab some cornstarch from the kitchen and sprinkle it on. It will stop the itch and promote healing.

The Bathroom

HAIR CARE

Do a Bang-Up Job

❏ Time to trim those bangs? Don't call the stylist; grab the masking tape. Dampen your hair just a little and comb your bangs straight down. Place a piece of tape over them, just above where you want to trim them, pressing down lightly. Now use the bottom of the tape as a guide and trim along it. You may want to use quick-release masking tape; it's a little less likely to leave a residue on your hair or to pull when you remove it. Make sure not to get your hair too wet, because when it's plastered against your skin, it looks a lot longer than it does when it's dry, and you'll be liable to cut it too short. (Besides, if your hair is *too* wet, the masking tape won't stick.)

Give Yourself a Powdered Wig

❏ Sometimes, when you're short on time or aren't feeling well, a normal shampoo is out of the question. What you need is a quick fix. Just grab the cornstarch from your kitchen cabinet. Sprinkle some into your hands, vigorously rub it into your hair, and brush. The cornstarch will absorb the dirt and oils so that you can brush them right out. (Tonight might be a good time to wash that brush, though.)

❏ Baby powder works the same way. But use the kind made from cornstarch; it's more absorbent than talc.

Offer Your Hair Some Lemon-Aid

❏ You work in a library, but you want your hair to look as if you spend all your days in the sun. Here's how to achieve that look on your weekend off. Combine some lemon juice and water and place it in a spray bottle. Spray it in your hair and comb it through, then go out in the sun for a couple of hours. The lemon juice will gradually lighten your hair. (This works only for folks who are already blondish.)

Blonds Have . . . Green Hair

❏ Have you detected a greenish tint to your hair after you emerge from the town swimming pool? It's a reaction to the chemicals in the water. But fear not, there is a solution to this problem. Before you shampoo, rinse your hair with a little red wine. Any kind will do—the cheaper the better. After you wash and dry your hair, the green will be gone.

Don't Be Dull

❏ If you use the same shampoo, conditioner, or other hair care product day after day, you may notice that a residue begins to build up on your hair, making it look dull. You can cut through that residue and restore the natural shine with vinegar. Before your next shampoo, combine equal parts vinegar and warm water. After you've washed the shampoo out of your hair, finish by rinsing with the vinegar mixture. The acid in the vinegar, which is quite mild, will cut through the residue, allowing your hair to shine again.

Rosemary Will Baby Your Hair

❏ When you rinse your hair with vinegar, you can make the smell a little more appealing by infusing it with

The Bathroom

The Inside Story

Bobby Pins

How did bobby pins get their name? To wear the enormous wigs that were popular in seventeenth-century France, a person had to have his hair cut short or curled ("bobbed") very close to the head. Thus, the hairpins used to create the curls became known as "bobbing" pins. Over time, the name was shortened, and cutened, to "bobby" pin.

The Bathroom

some fragrant herbs—mint, rosemary, or any herbal scent you like. In a glass container with a lid, combine equal parts water, vinegar, and dried herbs. Set the container in a sunny window for a couple of weeks. Strain, then use the liquid to rinse your hair. In addition to looking lively and shiny, your locks will smell good, too.

Lose the Soap

❏ Alternatively, rinse the soap residue from your hair with a mixture of one part lemon juice and three parts water.

Accept This One Condition

❏ Have you seen what they're charging for a good hair conditioner? It's criminal, so don't be swindled; make your own. You probably already have all the ingredients on hand. Combine 3 tablespoons honey and 2 tablespoons olive oil. About 35 minutes before you're ready to wash your hair, place the mixture in the top of a double boiler and heat slowly over medium heat. You want the concoction to be very warm, but not so hot that you can't comfortably put your hand in it. Rub the mixture into your hair, then wrap your head with a hot, wet towel. Wait about 30 minutes, then wash your hair as usual. This mixture is especially helpful for dry hair.

Hold the Mayo

❏ Dry hair? Don't despair. If you have a jar of mayonnaise on hand, you have a perfect hair conditioner. Once a month or so (more often if your hair is exceptionally dry), slather lots of mayonnaise in your mane, then wrap your head with a towel. Leave the towel on for about 30 minutes, then wash as usual. The oils in the mayonnaise will condition your hair, while the vinegar, a main ingredient in mayonnaise, will cut through the shampoo residue, giving your hair a healthy shine.

Holy Guacamole!

❏ When your hair is in bad shape—overprocessed by coloring or perms or really dry—don't reach for the expensive, commercial hot oil treatments. Instead, make your own. Combine ¼ cup mayonnaise and 2 table-spoons mashed avocado. Smooth the mixture through your hair, then cover it with a hot towel or shower cap. Both the mayonnaise and the avocado are loaded with fat, and they will moisturize your hair. Leave the mixture on for about 30 minutes, then shampoo as usual.

The Bathroom

Earn Your Strips

❏ Coloring gray hair with a home rinse? It doesn't have to be an all-or-nothing proposition. You can leave a few natural light streaks at the temple by using some clean scraps of aluminum foil. Before applying the color, just wrap the foil around the hair segments that you want to keep their original shade.

Keep That Perm Right Out of Your Eyes

❏ One of the creepiest feelings in the world is the slow trickle of home permanent chemicals making their way to your eyes, ears, or neck. To make an excellent barrier, dig out some sanitary minipads that have an adhesive backing. After your hair is up in the bonnet or on the pins and curlers, and before anyone applies anything liquid, attach the minipads sticky side down to the forehead, temples, and back of your neck. Laid lengthwise at the edge of your hairline, they will stop all drips from reaching your face or collar. (Be sure to remove all makeup before trying this, or the pads may not stick.)

> ## Hidden Treasures
> ### Devil's Advocate
>
> I know some people hate the plastic bags that you get at the grocery store, but I love them. They fit perfectly into the small wastebasket in my bathroom. I never have to buy can liners.
>
> **–Tom Cavalieri**
> *Long Island City, New York*

Bubble, Bubble, Her Hair's in Trouble

❏ How is it possible for a child with bubble gum to blow a bubble so big that it lands in her hair? Her *long, long* hair, which then becomes thoroughly tangled in the stuff. We don't know, but we do know how to solve the problem. Coat the child's locks with peanut butter, then

carefully comb out the goo. The peanut butter will re-duce the stickiness so that you can remove the gum.

FOOT CARE

Brew Your Own Foot Deodorizer

❑ Stinky feet? Don't sweat it. Just boil about a quart of water and add 4 or 5 tea bags. Let the tea steep for 5 to 10 minutes, then let the mixture cool. Remove the tea bags, pour the tea into a bucket or dishpan, and soak your feet in it for about 30 minutes. Then dry them off without rinsing. Foot odor is caused by the bacteria in perspiration. The tannin in the tea is an astringent and will help close your pores, which will have the dual effect of drying your feet and preventing further perspi-ration.

Kick That Athlete's Foot

❑ Athlete's foot may be one of the most irritating afflic-tions known to humankind. But take heart! Relief is in sight, and it's in your kitchen cabinet. Sprinkle the in-sides of your shoes with cornstarch. And after you get out of the shower, dry your feet well and sprinkle them thoroughly with more cornstarch. The cornstarch will absorb moisture, the prime culprit in the development of the fungus.

Make Yourself a Dog Brush

❑ So what does one do with an old hairbrush with nat-ural bristles? If the bristles are still intact but have just become a little too soft, save the brush. It will make a terrific foot scrubber. Wash it well to remove any residue from shampoo or hair spray, then keep it in the tub with your back brush. After a long day in the garden, mowing the lawn, hiking, or golfing, you can give your tired dogs a good scrubbing.

Go Soak Your . . . Feet

❑ Soothe tired, aching feet with a hot oil soak. Pour into a pan enough vegetable oil to cover your feet. Heat the oil until it's warm but not too hot to touch. Then pour the oil into a bucket or dishpan and place your feet inside. While your feet soak, give them a good massage. The oil will moisturize and soften hardened skin and calluses. When the oil cools off, pour it into a jar with a tight-fitting lid. You can use it again to soak your feet another day. Label it clearly, though, lest a family member uses the oil to make french fries.

The Bathroom

SIMPLE FIRST-AID

Start a Splinter (Removing) Group

❏ Splinter? Don't pick up the tweezers just yet. Soak the afflicted area in some corn or olive oil, which will soften the skin. The splinter may work itself out within three to four minutes.

---

14 Uses for the Cotton from Medicine Bottles

Since drug companies are clever enough to stuff cotton into the tops of all our medicine bottles, the least we can do is prove our own craftiness by recycling those little white wads. Use those odds and ends of cotton:

1. To remove makeup.
2. To add a pleasant scent to any room. Add a couple of drops of perfume to the cotton and tuck it into a heating vent.
3. As applicators for makeup.
4. To touch up shoe polish.
5. To remove nail polish.
6. To fill holes left by picture hangers.
7. As earplugs.
8. To dust your plants (tops of leaves only, please).
9. As stuffing for a homemade pincushion or stuffed animal.
10. To clean dust from your computer monitor and keyboard.
11. To clean your phone. Just dip the cotton in a little vinegar.
12. To adjust the size of too-large shoes. Stuff the cotton into the toes.
13. To place between your toes when you give yourself a pedi-cure.
14. For Christmas crafts. Glue the cotton on a cardboard cutout to create a snowman for your holiday decorations.

The Bathroom

Cover Up the Problem

❏ Another way to handle a splinter is to cover it with a piece of adhesive tape. Leave the tape on for a couple of days, and you'll probably be able to remove the splinter along with the tape.

Serve Tea to Your Puffy Eyes

❏ It's happened to almost everyone. You eat a few too many potato chips or go a little too heavy on the soy sauce. Then, next morning, your eyes are all puffy and look as though you've been up all night crying. Help your eyes get back to normal with a little tea. After you finish your morning cup, grab the leftover (cooled) tea bags. Squeeze them out, then lie back with one bag on each closed eye. The swelling will go down in 10 to 15 minutes.

Cook Up Relief for a Sunburn

❏ So you didn't apply the sunscreen too carefully, and now your nose looks like Rudolph's? If you've made gravy lately, there's a quick fix in your kitchen cabinet: cornstarch. Make a paste of about 2 teaspoons cornstarch and 2 scant teaspoons water (more of each if you have a big honker), then spread it on the affected area to relieve itching and burning.

❏ Alternatively, make a paste of about 1 tablespoon powdered milk (whole, low fat, or nonfat) and 2 tablespoons water, then add a scant pinch of salt. Dab it on the burn for some soothing relief.

If the Teapot Was Too Hot This Morning

❏ You can ease the pain of a minor burn (say, from a hot teapot or steam iron) with an ordinary tea bag. Dip the bag in a cup of hot water to moisten it. Let the moistened bag cool briefly, then dab it on the burned area. The tea will have an analgesic effect and relieve the pain.

❑ Leftover tea works well on its own, too. If you didn't finish yours this morning, moisten a washcloth and dab the leftover liquid on the burn, or spritz it on with a water mister. But be sure to use only tea that has no honey, cream, sugar, or lemon added. Those other ingredients may actually irritate your burn.

The Bathroom

Let Poison Ivy Take a Powder

❑ Stop the itch of poison ivy with powdered milk. Make a thin paste of water and powdered milk (low fat or whole) and spread it on the trouble spots. It should end the itching posthaste.

Nip the Shaving Nicks

❑ One slip, and you end up with a shaving nick. For years, a bit of toilet paper on the cut has been the remedy of choice, but it's far from perfect. When you pull the paper off, you usually take the tiny scab with it, opening up the cut again. Here's a better way to stop the bleeding. Scoop up that little glob of shaving cream that's always left on the nozzle and dab that on the cut. It will stop the bleeding, but it won't stick or pull when you remove it; it will just dissolve.

The Laundry Room

S ure you can buy a thousand products designed to make your whites whiter, your
brights brighter, and the whole job easier.
But there's probably a better, less expensive way.
Got a little lemon juice? Meat tenderizer? Vinegar?
How about a few rags, a toothbrush that's seen
better days, and a worn-out sneaker or two? If
so, you're ready for laundry day.

In the following pages, you'll find ideas for organizing the laundry room and handy helpers for
anyone whose laundry room is actually the local
Laundromat. We've included plenty of tips, too,
for coping with stains ranging from spilled tea to
smudged ink. Just one note of caution: Before you
try any stain removal technique on the front of
your best blouse, be sure to test it first on an inside seam. That's to make sure you won't be removing the color along with the stain.

Now, do you have that meat tenderizer ready?
Read on!

HANDY HELPERS

Make a Case for Your Laundry

❏ Of course, you need to put your dirty laundry some-where, but where? Certainly not in a store-bought laundry bag. Instead, grab an old pillowcase and several old shoelaces. Knot the shoelaces together to form a long string. Open the edge of the top hem on the pil-lowcase and thread the shoelaces through it to form a drawstring. You have an instant, washable laundry bag. An added bonus: This is especially good for delicate items, because you can leave them right in the bag to wash them. The bag will keep them from snagging on the zippers and hooks of other garments.

When the Bottle of Detergent Is Bigger Than the Washing Machine

Everyone knows that generally, the larger the bottle or box of laundry detergent you buy, the lower the unit price will be. So if you have room to store the larger size, it almost always pays to buy detergent in quantity. However, if you don't have space in your laundry room for the super-economy-size package or you find it too big and heavy to deal with, you'll need to find a container for a reasonable amount of detergent so that it's accessible when you need it. Here are a few containers that make terrific detergent holders.

1. One- and two-liter plastic soda bottles. These take up less room than gallon-plus bottles of liquid detergent and bleach. And with the help of a funnel, you can refill them easily.
2. Dishwashing liquid bottles. The pop-up, squirt-style cap is especially good for pinpoint applications of liquid detergent to treat heavy concentrations of dirt and grime.
3. Pump spray bottles. Filled with diluted detergent, these containers make it easy to apply a presoak solution to a stain.
4. One-gallon plastic ice cream tubs. They're perfect for holding manageable amounts of your favorite powdered detergent.

Getting the Hang of It: Drying Clothes in Limited Space

If you don't have the floor space for a drying rack, even one that folds away when it's not being used, look around. You might see some potential drying space right over your head. Here are some possibilities.

1. Wet clothes are going to drip; they may as well drip someplace waterproof. Hang them over the shower curtain rod in your bathroom. Or run a length of nylon cord from the showerhead to the far end of the curtain rod and hang dripping clothes from there.

2. Hang clothes from exposed pipes in your basement or boiler room. Just make sure the pipes don't leak, or you'll need to refer to the section on rust stains elsewhere in this chapter.

3. That old umbrella may be useless for keeping you dry, but you can still use it to dry your unmentionables. Peel away the fabric, leaving the metal skeleton, and you have a collapsible lingerie dryer. Hang it, opened up, from the shower curtain rod or from pipes in your basement. (This idea is *not* for the superstitious!)

Hamper Those Laundry Problems

❑ One of the worst things that can happen on laundry day is to sort out the clothes and find that the cloth you used to mop up grape juice and greasy food spills has spent the week in your hamper right next to your brand-new white blouse. Now they *both* need stain remover. Prevent this by keeping an old mesh grocery bag hanging from the knob of a kitchen drawer or from a convenient hook. Toss wet washcloths and dish towels in there during the week. Then on laundry day, they will be dry and ready to wash.

Shell Out for Laundry Detergent

❑ Sure, laundry can be a chore, but there's no reason you can't get some enjoyment out of it. Remember that time you made a trip to the shore and collected all those seashells? Use a large one to scoop powdered laundry detergent into the washer. Make sure the shell has been rinsed and dried off before you use it, measure to see just how much it holds, and then start scooping. Who said doing laundry was no day at the beach?

Get the Scoop on Detergent

❑ Alternatively, a clean yogurt container or an old plastic mug will make a perfectly good detergent scoop.

The Laundry Room

Be Sneaker Savvy

❑ Next time you wash a comforter, sleeping bag, parka, or any other item that has loft, toss an old sneaker into the dryer with it. The bouncing sneaker will lift the loft of your down-filled washables.

❑ Alternatively, toss a clean tennis ball in the dryer with your down-filled items to help restore the loft.

FABRIC SOFTENER AND STATIC CLING

Reach for the Rag Bag

❑ Who needs those expensive, disposable fabric softener sheets that you put in the dryer? You can make your own with less expensive liquid softener. Normally, you'd use about half a cup of liquid fabric softener in the rinse cycle, but you can be even more economical by putting about a teaspoon of that same liquid on a clean rag and throwing it in the dryer with the rest of the laundry. Your clothes will be as soft as if you'd used store-bought dryer sheets.

Add Vinegar and Toss Lightly

❑ Like your clothes to come out of the wash soft and smelling fresh? Add approximately half a cup of white vinegar during the rinse cycle.

The Laundry Room

(If you have hard water, you may need to add a little more.) That'll do the trick just as well as any commercial product.

Bring Those Socks Out of Hiding

❑ Static cling is public enemy number one when it comes to hiding stray socks. They're usually out of sight somewhere they're not supposed to be, such as stuck to the roof of the dryer drum or hidden inside a pant leg. If you hate perfumy fabric softener sheets or, worse yet, hate the thought of buying them, try this approach instead. A few minutes before you take your clothes out of the dryer, toss in a damp cloth. That little bit of extra moisture will cut down on static cling and make your laundry easier to fold.

THE LAUNDROMAT

Become a Quartermaster

❑ If you use a coin-operated Laundromat, you know that all the quarters in your house seem to disappear on laundry day. One way to make sure there's always laundry money around is to keep an old plastic laundry detergent bottle near where you empty your pockets of change. A large economy-size bottle will work best. Cut a slice out of the soft plastic side with a sharp knife, making sure the slit is large enough for you to slip quarters through it. When you're ready to do the laundry, just remove the cap from the top of the bottle and pour out as many quarters as you need.

Make Your Laundry Take a Hike

❑ If you take your laundry to a Laundromat, you know that carrying a large sack of clothes can literally be a pain. Try using your backpack or day pack instead. It'll save wear and tear on your back, and the side pockets are handy for toting bottles of bleach or detergent. If you don't like the idea of your dirty laundry rubbing against the inside of your pack, place a big trash bag inside the pack, then add the laundry.

5 Uses for Dryer Lint

And you thought it was destined for the trash. Not so fast! Here are some better possibilities.

1. Packing material. Place the item you want to mail in a re-sealable plastic bag. Place that in a larger envelope and fill the extra space with lint.

2. Draft dodgers. Stuff your extra lint into a leg cut off an old pair of panty hose, then use your homemade draft dodger to fill the space between the sill and sash during those windy nights.

3. Doll stuffing. Save up the lint, and the next time you make a stuffed doll or animal for a child, you'll have the stuffing on hand. (If you know the child is sensitive to dust, you may want to skip this one—and start saving the cotton from aspirin bottles instead.)

4. Clouds for that school art project or diorama. A little glue will affix the lint just fine.

5. Shoe stuffing. Shoes too loose? Sore toe? Stuff some dryer lint into the gaps, and you'll be walking easy.

Bring a Stuffed Shirt to the Laundromat

❏ If you have only a very little laundry to do at the Laundromat, tie together the arms of a long-sleeved T-shirt and fill the shirt with your laundry. Tie up the bottom by the corners, as you would a trash bag, so that your clothes won't fall out. Toss the shirt in the washer, and you won't have a laundry bag to worry about. Then you can carry the clean, folded clothes home in a pile or tuck them back inside the clean shirt.

GUM STUCK TO CLOTHES

Be Cool, Bazooka Joe

❏ Well, you've won the bubble-blowing contest, but you have a shirt covered with Dubble Bubble for your trouble. Now you need a way to remove the gum. Put some ice in a plastic bag. From the inside of the garment, hold the ice pack against the spot with the gum

The Laundry Room

for about 10 minutes. When the gum hardens, peel it off or scrape it off with a knife.

STAINS

Keep Off the Grass

❑ Got grass stains on your knees while you were working in the garden? Rub the stains with glycerin. And where, you might ask, can you find glycerin? Well, check your medicine chest. You may find it in a constipation suppository or a skin-softening lotion. First, make sure you're using pure glycerin; other ingredients might add to the stain. If you're dealing with glycerin hand lotion, you can just pour it onto the stain. If you're using a solid glycerin suppository, which has a consistency somewhere between that of a Gummi Bear and soft wax, rub it into the stain. Don't worry about getting some on your hands; it's good for the skin. Let the glycerin sit on the stain for an hour, then wash the garment as usual.

Rust: Hold the Bleach

❑ What are those yellow spots on that white shirt? One cause of yellow and brown stains in laundry is rust that develops from iron deposits in your water supply. You might be tempted to bleach them away, but household chlorine bleach can cause the iron in water to precipitate out into fabrics, leaving additional stains. Instead, treat the stains with a solution of equal parts lemon juice and water, letting the mixture sit for a few minutes. Then hand-wash the garment.

❑ Stains from contact with rusty metal will need more aggressive treatment. You can get that by applying full-strength lemon juice directly to the stains as soon as possible, then washing as usual.

Ride the Rusty Steamer

❑ Unfortunately, you may not always have the chance to do laundry right away. For a rust stain that has already set, try this. After you soak the stain with lemon

6 Laundry Aids from the Kitchen Cupboard

Who needs all those whiteners, brighteners, and stain removers that fill the laundry aisle at the grocery store? You already have all of the above right in your kitchen—you just have to know what to look for.

1. Lemon juice. Diluted or straight, it's a safe treatment for fruit juice and rust stains. Pretreat stains with the juice as you would with a commercial presoak, then wash as usual.

2. Baking soda. Use half a cup in the wash to eliminate odors and soften clothes. It's gentle enough for diapers, too.

3. White vinegar. Use it to eliminate odors and soften hard water. Add a cup to the rinse cycle for a full load.

4. Meat tenderizer. For milk, blood, chocolate, and other protein-based stains. The special enzyme it contains—the one that tenderizes meat—works to break down many proteins. To treat a fresh stain, sprinkle enough on the problem area to cover it, then let it sit for about an hour. Brush off the dried tenderizer and wash as usual. To work on a stain that's set, make a paste (2 or 3 drops water and 1 teaspoon tenderizer) and work it into the stain. Let it sit for an hour before laundering.

5. Sour milk. It's slightly acidic and has bleaching qualities as well. An old trick for whitening shoelaces—one that still works today—was to soak them in sour milk. About half a cup will do for an average pair of sneaker shoelaces. Rinse them off and launder with the rest of the whites.

6. Salt. It can do more than just make your food taste better. Its absorbent quality is the reason you can treat a fresh grease spill by sprinkling on enough salt to cover the entire stain. When it dries, brush it off, and you'll brush off most of the stain with it. Or you can loosen an *old* grease stain by rubbing salt into it, loosening the grease before washing as usual. And it's abrasive, so you can use it to attack rust stains. Mix salt with white vinegar to make a paste, then rub the mixture into the stain before washing as usual.

juice, hold it over a steaming teakettle until the stain is thoroughly steamed. This may loosen the stain's hold on the fabric and enhance the bleaching action of the lemon juice.

Bleach: A Story of White Knights

These days, we use chlorine bleach for just about any disinfecting job. And as a whitener, it's second to none. But people weren't always so lucky.

The ancient Egyptians soaked their linen fabrics in harsh alkaline lye, transforming them from their natural off-white color to bright white. It was an effective process but a tricky one. The harsh lye, if left too long, could destroy the fabric.

In the thirteenth century, the Dutch were known as master bleachers. Most European fabrics used for white garments were sent to Holland to be bleached in a process not all that different from the one the early Egyptians used. After being soaked in lye, the fabric was stretched out in the sun to dry and lighten, then put through the entire process once again. Finally, to fix the bleaching agent and stop further deterioration of the fabric, the material was soaked in buttermilk or sour milk.

It wasn't until 1774 that chlorine gas was discovered. Within a few years, Count Claude-Louis Berthollet figured out that the gas, dissolved in water, was a powerful bleaching agent. When combined with lime and potash, it became known as *eau de Javel,* named for the Quai de Javel chemical works in Paris. It soon became the accepted way to bleach fabric. And so, you'd think, the problems of laundresses the world over would have been solved.

Wrong. Unfortunately, the count couldn't be bothered with such common activities as manufacturing. He left that to all those hapless professional laundresses, who had to obtain their own chlorine gas, lime, and potash and mix it themselves as best they could. Usually, the process burned their eyes, noses, and hands.

Fast-forward to 1799, when Scottish chemist Charles Tennant whipped up his own mixture of the count's magic bleach and then dried it into the very first powdered version. Finally, laundry workers were able to do what homemakers and college freshmen now take for granted: They could just measure out the powdered bleach and pour it into the wash water. Suddenly, the world got a whole lot brighter.

A Spot of Tea?

❏ On your blouse? Rub the stain with some glycerin, a primary ingredient in many skin-softening lotions and constipation suppositories. Check your medicine cabinet; you may already have some. When you lay your hands on it, make sure the product is pure glycerin; other ingredients might add to the stain. Pour glycerin hand lotion onto the stain or rub the solid suppository right on it. Let the glycerin sit for a few minutes, then wash the garment as usual.

The Laundry Room

Take Vinegar with Your Tea

❏ You gave up milk and sugar in your coffee and tea, and now that sacrifice is paying off in the laundry room. It's a lot easier to get coffee and tea stains out of washable garments if there's no milk or sugar involved, because either of these adds a protein component to the stain that makes it tougher to remove. So if the coffee you spilled on your washable skirt was black, when you do the laundry just make up a solution of 1 quart warm water, ½ teaspoon dishwashing liquid, and 1 tablespoon white vinegar. Soak the stain in this solution for 15 minutes. Rinse the garment with cold water, sponge the stained area with alcohol, and launder as usual.

Add Cream, Sugar—And Alcohol

❏ If you take cream and sugar in your tea or coffee, you'll need to act fast to prevent any spill from becoming a permanent stain. In that case, immediately flush the stain with cold water to prevent it from setting. Then mix up a solution of 1 quart warm water, ½ teaspoon dishwashing liquid, and 1 tablespoon white vinegar. Scrub the stain a bit before letting it soak in the solution for 15 minutes. Rinse the garment with cold water, sponge the problem area with alcohol, and toss the garment in with the rest of the wash. You may need to use chlorine or color-safe bleach to remove any remaining spots.

Treat It Tenderly

❏ For those who like milk or cream with their caffeine, here's another way to deal with a coffee or tea stain.

The Laundry Room

Make a paste of 1 teaspoon unflavored meat tenderizer and a few drops water, work it into the stain, and then launder as usual. Breaking down the milk in the stain will make it easier for your usual detergent to remove the coffee or tea.

That Beer Stain Is Outta Here

❏ It's a long fly ball; it's going, going, gone! As you leap up to watch the ball sail over the fence, you spill beer all over your pants. Don't worry; beer is not a major-league stain if your clothes are washable. When you get home from the ballpark, combine ⅓ cup white vinegar and ⅔ cup water. Soak the stain with the solution, then blot the area with a clean towel. This will neutralize the stain and eliminate the smell. Follow up by washing the garment as usual.

Order Seltzer to Go with the Wine

❏ If you get a little tipsy and tip your wineglass onto your best dress, you don't have to wait until you get home to treat the stain. Immediately pour a little club soda or seltzer over the stain, then blot it with a clean napkin or paper towel. Wash the garment as soon as possible.

Oh, Fudge, Another Stain

❏ If your hot fudge sundae drips on your clothes, rub the stains with glycerin. You may already have glycerin in your bathroom in the form of either a constipation suppository or a skin-softening lotion. Make sure the product you have on hand is pure glycerin, so you don't make the stain worse. Pour glycerin hand lotion on the stain or rub the suppository directly into the problem area. Let it sit for a few minutes, then wash as usual.

Don't Fret over Fruit Stains

❏ If the cherry falls off your sundae and onto your shirt, it'll ruin your Monday—unless you act fast. To treat any fruit stain, rinse the affected area with cold water immediately. Then dab it with a solution of one part white vinegar and two parts water. Rinse again with cold water and air dry if possible.

Treat a Juicy Problem

❏ A fruit juice stain that's not treated immediately can be tough to get out later. To handle a stain that has set before you get to it, pretreat the problem area with white vinegar. Let it sit for 15 minutes, then rub in a little laundry detergent before tossing the garment in with the rest of the wash.

The Laundry Room

Remove the Real (Stained) Thing

❏ They might be soft drinks, but the stains they produce can be hard to remove. One approach is to soak the affected area immediately in cold water, apply rubbing alcohol to the stain, and then launder as usual.

Sop Up the Grease

❏ You can remove greasy stains with an absorbent such as baking soda, cornmeal, or cornstarch. Just sprinkle the absorbent over the stain. When it begins to cake up, brush it off. You'll be brushing off the stain at the same time.

Chalk Up One Way to Cope with an Oil Spill

❏ If you splash salad oil on your clothes, make the stain easier to remove later by treating it with a stick of white chalk immediately. If you're in a restaurant, ask the waiter whether he has a piece you can borrow. (Some use chalk to write the daily specials on a blackboard.) Just rub the chalk right on the stain. If the powder doesn't seem to come off onto the fabric, scratch a little of it off the stick with your fingernail or the edge of a knife. When you get home, wash as usual.

A Different Twist

Fizz Away Food

Hmmm . . . Grandma's blueberry pie, all over your white cloth napkin. To get the napkin clean, borrow something else from Grandma. Effervescent denture cleaning tablets can be used to remove food stains from some washable fabrics. Select a container that's large enough to hold the stained portion of the fabric and fill it with warm water. Add the tablets in the recommended proportion and immerse the stained article. Let it soak until the stain has dissolved.

Don't Be a Grease Monkey's Uncle

With all the fix-it work I do, it's not unusual for me to end up with a grease spot on my work clothes. I want to get rid of the spots, but I don't want to spend a lot of time doing laundry, so I was glad to hear about a good way to get grease out of clothing. Just apply a little mechanic's water-free hand cleaner, such as Goop, to the stain before you put the garment in the wash. The cleaner will do the same thing for your shirt that it does for your hands. And anything that gets me out of the laundry room faster is fine by me.

Powder Your Clothes

❏ You can get rid of a grease spot on fabric without cleaning the entire garment. Just sprinkle a little baking powder or talcum powder on the spot. Shake or brush the powder off after the grease has been absorbed.

Blood: Cut to the Cleanup

❏ If you get a paper cut at work and end up with a drop of blood on your blouse (or your paperwork), moisten the spot immediately with your own saliva, then blot it with a clean cloth or paper napkin. That will prevent the stain from setting before you get home. Why saliva rather than water? Saliva contains digestive enzymes that break down protein—and the protein in blood is what makes it so hard to remove.

Call for First-Aid

❏ When you see blood, it's always a good idea to get out the first-aid kit, and not just for a bandage. You can treat a spot of blood on white fabric, after you rinse and blot it, by dabbing it with a little hydrogen peroxide on a cotton swab.

A-Salt That Bloodstain

❏ Bloodstains need to be treated right away. To save yourself more work later, immediately soak a bloodstain in a solution of 1 cup water and ½ teaspoon salt.

Get the Red Out

❏ To get rid of bloodstains, add a generous splash of ammonia to a sinkful of cold water. (Don't use hot water, which will set the stain.) Immerse the stained fabric in this solution and let it soak for about 30 minutes. Then rinse it with cold water. You may need to follow up by scrubbing lightly with dishwashing liquid, but the ammonia will eliminate the bulk of the stain, even if you don't get to the problem immediately.

Try Moo Juice Magic

❏ To wash a bloodstain that wasn't treated immediately, especially on a brightly colored or white fabric, soak the stain in milk before you throw it in with the rest of the laundry.

If You Hit the (Nail Polish) Bottle

❏ If you have a minor mishap while putting on your nail polish, don't forget nail polish remover. If you're dealing with natural-fiber clothes, dab the stain from behind with the remover, then blot the area with a clean cloth. (Don't try this with synthetic fabrics, because the nail polish remover will eat right through them.)

A Kiss Is Still a . . . Stain?

❏ To get rid of a lipstick stain on fabric, coat the problem area with hair spray. Let it sit for a couple of minutes, then carefully wipe off the excess spray—and the lipstick. Follow up by laundering as usual.

Pencil Marks: Get to the Tooth of the Matter

❏ If you get a pencil mark on your cuff (or any other part of your clothing), use an old, clean toothbrush to apply a little diluted window cleaner to the stain. Then toss the garment in with the rest of the laundry.

The Laundry Room

The Laundry Room

❏ Another way to remove a pencil mark from fabric is to treat it with a solution of ½ cup water, 1 tablespoon alcohol, and 2 or 3 drops dishwashing liquid. Apply with a clean toothbrush, then rinse and launder as usual.

Ink: Hair's a Solution

❏ Leaky pen in your pocket? Check the label on that can of hair spray in the bathroom. A main ingredient of most brands is alcohol, which acts as a solvent on ink. If the label says that's true of your spray, just apply it full force to the ink stains before laundering.

Cray-Off

❏ When the kids come home from school with crayon on their clothes as well as their artwork, don't hang those decorated shirts on the refrigerator. Instead, remove the crayon marks like this. Lay the garment stain side down on a paper towel. Spray from the back with WD-40. Let this sit for a few minutes, then turn the fabric over and spray the stain itself. Apply a mild dishwashing liquid and work it into the stain. Use an old toothbrush if the fabric isn't too delicate. Sandwich the problem area between clean paper towels to absorb the stain. Remove the towels and wash the garment separately with laundry detergent, setting the machine to wash in hot water (if the fabric can handle the heat) and rinse in warm or cold water.

Crayon, Spray Off

❏ If a young artist leaves a crayon in her pocket that finds its way into the dryer, that can cause loads of trouble. You need to remove the crayon residue from the dryer drum. To do that, spray a clean rag with WD-40 and wipe the drum with it. (Don't spray WD-40 directly into a hot dryer, as the aerosol might ignite.) Run a few clean rags in the dryer on a medium setting for 10 minutes to remove any residue before you put in another load of clothes. The dryer will be as good as new.

Don't Sweat It

❏ Perspiration stains are tough, so tenderize them. Before you wash that sweat-stained shirt, dampen the stains and sprinkle meat tenderizer on them. Then go ahead and wash as usual.

Never Let Them See Your Sweat

❏ Another solution to perspiration stains is right there in your kitchen: salt. Add a handful to a quart of water, then soak the offending item for an hour. Wash as usual, and you'll never know which outfit you broke a sweat in.

The Laundry Room

Write Off That Collar Ring

❏ When you get those dark lines around the collar of your white or light-colored cotton shirt, don't panic. Rub

---

The Inside Story

The Snip Heard Round the World

Like many housewives before her, Hannah Lord Montague hated to wash her husband's shirts. It seemed such a waste to wash the whole shirt when her husband sat at a desk all day. The only part of the shirt he actually dirtied was the collar. One day in 1827, she decided to take drastic measures. She got out a pair of scissors and cut the collar off every one of his shirts. It was a simple act of desperation, and it let her wash the collars separately, then reattach them after they'd dried.

Word spread pretty quickly that Mr. Montague's collars were the cleanest in Troy, New York. Soon Hannah had her own business, selling clean collars to area housewives. And before long, this small innovation revolutionized men's fashions. The detachable collar became a mark of social status throughout nineteenth-century America.

In fact, the town of Troy earned the nickname "Collar City" because it was the center of the industries that manufactured and cleaned them. Hannah Lord Montague eventually sold her business to one of the big shirt manufacturers in town. She made a bundle—presumably enough to hire someone else to clean her husband's shirts.

The Laundry Room

a piece of white chalk into the stain and let it sit overnight. Then launder the shirt as usual. The chalk will absorb most of the stain.

IRONING

Just in Case You Need to Iron

❑ If you don't have room for a full-size ironing board or don't use one often enough to warrant having one around, try this. Store an old bath towel—one that's both heavy and clean—folded up inside a hard-sided briefcase. Stow the whole thing under the bed, in the closet, or between the washer and dryer. When you need to iron something, open the briefcase flat on top of the bed with the outside surface up. (Or if the washer and dryer are close enough, set up the opened case so it straddles the two appliances.) Cover the briefcase with the towel, and you have an instant ironing board.

❑ Prefer a larger surface for your improvised ironing area? Substitute a hard-sided suitcase. If it's deep enough, you can store the iron inside as well, but be sure to let the iron cool and empty any water from it first.

Withdraw Those Deposits

❑ If you live in an area with hard water, mineral deposits can build up in the steam vents in the soleplate of your iron and the spray nozzle up front. When you're ironing clothes and start to notice spots that weren't there before, try this. Pour equal parts distilled water (or other bottled water) and vinegar into your iron's reservoir. Turn the iron on and make it steam and spray until the reservoir is empty. The iron will be as good as new.

Purify the Sole

❑ To clean the surface of an iron that doesn't have a nonstick coating, turn the iron on. While it's warming, place a brown paper bag on the ironing board and sprinkle table salt on it. When the iron is hot, run it over the salt. This will gently scrub the soleplate clean. Let

Start a Lint-Lease Program for the Birds

Here's a novel and practical outdoor tree decoration that's best created whenever birds are building nests in your neck of the woods.

Ransack the laundry room and your sewing basket to find material that you can convert into 3-inch squares of mesh. Consider cheesecloth, old mesh tank tops or beach cover-ups, mesh grocery bags, scraps from mesh coverings for sponges, or defunct goldfish or fishing nets. The idea is to get material with holes that are large enough to let pieces of lint through but small enough that the lint won't fall out in huge hunks. Lint? Yes, that will provide the stuffing for these "ornaments," which will give birds soft material for their nests.

Wrap a small amount of lint from the clothes dryer in each square of mesh, then tie it with a scrap of ribbon, colored thread, or string. Use more string to fasten it to an outdoor tree branch, high enough from the ground so that birds that light won't be attacked by local cats. You've just given your feathered friends the perfect nesting insulation.

the iron cool, then wipe off any residual salt with a damp cloth.

Add Starch to Your Ironing Diet

❏ Here's a recipe your grandmother might have used to starch your grandfather's collars. Make your own spray starch by mixing approximately 1 tablespoon cornstarch and ¾ cup cool water. Using a spray bottle, spritz the mixture on your clothes as you iron. Give the bottle a shake every so often to keep the starch in solution. The more you spray, the more stiffly starched the garment will be.

The Living Room and Family Room

Whether your living room and family room are two separate rooms or combined into one, decorating this special part of your home needn't be a daunting task. You can furnish attractively on a budget (use an old trunk as a coffee table), add accents with a personal touch (display favorite photos in an old window frame), and bring outdoor objects inside for a pleasant surprise (turn a wooden ladder into an indoor trellis for your favorite ivy). And if everything doesn't look quite perfect to begin with, well, we'll tell you how to take care of the scratch in the end table, the spot on the wall-to-wall carpeting, and even the blister in that veneer.

Remember, the most attractive rooms are those you've decorated yourself. They are the most personal, the most unusual, the most welcoming. As for the fact that those decorations are also the least stressful on the budget—well, just think of that as a bonus.

WALL DECORATIONS

Be a Shutterbug

❏ Create an interesting accent for a wall in your living room or family room by hanging up a pair of old, weather-beaten wooden shutters—perhaps a pair that's been hiding in the back of the garage. They're sure to spark conversation among your guests.

The Living Room and Family Room

Go for a Photo Finish

❏ To dress up an old wooden picture frame that's seen better days, try this technique. First, remove the glass from the frame. Now, working with leftover gift wrap or wallpaper, cut a strip to exactly cover each piece of wood in the frame. Glue the strips in place. Wait for the glue to dry, then paint over the paper with clear varnish to protect the paper and give the frame a more finished look. Let the varnish dry, then reinsert your photo and the glass. Your special picture is ready to hang.

Cut a window in your mat to let each photo show through, and glue the photo in place behind the mat (A). Then mount the mats in the spaces of an old window frame (B).

Frame to Please

❏ Need a picture frame for several favorite vacation photos or pictures of the grandkids? Turn an old wooden window frame—one with several "lights," or openings—into a picture frame without even using glass. First, measure each frame opening. Next, choose construction paper, poster board, a colorful department store shopping bag—whatever nice paper you have on hand—for your homemade mats. If the paper is lightweight, glue it on top of a sheet of cardboard to increase its strength. Place each photo on the back of its mat, exactly in the spot where you want the image to show through. Trace the edges of the photo with a pencil and cut a window in the mat, making the window fall one-eighth inch inside

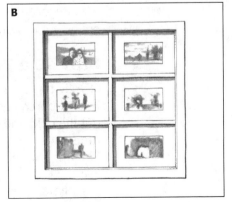

Items the Retired Athlete Can Display on the Wall

Got a sports enthusiast in your family? If so, your house may be filled to the rafters with retired equipment—stuff that your sports buff no longer uses but can't part with. Instead of having a yard sale, hang these relics of glory days on the wall of your family room or living room as part of your decorating scheme. Any of these will enhance your home's decor.

1. Canoe or kayak paddles
2. Tennis rackets
3. Golf clubs
4. Snowshoes
5. Hockey sticks
6. Old bridles and crops
7. Fishing rods and lures
8. Baseball hats
9. Skis

your penciled photo outline. To make a precise cut, use sharp scissors, a single-edge razor blade, or a knife. Now glue the front of the picture to the back of the mat so that you look through the opening to the image.

Secure the mat to the window frame with tiny nails such as brads or even thumbtacks. Repeat the process for each picture. Now tap an old serrated picture hook into the back of the window frame and hang your masterpiece with pride.

Combine Photos and Fabric

❏ Alternatively, glue or staple fabric to a sheet of cardboard to create a mat for each photo. There's no rule that says all the mats have to be alike. For a truly special wall decoration, have fun using up scraps of fabric to create a crazy quilt and photo display all in one.

Provide a Bit of Yankee Comfort

❏ A living room with a glass door opening onto an unheated porch can get mighty chilly in the winter. Keep out the cold and give the room some color at the same time by tacking a comforter to a broomstick and hanging the whole thing over the door. Come spring, just take your makeshift insulation down, roll it up, and store it away for next year.

Wall Decorations

Dress Up Your Living Space

❏ Looking for an attractive way to show off your collection of antique clothing? Remember, a "collection" doesn't have to be expensive. Great-Grandma's old dresses from that trunk in the attic will do very nicely. All you need is an old wooden curtain rod mounted on the wall of your living room or family room. Just slide the arms of each dress, coat, or shirt onto the rod and bunch them together a little. Then hang up your display. Wouldn't Great-Grandma be surprised?

The Living Room and Family Room

Here's a Blue-Ribbon Idea

❏ Got an athlete in your family who brings home ribbons from competitions? Don't hide them, hang them. Create a border around your family room by hanging the ribbons, evenly spaced, on the walls near the ceiling. Clear fishing line, anchored at each end by tacks, will make a good hanger.

WINDOW TREATMENTS

Your Best Bet?
Two Sheets to the Wind(ow)

❏ Don't want to pay for custom-made draperies? Look in the linen closet. A nice pair of flat sheets can be turned into curtains with ease. Just measure your window and the sheets. Next, look at the way the top edge of each sheet (the edge closest to your pillow) is put together. If there's an opening along the side, you're in luck. All you have to do is slide a curtain rod through this ready-made pocket. And if the length is right, you may not even need to hem the bottom.

If the edge is stitched shut, don't despair. Turn the top edge down, along the reverse side of the sheet, about three to five inches. If you are sewing by hand, just hem the turned-down edge to the sheet and slide your curtain rod through the opening in the side. If you are using a sewing machine, you may want to stitch a channel along the turned-down flap wide enough to accommodate your curtain rod while leaving a ruffle above.

Tie back your new homemade curtains with strips of fabric cut from pillowcases that match or complement

The Living Room and Family Room

the sheets. Screw a cup hook into the trim on each side of the window. Then grab four paper clips from your desk drawer. Hand-stitch one end of a paper clip to each end of each fabric strip, about one-half inch from the edge (so that part of the paper clip is hidden from view). Wrap your new ties around the curtains, slipping the paper clips onto the cup hooks.

Branch Out

❏ If you're lucky enough to live in an area where you can forage for dead birch branches, take a walk in the woods and pick up a few to use as rustic curtain rods in your living room or family room. (This works best with curtains that hang by tabs rather than traditional rod pockets. Look for branches that are slender enough to slide easily through the tabs.) Remove protrusions that may snag the fabric, but leave the bark intact; its silvery hue will enhance the color of your curtains. Rest the branch on a pair of old wooden or iron mounts. Or take a pair of old spoons, drill a hole in each one near the end of the handle, and bend it into a U shape. Screw both to the wall or wood trim as mounts. This is a good approach for informal settings such as summer camps.

❏ If you don't live in birch country but still want that rustic look, search for several dead branches of uniform size. Break off any protrusions along the branches so they will slide easily through curtain tabs or rod pockets.

Get Caught on the Beltway

❏ Pluck your old costume jewelry necklaces and chain belts out of the bureau drawer and use them to tie back curtains in your living room or

---

If the Sheet Fits, Hang It Up

Not sure whether those extra sheets are the right size for the window you're decorating? Sizes vary somewhat from one manufacturer to another, but here are some general guidelines.

Twin: 70 inches wide by 96 inches long

Full: 81 inches wide by 96 inches long

Queen: 90 inches wide by 102 inches long

King: 108 inches wide by 102 inches long

When measuring your sheets for width, keep in mind that a pair of curtains should be twice as wide as the window to allow for gathering.

Window Treatments

A Room by Any Other Name . . .

Before 1700, many American homes didn't have separate rooms for entertaining guests. In fact, most families lived in two cramped rooms. But during the eighteenth century, the idea of the "best room" evolved—a room where families could greet guests and host formal gatherings such as wedding receptions, christening parties, and funerals—much like today's living room. They also wanted to be comfortable. So the family parlor, or "back" parlor, emerged as a room for everyday use. Here, family members read and sewed by the fire or visited with their closest friends, just as they do today.

family room. Choose similar styles—they don't have to match—and loop one around each curtain. Then secure each one to the wall or woodwork just as you would a standard fabric curtain tieback.

Be a Scarving Artist

❏ Tie your curtains back with old silk scarves or cotton bandannas. You don't need a matching pair—just choose two that have complementary fabrics, colors, or patterns. Secure them to the wall or woodwork with tacks that are hidden beneath the folds of fabric.

Hang Up the Tools

❏ Fill your family room with country charm by making curtain rods from long-handled lawn or household tools. Slide a pair of tab-style curtains onto a handle cut from a broom, hoe, rake, or the like. Then set the improvised rod on a pair of wooden or wrought iron curtain rod mounts above the window. If necessary, prevent the rod from slipping out of the mount by securing it with twine, household wire, or leather shoelaces. If you don't have suitable curtain rod mounts on

The Living Room and Family Room

hand, make your own out of a pair of old spoons. Drill a hole in each spoon, placing the hole near the end of the handle, then bend the spoon into a U shape to hold your new rod. Mount each spoon with a screw on the window trim or wall.

Tell a New Leatherstocking Tale

❏ Tie back the curtains in your living room or family room with a pair of old leather shoelaces. Mount a cup hook or thumbtack on the window trim or wall to secure each lace. If the laces are a bit dry, you may want to recondition them first by rubbing them with a little olive oil. Be sure to rub it in thoroughly so that you don't end up with oil all over the curtains.

FIREPLACES AND WOODSTOVES

Notify the Next of Kindling

❏ If you're looking for a kindling container, try a flowerpot. Place one next to the woodstove or fireplace and fill it with sticks of wood, ready to use anytime you want to light a fire.

Rock the Cradle

❏ Where can you keep firewood when it's not in the fireplace or woodstove? Try an old-fashioned wooden cradle (doll size for kindling, full size for logs). Rest your quaint container right by the hearth.

OTHER DECORATING TOUCHES

What's Cooking?

❏ Looking for a heavy-duty holder for all those magazines, catalogs, and newspapers? An old enamelware cooking pot (especially the kind with a spatterware design) can do effective duty outside the kitchen if it's big enough. Slide the pot under a coffee table or end table, where it's out of the way but easy to reach, and pile your publications in it.

❏ Alternatively, put your periodicals in an old lobster pot. Or use an old wooden cradle.

Pack It In

❏ If magazines, newspapers, and toys seem to be scattered around your living room or family room, contain them with those old wooden packing crates that have been stacked in your basement. Dust off the crates, rub a little lemon oil into the wood with a rag, then fill them with all that stuff.

❏ Another approach is to use an old wooden picnic basket. The basket has an added benefit: Once you close the lid, all the clutter is hidden.

Try a Little Flower Power

❏ Need a place to toss your trash? A large ceramic or porcelain flowerpot works well as an attractive wastebasket in your living room or family room. Or use a

The Living Room and Family Room

10 Bookends You Don't Have to Buy

You needn't buy expensive bookends to hold your tomes together on the shelf. Instead, rummage around the house for items that are weighty and attractive. You're bound to come up with something more unusual than those brass numbers you see in catalogs and department stores. Here are a few ideas.

1. Small jars filled with beads, shells, marbles, or colored sand
2. Decorative beer steins
3. Ceramic pitchers
4. Crockery
5. Duck decoys
6. Piggy banks filled with change
7. Small baskets filled with gourds (Shellac the gourds to preserve them.)
8. Doorstops
9. Dolls or teddy bears (Try ones that are tall enough to slide into the bookshelf in a sitting position, with their heads barely touching the bottom of the shelf above.)
10. Stirrups

small wooden packing crate. Place the pot or crate where people can reach it, then toss a crumpled piece of paper into it, so that new guests will know that it is indeed for trash.

Apply to the Ivy League

❏ Turn a discarded wooden ladder into an indoor trellis for ivy. Clean up your ladder, haul it inside, and stand it against a wall in your living room or family room (choose a spot where it will receive light). Wrap the tops of the two rails that stand against the wall with fabric so that the ladder won't damage the paint or wallpaper. Place one or two pots of ivy on the floor at the base of the ladder, then use the ladder to train the ivy upward as it grows. (If your new trellis is too tall for the room, saw it down to size.)

Take Me to Your Ladder

❏ Alternatively, drape quilts, throws, afghans, woven rugs, or other large pieces of fabric over the rungs of your ladder to create a colorful look. This is a great way to store quilts and throws when you aren't using them.

Don't Let Cattails Get Ratty

❏ A bunch of cattails, collected from the wild, makes an attractive addition to the living room or family room.

But how do you preserve them? Just give each cattail a thorough coating of hair spray, and your wild bouquet will last indefinitely.

Put Reading Material on the Rack

❏ Get magazine and catalog clutter off the floor by mounting an old towel rack on the wall, within reach of the couch or an armchair. Hang a selection of current magazines and catalogs on the rack by opening each to the center spread, then draping it over the rack so it hangs from its spine.

Feeling Quilty?

❏ If you want a wider magazine holder, retrieve the quilt rack that's been languishing in the attic. Mount the rack on the family room wall and hang your favorite periodicals from it.

Here's a Jewel

❏ Display your prized collection of shells, marbles, miniature figurines—or anything else you can think of—

9 Reusable Items for Sorting Things Out

If you find clutter creeping into your living room or family room, contain it! Here are just a few of the many household items you can use to stash coasters, matches, cocktail napkins, napkin rings, candles, and other things you want to put your hands on at a moment's notice but don't want scattered around the room. The "hidden" benefit is that all of these storage containers look decorative sitting on a mantel, end table, coffee table, or plant stand, or simply stacked in a corner.

1. Old cigar boxes
2. Baskets that flower arrangements come in (Leave the plastic liners in the baskets. They're great for holding loose stuff.)
3. Laundry baskets or other large baskets, either wicker or plastic
4. Old hatboxes
5. Old drawers from small pieces of furniture
6. Old jewelry boxes
7. Utensil holders, made of wood or basket material
8. Large wooden bowls
9. Old bread boxes

in your grandmother's old glass-top jewelry box. Place the box on your coffee table or an end table, and you can store coasters, cocktail napkins, or fireplace matches in the drawer beneath the display section of the box.

Call the Welcome Wagon

❑ Looking for a playful but attractive place to put your collection of dolls, stuffed animals, or antique toys? Roll a child's wagon—metal or wooden—into the family room or living room and arrange your childhood treasures in it.

Try a Win-Some Solution

❑ A collection of games and puzzles tends to grow as a family grows, and it can be tough to cram all those odd-size boxes into the hall closet—let alone get at the one you want to pull out later. Forget the "games closet." Instead, bring that cast-off wooden snow sled down from the attic and place it on an old rug (so the runners won't leave rust stains on the carpet) in a corner of the family room. Plunk the games on top, and they'll be ready when you are.

Stand Tall

❑ To get your collection of framed photos out where you and your guests can enjoy them, place them on a plant stand—wooden, iron, or wicker—in the living room or family room.

Engage in Child's Play

❑ Once your children are grown, use their old kid-size table and chairs to display collectibles in your living room or family room. It's a charming way to show off dolls, teddy bears, miniature china, and so forth.

My Way

Block–And Tackle

My three boys are pretty tough on toys. They also drink a lot of fruit juice. So when I wanted a set of lightweight blocks for them to play with, I started collecting the heavy-duty cardboard boxes that hold a dozen of those individual juice drinks. I taped the boxes shut with duct tape and had instant blocks. They're so sturdy the kids can even stand on them.

–Jackie Cahill
North Hampton, New Hampshire

MULTIPURPOSE ROOM DIVIDERS

The Living Room and Family Room

Shutter Up

❏ Separate your living room from your family room with those tall wooden shutters that have been stacked in your basement for years. Clean them up, repaint them if they need it, and connect each pair with door hinges so that they'll stand on their own. Then place a row of them where you want your room to be divided.

See Things Through

❏ To create a see-through room divider, try cleaning up a few old storm windows and repainting the frames. Then hinge pairs of them together to make a divider of the length you need. They're sturdy enough to stand on their own when angled properly, and they'll add interest to any room.

FOUND FURNITURE

Let the Games Begin

❏ Make an auxiliary end table by placing a heavy game board—such as a marble chessboard or wooden

---

The Inside Story

This Rocker Doesn't Roll

These days, nearly every living room or family room has a rocking chair. But today's chair—a uniquely American piece of furniture—actually started out as a cradle. If babies were comfortable rocking, early Americans reasoned, why not adults? So colonial Americans, including Ben Franklin, experimented until they came up with an upright design that wouldn't flip over. That design—with many variations, of course—has endured for more than two hundred years.

The Living Room and Family Room

checkerboard—on top of a stool or low plant stand that's around 18 inches high. This works best if the top of the stand is wider than the game board so the board isn't easily knocked off.

Bring the Office to the Living Room

❏ Looking for a place in your living room or family room to hide toys, videos, CDs, even hats and mittens? An old wooden filing cabinet—either a short or a tall one—works perfectly. If you use the short type, slide it next to the couch or armchair, and it will double as an end table.

Please Pass the Jelly

❏ To keep videos or CDs organized and contained, store them in an old wooden jelly cupboard. Its tall, narrow shape is perfect for the job.

That's Enter-tunement

❏ Instead of buying a new entertainment center, store your stereo equipment in the lower portion of that old-fashioned dry sink that used to be in the dining room. First, measure the depth of the cupboard to be sure your stereo will fit. Next, determine where, along the back of the cupboard, you want to thread the stereo wires. If it's

Earl's Favorites

She's a Doll

Not so long ago, I heard about a little girl who thinks the way I do when it comes to reusing old things. When her parents bought a new TV that was too large for their old TV cabinet, she piped up, "I know! Let me use the old TV cabinet for my doll clothes! It's just the right size for all my things." Her parents liked the idea, and now it's easy for the girl to pick up her doll clothes and store them behind those cabinet doors.

Found Furniture

4 Great Homes for Your Old Furniture

What can you do with your cast-off furniture? Don't despair. Here are some places that might love to use your comfy but worn couch—or armchair, coffee table, even curtains.

1. Salvation Army. This organization of good Samaritans will actually pick up your used furniture and cart it away, either for charitable donation to someone who needs it or for resale at one of its thrift stores. All you have to do is call (look under Salvation Army in the White Pages of your phone book) and arrange a date and time for pickup.

2. Homeless shelters and shelters for battered women and children. Often these shelters are located in houses or apartment buildings that have common areas—and they need donations of couches, tables, chairs, rugs, even curtains. Look for the appropriate phone numbers in the White Pages under the name of your town, or in the "Community Service Num-

bers" section at the beginning of your phone book. Be sure not to call any emergency numbers. Note that for security reasons, a shelter for battered women and children may not be listed in the phone book. But the mayor's office, police chief, or a pastor may know how to contact a shelter and arrange for delivery or pickup of your donation.

3. Senior centers or youth centers. Either of these may need your living room or family room furniture. Look for appropriate phone numbers in the "Community Service Numbers" section at the beginning of your phone book, or in the White Pages under the name of your town.

4. Offices of nonprofit organizations. A local church or synagogue, or any group with an office and a tight budget, may welcome your donation of furniture for its conference rooms, offices, and the like. Just call the office during regular business hours and ask whether the organization could use your furniture.

truly an old piece of furniture, the back is likely to have knot holes. Perhaps you'll be lucky and the knot holes will be perfectly placed so you can pass the wires through them. Otherwise, you may need to drill a hole

Spit-Backs: A Family Tradition

My family has had a long-standing tradition of trading what my grandmother called "spit-backs," all sorts of items that were passed from one family member to another. Spit-backs were often used for purposes that were entirely different from those for which they were originally intended. My dad used his mother's old rugs to cover ceiling fans in the attic during the winter. I stored office supplies in an antique console table that was once my grandmother's. In our master bathroom, my husband and I hung a carriage lamp that my parents had had made for the exterior of their house.

My home is filled with these things. Recently, an old friend came to visit our new house. As she walked into the living room, she stopped still at the center and looked around. "I feel like I'm standing in your parents' living room," she commented. I laughed. "You should," I replied. "This is all their old stuff!"

–Linda Buchanan Allen
Exeter, New Hampshire

in the back. (Don't do this with a precious antique!) Then slide in the stereo and turn on the tunes.

Not for Medicinal Purposes Only

❏ All those little living room/family room necessities—matches for the fireplace, coasters, candles, light bulbs, even the TV remote—are a tremendous source of clutter if you don't keep them contained. The answer: an old-fashioned wooden medicine cabinet. Hang your cabinet on a wall near the fireplace, TV, or wherever you can reach it easily, and pop all those essential odds and ends inside.

Play Your Trunk Card

❏ Want a coffee table that does double duty as a storage container? Carry that old wooden trunk down from the attic to your living room or family room. Fill it with a combination of toys, games, videos, cocktail napkins, coasters—whatever you want to keep on hand, but hidden.

FURNITURE SCRATCHES AND STAINS

The Living Room and Family Room

Go Nuts over Scratches

❏ While cleaning up after last night's party, you go to clear the last odds and ends off the wooden dinner table and notice a scratch that wasn't there before. You also notice that the only things left in the bowl of party mix you served are the Brazil nuts. The good news is that these little gems are perfect for repairing small scratches in wooden furniture. Simply break open one of the nuts and rub the meat over the scratch so that the oil can mask and repair it.

Cover Those Scratches—With Coffee

❏ To conceal a superficial scratch in an old wooden table, make a thick paste of instant coffee and water, then rub the mixture into the scratch. This is not an appropriate treatment for a family heirloom, but if you need a quick cover-up for a piece that's not tremendously valuable, it's a good approach.

Color inside the Lines

❏ Another way to cover minor scratches in wooden furniture is to go over them with a wax crayon of the appropriate color. Then polish the area with the tip of your finger to blend in the coloring.

Who Forgot to Blow Out the Candles?

❏ If melted wax drips onto a wooden table, get out your iron. Turn it on and, while the iron is heating up, gently peel off as much of the wax as you can. Then place three or four layers of paper towels or brown paper grocery bags on top of the wax that remains. Hold the hot iron half an inch or so over the paper, but don't actually touch the iron to the paper (doing so could burn the sur-

A Different Twist

Edge Out That Candle Wax

If you're stuck with melted candle wax on a wooden table, scrape it off with the edge of a child's wooden building block. Use the sharpest edge to nudge the wax off the surface.

The Living Room and Family Room

face of the table). As the candle wax melts, the paper will absorb it. Remove the paper and repeat the process if necessary.

Don't Hold the Mayo

❏ To remove crayon marks from wooden furniture, head to the refrigerator and grab a jar of mayonnaise. Rub some mayo into the crayon marks. Let it soak in for a few minutes, then rub the area clean with a damp cloth.

Brush Regularly

❏ If you discover a small white stain on the surface of a piece of wooden furniture, get out the toothpaste (not the gel type). Squeeze a dab of paste onto your fingertip and gently rub it into the stain, then wipe the area clean.

---

3 Instant Cover-Ups for Furniture Scratches

What article of furniture doesn't suffer a regrettable scratch or ding from time to time? Cabinets, chairs, and tables often get gouges across prominent surfaces, putting light-colored scars through the varnish and stain. Some clever use of common household materials can often cover up these defects and save you the effort of a total refinishing job. Try these furniture savers, always being careful to test them first in an inconspicuous spot.

Shoe polish. Choose oxblood, or reddish, shoe polish for cherry furniture, tan or natural polish for light wood. For scratches in dark wood, select a polish that matches the lightest tones in the finish. Once you've identified the appropriate color, apply it to the scratch with a cotton swab.

Iodine. For cherry-colored wood, try applying dark iodine (the stuff typically used on cuts) full strength with a small sable artist's brush. For light wood, dilute the iodine by mixing it with an equal amount of denatured alcohol.

Felt-tipped markers. Colored office markers or artist's markers in appropriate shades often come in handy for touching up furniture finishes.

---

106   **Furniture Scratches and Stains**

O Soda Mio

❏ You can also remove a white stain from the surface of wooden furniture by sprinkling baking soda on a damp cloth and rubbing the stain. Then wipe the soda off with a clean cloth.

Put a Little Dressing on That Stain

❏ To treat water rings on shellac, rub the affected area with mayonnaise or salad oil, then leave the "cure" in place overnight. By the next day, the oil in either of these foods will displace the moisture in the ring, causing the unsightly stain to disappear. Just wipe off the excess.

Give Old Paper a Lift

❏ Paper that sits on a piece of furniture for a long time—say, under a lamp—sometimes gets glued to the finish. To remove it, soak the paper with cooking oil, let it sit for five minutes, and carefully lift the paper.

Add a Dash of Salt

❏ When upholstery gets splashed with red wine, cover the fabric immediately with a generous coating of salt. Then blot up the wine and salt and finish up with a sponge dipped in a solution of a gentle laundry soap (such as Woolite) and cool water.

FURNITURE REPAIRS

Try a Joint Resolution

❏ As wooden chairs age, it's very common for the joints between legs and stringers to loosen and come apart. Usually, this happens because the glue has dried out and the wood has shrunk. The solution is to disassemble the joint, clean off all the old glue, and reassemble everything with new glue. However, the repair won't last if the dowel and socket are not a tight fit. To increase the thickness of a dowel that has shrunk over time, wrap it in ordinary cotton kitchen cord—the kind used for trussing up a turkey or roast beef.

The Living Room and Family Room

When You're Strapped for a Clamp

❑ Bungee cords—those large elastic straps with hooks used by backpackers and cyclists—make great light-duty clamps for furniture repairs. They're particularly useful when you're regluing chairs. Bind one or more cords around the legs to keep gentle, constant pressure on the joints while the glue dries.

❑ Alternatively, cut strips of rubber from old bicycle or automobile inner tubes and use those as temporary furniture clamps.

Iberia Was the Mother of Invention

❑ A time-honored device for clamping furniture parts for gluing is a Spanish windlass—which you can easily make from old cloth belts or strips of strong cloth. Just cinch the belt or cloth loosely around the parts to be

Here's a clamp with a special twist. Use a dowel to tighten the strips of your impro-vised clamp and hold the furniture parts securely in place.

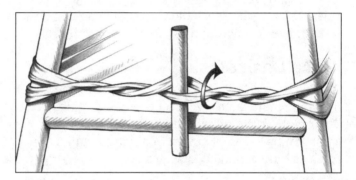

joined, making a continuous loop. Then insert a strong dowel or stick into the loop and carefully tighten it until the parts are under the right pressure. Think in terms of tightening a tourniquet. (You can usually maneuver the stick under another part of the chair or table to secure it.) The windlass is better than an iron clamp because it is light, easily adjusted, and less likely to leave marks in the wood.

Iron Out Veneer Problems

❑ The tops of tables, desks, and sideboards are often made of veneer—that is, a paper-thin sheet of highly de-sirable wood such as walnut that is glued to a less at-tractive, but more stable, material such as plywood.

Through age and use, veneers sometimes pop up in a blister. You can often re-adhere small veneer blisters with an iron. Place a piece of heavy writing paper on the blister. Then gently press the blister flat with a warm iron (don't use any steam). Once the veneer is flat, hold it in place with a heavy weight until it cools. If the underlying glue is still good, the iron will soften it and re-anchor the veneer.

Drag It Out

❑ When doing meticulous wood surfacing—leveling a veneer repair on furniture, for example—one of the best tools you can use is a blade from a drywall knife. Take a fresh blade in two hands and drag it over the wood while keeping the blade perpendicular to the surface. It's better than any sandpaper.

FURNITURE REFINISHING

Spray On, Wipe Off

❑ If the furniture you're restoring has splashes of paint you want to remove, you can probably find an alterna-

The Living Room and Family Room

tive to regular paint stripper right under your kitchen sink. Believe it or not, alkaline-based oven cleaner is an effective paint stripper. The chemicals that soften the old grease in your oven can just as easily soften the oils in old paint. Be sure to observe the cautions on the label and test first to make sure the product does not alter the look of the wood. The cleaner will remove the original finish along with the paint, but hey, you were going to refinish the piece anyway.

8 Helpers Every Refinisher Should Have

The many layers of paint on a piece of antique furniture may conceal fine wood and interesting details. A clear varnish would allow the piece's natural beauty to show through—but first you have to get rid of all that old paint. Just the thought of trying to strip the finish from complicated surfaces—such as concave moldings, turnings, carvings, and other elaborate surfaces—can be enough to move that refinishing project to the bottom of the "Someday I'll Get to It" list. You can't clean these features with a putty knife, and you may damage them in the attempt. But handy Yankees have their ways. Try adding these common household items to your refinishing kit.

1. Old spoons of all sizes and shapes. The bowls of the spoons are great for working on the curves in moldings.
2. Heavy packing cord. Use this to "floss" turnings of all kinds, especially deep insets. Run the cord back and forth along the indentations, just as you would use dental floss between your teeth.
3. Old toothbrushes. They're ideal for all kinds of detail work.
4. Ice pick or awl. These are the universal tools for cleaning hard-to-reach spots.
5. Fruit and shellfish picks. These are terrific for detail picking and scraping.
6. Old dental tools. Hey, they were designed to get into small crevices.
7. Automotive parts–cleaning brushes. They're useful for applying stripper, because the polypropylene bristles won't dissolve in solvents.
8. Plastic food wrap. Placed over applied stripper, it contains the solvent so that it won't evaporate prematurely.

Scrub It—Don't Scar It

❏ Sometimes in the process of cleaning or lightly refinishing varnished or painted furniture, you want a little gentle abrasion on the surface—either to remove encrusted dirt or to deglaze the finish in preparation for the next coat. Try rubbing the surface with fireplace ashes, toothpaste (not the gel type), or baking soda on a clean cotton cloth. Any of these will provide the abrasion you need without roughing things up too much.

The Living Room and Family Room

Work with Sandpaper in the Round

❏ It can be tricky using a flat piece of sandpaper to get the old finish off a rounded surface. A better idea? Cut a slit down the length of a six-inch section of garden hose. Wrap a sheet of sandpaper around the cylinder, inserting the ends into the slit. Secure the whole thing with a narrow strip of duct tape and start sanding.

CARPETING

Take Time for That Nap

❏ You recently moved a heavy piece of furniture from its long-standing place in the living room or family room, leaving the carpet nap flattened where the furniture used to stand. No problem—just place an ice cube or two on the matted area before you go to bed, and by morning the nap should be as fluffy as ever.

Oh, Those Ink Spots!

❏ Somebody's pen leaked on the carpet. Sprinkle the ink stains with cream of tartar, then with lemon juice. Let the mixture sit for one to two minutes, then remove it by rubbing gently with a clean scrub brush. Follow up by dampening a sponge with warm water and blotting the spot. (Don't saturate it.) Repeat if necessary.

Squeeze the Fruit Juice Out of the Rug

❏ Did someone spill fruit juice on the living room rug? Head for the medicine cabinet and grab the shaving cream. Squirt just a dab into your hand, then spread it over the stain. Let it sit for a few minutes, then dampen a sponge with water and dab the shaving cream with it. Repeat if necessary, but take care to use as little shaving cream as possible each time, so that you don't create a new stain.

Solve This Pet Problem

❑ Your young puppy or aging kitty has had an accident on the carpet, and you're worried about urine stains.

First, blot the dampened area as much as possible with dry paper towels. Next, combine 1 tablespoon white vinegar and 2 tablespoons dishwashing liquid. After testing first in an inconspicuous area to be sure your treatment won't discolor the rug, dab the mixture onto the stain with a damp sponge. Let it sit for 15 to 20 minutes, then use a sponge dampened with warm water to get up any residue. Be sure to blot, not rub, to avoid further damaging the carpet.

The Living Room and Family Room

OTHER CLEANING

Dust Off Your Wardrobe Rejects

❑ There's nothing better for dusting and polishing furniture than soft cloths, and some of the softest cloths around are pieces of old clothing. You probably already save old diapers and T-shirts—especially those made of 100 percent cotton—and recycle them for housecleaning. But have you thought about holding on to all-cotton gloves and socks? Turn these inside out and slip them over your hands; they make wonderful dust mitts.

It's a Close Shave

❑ Dust your delicate collectibles—such as figurines, dolls, antique toys, and miniature china—with an old-fashioned shaving brush. The bristles are soft and will gently remove dust from the crevices.

Brush Up Your Dusting Skills

❑ For a quick duster that will get into small spaces, grab an old paintbrush. Choose the size according to the task, and you'll have an effective cleaning tool for everything from knickknacks to pleated lamp shades.

My Way

Little Drummer Girl

One day, when a friend of mine came to play, we wanted a set of drums. So we found a couple of empty cardboard shoe boxes for drums and some sticks in the backyard for drumsticks. Then my friend had another bright idea: He popped the legs off a Barbie and used them as drumsticks! Now I play my shoe box drums all the time—but I still use the sticks from the backyard.

—Tegan Wedge (age nine)
Weston, Massachusetts

The Living Room and Family Room

At Last You Have Permission to Write on Walls

❏ If you have a gouge or mark in patterned wallpaper, you don't need to call an expert. Instead, take those fine-tipped markers out of the kitchen or office drawer and make the repair yourself. Choose colors that most closely match the colors in your wallpaper and carefully fill in the problem. No one will ever notice.

Color It Repaired

❏ For damaged areas that need a white fill-in, try the white correction fluid designed for office use.

A Different Twist

Tickle Those Ivories— With Yogurt

Don't let yellowed piano keys give you the blues. Just grab a container of plain yogurt from the refrigerator, use a clean rag to spread it in a thin layer over the keys, and wipe it off with another rag. You'll be amazed at the difference.

You Didn't Want Faces on Those Wallpaper Flowers?

❏ Did a young family member or visitor get a little carried away with his crayons and decide to improve on your wallpaper? Not to fear! Just heat the wax with a blow dryer, then wipe it away once it has softened.

Get That Grease

❏ To clean grease spots off wallpaper, gently rub talcum powder on the spot, using your finger or a clean cloth. Repeat as necessary. This will work not only on vinyl wallpaper but also on more fragile wallpaper that's actually made of paper.

Gone with the Wind(ows)

❏ Wipe your windows squeaky clean with a little vinegar on a clean cotton rag. You'll get a clear, streak-free finish.

Spread the Good News

❏ To brighten up dingy mirrors or windows, crumple up yesterday's newspaper and rub it vigorously over the glass. The ink in the newsprint will act as a cleaning agent on the glass.

Where There's Smoke, There's Staining

❏ Are smoke stains marring your old marble mantelpiece? Make a thick poultice of baking soda and water, smear it over the stains, and wipe it off. Buff the area with a clean, dry cloth if necessary.

Brass: Apply Ketchup with Relish

❏ Polish tarnished brass candlesticks—or brass hardware on furniture—with ketchup. Rub the ketchup onto the brass with a cloth, then wipe it off. Buff with a soft, dry cloth.

Unwax Those Floors

❏ Banish built-up wax from wood floors with paint thinner. Make sure the room is well-ventilated before you begin this process. Wipe a small area of the floor with a rag moistened with paint thinner, then dry the area with another rag. Work on one small area at a time, so that you can apply the thinner and wipe it off before it dries.

Radiators: Let Off Steam

❏ If your old steam radiator has a clogged valve, clean it with vinegar. First, shut off the valve, then turn it counterclockwise to remove it. Place the valve in a pan of vinegar and boil it on top of the stove for 20 minutes. By then, the calcium deposits blocking the valve will have dissolved.

The Living Room and Family Room

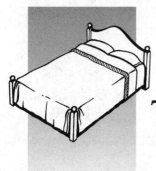

The Bedroom

M ost of the people who visit your house won't see your bedroom, but you still want its decor to express your special quirks and passions. How can you create a unique, comfortable room without breaking the bank? It's simple: Decorate and furnish with a personal touch, using things you already own. A wooden stool can become a nightstand, a picket fence can simulate a headboard, and a piano bench can be turned into a luggage rack. After all, what could be cozier and more personal than treasured items that you've been holding on to forever?

Once you've prettied things up, you'll need to get them organized. In the following pages, you'll find plenty of quick and easy ways to straighten out those drawers and closets, and even to double their storage capacity. We offer ideas for polishing up your fashion image, too. Before you're through, both the room and your wardrobe will be completely rejuvenated. And *then* we'll tell you how an old tennis ball can help you deal with that problem snorer who shares your bed.

DECORATING IN GENERAL

Climb the Ladder of Decorating Success

The Bedroom

❏ Here's a unique way to feature the family photos in your bedroom. Hang a small wooden ladder on a blank wall, using heavy-duty hooks screwed into the studs. Then hang one or two framed photos inside the "frames" made by the ladder rungs.

❏ Alternatively, hang dried flower wreaths, small wall hangings, or other decorative pieces inside the "frames" of the ladder.

Slide into Home Plate

❏ Display framed family photos on a dresser or night-stand by standing them on old wooden plate holders. Your pictures will appear more prominent and precious.

Stainless? It's a Steal

❏ If you like to display fresh flowers on your dresser or nightstand, try putting them in a vase that's a little different. Get out that old stainless steel thermos that's been hiding in the kitchen cabinet. Add water and arrange your flowers in it. You'll enjoy the bright colors of spring and summer against the soft patina of the old thermos.

Tea Up

❏ Alternatively, collect fresh flowers in a dainty ceramic or porcelain teapot, placed on your dresser or nightstand.

It Gives a Whole New Meaning to "Pushpins"

❏ Brighten up a bedroom throw pillow with costume jewelry pins—especially vintage ones you've had around for a long time. Arrange as

My Way

Tea for Two

I love to use baskets to store and display things around my bedroom. I have a couple of special dolls and a miniature china tea service, so I propped my dolls inside a flat-bottomed basket and set the tea service in the middle. People of all ages love my tea party in a basket!

–Lynne C. Beach
South Hampton, New Hampshire

Ringing In a New Day

The very first alarm clock in America was invented by a New Hampshire clock maker named Levi Hutchins in 1787. It was 29 inches high and 14 inches wide, with a pine case that had a mirror at the door. It looked much more like a grandfather clock than a modern bedside alarm. Hutchins rigged the alarm to go off at four o'clock each day, a time that could not be changed. He had no interest in selling his invention; he used it solely to wake himself for work—and that meant four o'clock every morning.

It's probably good that Hutchins didn't dream of a great market for alarm clocks. It wasn't until the late 1800s that people woke up to the idea of getting out of bed at an exact time every day. As factory jobs proliferated, so did the need to be up and out of the house at a certain time. In 1876, Seth Thomas in Thomaston, Connecticut, designed the first windup alarm clock. Unfortunately, the snooze button didn't come along for another century.

many pins as you like on the face of the pillow, fastening them securely in place so nobody gets jabbed. Don't worry, you can still wear the pins—just remove one when you want to spruce up an outfit and reattach it to the pillow when you're through. Your pillow will be not only decorative but also a great storage place for your pins.

Start a Cover-Up

❏ It's your prerogative to move photos, mirrors, and paintings from place to place on your bedroom walls. But if you don't like the tiny holes left in plain view, and if your walls are white, borrow an idea from renters trying to collect their deposit money: plain white toothpaste. Carefully squeeze a dab of it on your finger or onto a cotton swab, then fill the hole with it. Use a damp sponge to wipe off any that gets on the wall. The repair won't stand up to close scrutiny, but it will look perfectly fine from a few feet away.

The Bedroom

BUREAUS

Turn Back the Clock with a Teapot

❑ Going for a Victorian look in your bedroom? Create an "instant antique" runner for a dresser from a stained white linen napkin, scrap of white tablecloth, or white cloth place mat that has seen better days. Get an old-time look by steeping 3 tea bags in 2 cups boiling water for 20 minutes, then soaking your material in the mixture for 10 minutes. Wring it out, let it line dry, and iron it flat or leave it romantically crumpled.

Uno, Dos, Trays

❑ Collect clutter and protect the surface of your bureau from dings and scratches by placing a serving tray on top. That way, if you toss loose change, a hairbrush, or cuff links on the dresser, they won't slide off or nick the wood finish.

This Susan Isn't Lazy

❑ To keep odds and ends under control and save the surface of your dresser at the same time, put a lazy Susan from the kitchen to work in the bedroom. Place

---

8 Places to Toss Loose Change

When you empty your pockets at the end of the day, where do you drop those pennies, nickels, dimes, and quarters that you've accumulated? Instead of scattering them all over the top of your bureau, plunk them in an unusual container. Here are a few ideas.

1. Empty flowerpot
2. Antique teacup
3. Candy dish
4. Old-fashioned jelly glass
5. Porcelain soap dish
6. Ceramic ashtray
7. Large seashell from your last trip to the shore
8. Souvenir coffee mug

The Bedroom

the lazy Susan in the center of your dresser and arrange containers—perhaps a collection of old mugs that you're no longer using in the kitchen—on top. Use the containers to hold loose change, jewelry, cosmetics, and so forth. Just spin the lazy Susan around to reach any item you want.

Toss the Salad

❏ Toss shoulder pads, socks, and the like in a large stoneware mixing bowl or wooden salad bowl on top of your dresser. Or hide the bowl on a closet shelf.

It's Like Living in a Fishbowl

❏ Pop hair scrunchies or shoulder pads in a clear glass goldfish bowl on your dresser or a shelf in the bedroom. The bowl's shape will keep items from escaping, and

---

5 Uses for an Old Pillowcase

Does that Spiderman pillowcase seem a little dated now that Junior has graduated from high school? Just because it's seen its last pillow fight doesn't mean it is ready for the ragbag. On the contrary, here are just a few of the many ways you can still use it.

1. Laundry bag when traveling. It keeps the dirty clothes away from the clean ones and, unlike plastic bags, lets fabrics breathe.
2. Picnic bib for a young child. Open the seam opposite the end that's already open and pop it over the youngster's head so it rests on her shoulders. *Now* give her that ice cream cone.
3. Dustcover for a computer or other electronic equipment. Unlike plastic, it won't hold in the heat.
4. Stuff sack for a sleeping bag or other camping gear. If you want to get fancy, knot together a pair of shoelaces from old hiking boots and thread them through the hem of the pillowcase for a drawstring.
5. Container for a hard-to-wrap gift. Just plunk that soccer ball or bicycle helmet inside, gather the top together with a colorful bow, and hand it over.

---

you'll be able to see what you want to retrieve without having to fish around.

Be Letter-Perfect

❏ Catch hair accessories, stray buttons, and such in a wooden letter box or mailbox mounted on the closet wall or on a wall near your dresser. They'll be out of the way but still handy when you need them.

Have Buckets of Fun

❏ Collect hair accessories and other odds and ends in children's cast-off plastic sand buckets. Keep the buckets on a closet shelf, on your bureau, or wherever you want to be able to reach them easily.

❏ Alternatively, use one of those plastic sand buckets to store your cosmetics. The handle makes it easy for you to carry the bucket back and forth to the bathroom if necessary.

Scrunch Up

❏ Use hair scrunchies to keep pairs of socks together in the bureau drawer. Just wrap a scrunchie around each pair of socks. If you're especially fashion conscious, wrap a color-coordinated scrunchie around each pair. That way you can grab both in the morning when you're on the run.

Comb Your Hair, Wash Your Vase

❏ Don't like to fumble in your drawer for your comb and brush when you need them quickly? "Plant" them in a ceramic or porcelain flower vase on top of your dresser. The vase will add a charming touch, and you'll be able to grab your comb and brush in a hurry.

Let's Do Lunch

❏ Collect bedroom necessities in an old lunch box—especially if you still have a metal one from your childhood—and display the box on your dresser or nightstand. If the box isn't particularly decorative, keep it on a closet shelf or in a dresser drawer.

The Bedroom

Out Go the Knives, In Go the Nail Files

❏ Keep necessities in order with a plastic kitchen utensil tray in your dresser drawer. Put a comb and brush, hair accessories, or costume jewelry in each of the compartments and slide your drawer shut. When you open the drawer again, everything will be in plain sight instead of in one mishmash at the back.

Chip In for Off-Season Storage

❏ You could spend seven or eight bucks on cedar blocks to mothproof your sweater drawer or chest, but why do that when you can create the same effect for free? If you're a pet owner, you probably already have a few spare cedar chips—the kind sold in pet stores—lying around. Make a cedar sachet for your closets or chests by wrapping the cedar chips in cheesecloth or scraps of cotton cloth. Or plunk the cedar in the foot cut off an old pair of pantyhose. Place a small handful in the middle of the fabric and tie it up with some twine, ribbon, or yarn, or with another scrap of fabric. Change the chips every three to four months, and store the leftovers in a tightly sealed plastic bag or plastic container. The moths won't like it, but your sweaters will.

Eliminate the Sticking Points

❏ The next time the squeaking and sticking of a wooden drawer has you ready to pull out your hair, grab one of those old candle stubs that you couldn't quite bear to throw out and rub it along the underside of the drawer. That will keep it from sticking and will eliminate the squeaking.

Dress Up Your Drawers

❏ Cover up wear and tear on flat-front dresser drawers with leftover wallpaper, either from the bedroom or from another room. Measure, apply, and trim the wallpaper around the knobs and front of each drawer, just as you would when papering a wall. (Don't do this with a valuable antique!)

BEDS

Slumber under the Big Top

❑ Evoke the romance of a canopy bed without buying new furniture. Instead, make your own canopy from full-length draperies. Note that this procedure works best if you can push your bed sideways against a wall. First, take a spare hook designed to hold a hanging plant and screw it into the ceiling directly above the center of the bed. Bunch the top of one drape together in your hand and wrap a piece of wire tightly around the bunched fabric. Repeat the process with the other drape. Now thread a third piece of wire through the wires holding the drapes, looping it through several times and pulling it tight to hold the two drape tops together. Tie a wide fabric bow around the drapes so that the bow hides the wire. Loop a final piece of wire through the knot of the bow and slip it onto the ceiling hook. Spread your canopy over the head and foot of the bed, draping the ends over the headboard and footboard. If your headboard and footboard are too low (or if you don't have either), screw coat hooks into the wall to hold up the fabric ends, creating a framing effect. The

Secure the bunched-together top of a drape with wire. Repeat with a second drape, then wire the two together (A). Cover the wire with a fabric bow (B). Hang the beribboned piece from the ceiling and extend the ends of the drapes over the head and foot of the bed (C).

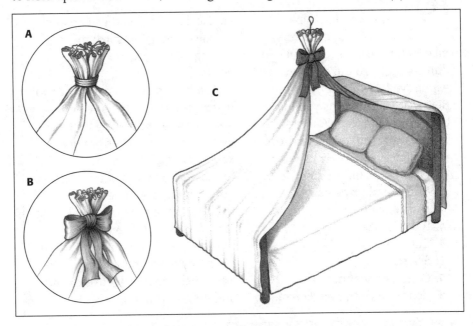

The Bedroom

draperies won't cover the whole bed, but they will suggest the cozy illusion of a full canopy.

And You'll Be All Set for Breakfast in Bed

❏ Make a luscious-looking bed by draping a clean fabric tablecloth over the blankets or on top of a plain bedspread. For an unusually palatable bedcover, place a round tablecloth at the center of the bed on top of another bedspread.

HEADBOARDS

Go to the Head of the Class

❏ Want a headboard with country style—without setting foot in an expensive furniture store? Cut a length of picket fence that's left over from your fencing project. (You can match the length of the picket fence to the width of the bed or make it longer, depending on your

---

10 Objects You Can Use to Make Throw Pillows

You want to whip together a few throw pillows for the bedroom, but you don't want to go out and buy expensive fabric. No problem! Below are a few items you may be ready to toss out. You can recycle them into pillows instead.

1. T-shirts
2. Oxford or flannel shirts
3. Bedspread (especially a chenille one)
4. Baby blanket
5. Curtains
6. Silk scarves
7. Cotton bandannas
8. Cotton or linen handkerchiefs
9. Neckties (Open these up and lay them flat to stitch them together.)
10. Tablecloth

Making a pillow is easy. Cut two pieces of fabric to the size you want. (If you are piecing together items such as neckties or handkerchiefs, stitch these together to make two pieces of the appropriate size.) Sew three edges together to form a pocket, with the fabric inside out. Then turn the pocket right side out and fill it with old panty hose, socks, rags, or the like. Stitch the fourth edge closed and fluff up your pillow.

Headboards

Earl's Favorites

Wake Up and Smell the Coffee

I love stories of efficiency, so I got a kick out of hearing about a couple who used to hate waking up to the blare of the alarm clock or clock radio in the morning. They took the coffeemaker from the kitchen, fixed coffee each night so it was ready to brew, and put the contraption on their nightstand. Their machine had a timer, so they set it for the time they wanted to wake up. (If your machine isn't that fancy, you could just plug it into an ordinary timer switch—the kind made to turn lights on and off at a certain time.) Now they wake up every morning to the smell of fresh coffee.

personal preference.) Clean it up and repaint it if you want, then secure it to the wall behind the head of your bed with screws or nails.

Pick the Lattice from Your Garden

❏ Enjoy sweet dreams of sleeping in a garden when you make a headboard from a leftover piece of garden trellis or lattice from your yard. Start with a piece that's at least as wide as the bed, wider if you prefer. Clean the wood and paint or stain it if you wish, then secure it to the wall behind the head of your bed with nails or screws. Add dried flowers at strategic spots if you want to dress things up a bit.

Bulletin! You're Not Bored

❏ Organize your busy life with a headboard made from a bulletin board. Just grab the corkboard you used to keep in the kitchen or office and mount it above the head of your bed. Post notes to yourself, a calendar, sale coupons, even cartoons or sayings you like to keep on hand, and you'll be reminded of many daily details before you drift off to sleep or as soon as you wake up. A

3 Great Homes for Old Blankets and Bedspreads

The kids have grown up and moved out, so you're turning their room into a guest room with a somewhat more sophisticated decor. Or you've moved to a smaller home with fewer bedrooms than your old home had. Whatever the reason, you've wound up with blankets and bedspreads you no longer need but you don't want to throw away. The Salvation Army and Goodwill are always looking for these items, but following are some other charitable organizations that also would welcome your donations. Before you call, make sure your blankets and bedspreads are clean and in excellent condition.

1. American Red Cross. The Red Cross conducts relief efforts all over the world and very likely has a chapter in your state. Call the office nearest to you and ask whether they need donations of bedspreads or blankets. (Look under American Red Cross in the White Pages of your phone book.)

2. Homeless shelters. Many need extra blankets and bedspreads. To make a donation, call the shelter for an appointment. (Look for the phone number in the White Pages under the name of your town, or in the "Community Service Numbers" section at the beginning of your phone book. Be sure not to call any emergency numbers.)

3. Churches or synagogues. Many accept donations of items to help families or individuals in need. To find out whether your blankets and bedspreads can be used, call a church or synagogue office during regular business hours (Monday through Friday).

side benefit: When thoughts of all those details keep you awake, you can just jot down a quick list, tack it on your headboard, and forget about it until tomorrow.

NIGHTSTANDS

Store It Again, Sam

❑ An old piano bench makes a great nightstand. If you limit the items you keep on top, you can easily store books and magazines inside, keeping the clutter out of sight but the reading materials at the ready.

Go Back to Stool

❏ Need a nightstand for a tight space? Try a wooden stool that's 18 to 30 inches high (a full-size bar stool will probably be too tall). If your stool is a bit the worse for wear, or if you want a softer look, drape a piece of fabric over the seat before you place your alarm clock and other items on it.

Don't Shoo This Shoe from the Table

❏ If you're one of those people who likes to have a glass of water on the nightstand but don't want to worry about jostling it or constantly leaving water rings on the wood finish, consider making a nightstand drink holder from . . . a shoe. A low-top tennis shoe or a lady's flat shoe with fairly rigid sides will work well. Just polish or machine-wash it, then cut a shoe liner–size scrap of towel to fit inside. If the shoe has laces, discard them and turn the tongue out. Choose a glass that the shoe will hold snugly but that will come out easily. If you like, hot-glue buttons, shells, or beads to the shoe in a decorative pattern that matches your bedroom decor.

❏ What if the shoe is intended to hold liquids for a youngster who's stuck in bed with the flu or chickenpox and could use some cheering up? Use a canvas shoe and ask a group of young friends to autograph the drink holder with an indelible marker.

FURNITURE ACCESSORIES

Create a Smoke-Free, Scratch-Free Zone

❏ If your four-poster or claw-footed bed rests on a hardwood floor, don't seek out special floor protector disks to keep the legs from scratching the floor. Instead, dig up all the cheap aluminum ashtrays you used to pick up at fast-food restaurants or trade shows when you were still smoking. Slip one under each foot, and your floor will be scratch-free.

The Bedroom

❑ Alternatively, use old soft drink coasters under the bedposts to protect the floor from scratches. Or substitute the lids from tubs of soft margarine or old 3½-inch computer disks.

Consider These Reflections on Vanity

❑ Don't drop big bucks at a furniture store for a new mirror to top your vanity or dresser. Instead, hang that mirrored medicine cabinet you removed from the bathroom when you were decorating, or the old-fashioned one you inherited from Grandma. You'll have not only a mirror but also extra storage space for cosmetics, hair accessories, and so forth.

GUEST BEDROOMS

Tell Visitors to Hang In There

❑ Bathroom space seems to shrink when overnight guests arrive. To minimize this problem, place a quilt rack in the guest room and invite visitors to hang their towels there. That way, everyone can keep track of their own, and you're less likely to find wet towels draped everywhere around the bathroom.

The Inside Story

Before There Were Murphy Beds

The small, three- by six-foot Oriental rug that lies alongside your bed may not come in a larger size. In fact, if the rug was made in Nepal or Tibet, it isn't a rug at all; it's a bed. The people of Nepal, Tibet, and some other countries roll out individual rugs to sleep on each night in the main room of the house. Then they roll the rugs back up for storage in a corner during the day. Since the average adult in these countries is shorter than six feet tall, the six-foot length is just fine. When you walk on the rug, your toes sink right into a thick pile that is much denser than that of other Oriental rugs—perfect for a good night's sleep.

Make a Case for Towels

The Bedroom

❏ Keep guest towels easy to reach and ready to use by rolling two of each size—bath, hand, and washcloth—and placing them in an old-fashioned, hard-sided suitcase. Before houseguests arrive, set the open suitcase on a bench or chair in the guest room, where your visitors will quickly find them.

Look to the Valet of the Dolls

❏ Make your overnight guests feel at home by filling a doll's suitcase with travel-size toiletries—shampoo, mouthwash, toothpaste, disposable razor, sewing kit, and so forth. Place the open suitcase on a dresser, nightstand, or someplace else where guests will readily find it.

❏ Alternatively, arrange these necessities in an empty flower basket, hatbox, ceramic bowl, child's lunch box, or the like.

Just Don't Plan the Recital for Tonight

❏ Your overnight guests will appreciate a luggage rack, so press a piano bench into active duty for this purpose. Put the bench in the guest room, in an easy-to-reach spot. If you're worried about suitcases scratching your bench, drape an old tablecloth, bedspread, or throw over it to protect the wood.

KIDS' BEDROOMS

How Dry I Am

❏ You need a diaper-changing table for only a few years, so why go out and buy one? Instead, use an old wooden dry sink. Cut a piece of foam rubber to fit into the sink, then cover it with fabric. This is where you'll change the baby. Store diapers and other supplies in the drawers or on cupboard shelves below.

Change with the Times

❏ It's too late? You already bought that diaper-changing table, and now your kids have outgrown it? Put it back

The Bedroom

to work in a youngster's bedroom. Remove the foam mattress from the top of the table and stash stuffed animals there, where the railing will contain them. Then slide some baskets (woven or plastic) onto the lower shelves, where your child can toss plenty of treasures.

Welcome These Clothes Encounters

❏ Make a headboard for a child's bed by attaching a wooden pegboard to the wall above the bed, with pieces of clothing hung from the pegs—pajamas, bathrobe, light jacket, favorite jeans, and the like. Your headboard not only decorates the wall above the bed, but it also offers a fun, easy way for the child to hang up clothes before going to bed.

Create Toy Story-age

❏ Toys and games will be simpler to store and retrieve in a child's bedroom if you put them in a child's shallow, plastic sled that's no longer used for its original purpose. Slide the sled under the bed for storage; pull it out when the youngster wants a toy.

My Way

Map Out a Plan

I wanted to decorate my son's bedroom walls, but I didn't want to invest in wallpaper. So I unfolded one of those huge National Geographic maps of the world, spread wallpaper paste on the back of it, and hung it on a painted wall just as I would have hung wallpaper. My son loved the new decoration—and learned a lot about geography as well!

—Robin Briden
Exeter, New Hampshire

Put G.I. Joe in His Place

❏ Collections of action figures, crayons, or play jewelry can provide a child with hours of fun, but a parent's heart can sink at the sight of all those tiny pieces. To keep collections under control, try storing them in old lunch boxes or day packs. That way, they're readily accessible, easily transported, and—best of all—quickly picked up when playtime's over.

Let Them Shovel through the Mess

❏ Make bedroom cleanup a simple task by letting small children collect their toys in sand buckets. Once the buckets are filled, they can occupy a shelf or a corner of the bedroom.

Kids' Bedrooms

❏ Alternatively, use plastic milk jugs for the same purpose. Cut off a portion of the top to create a wider opening in each jug, but leave the handle in place. This will create a toy collector that's light enough for a child to lift easily but big enough to hold lots of those odds and ends that seem to accumulate in every child's room.

The Bedroom

Take a Swing at This Dresser

❏ It's all too easy to lose the drawer knobs on a dresser in an active child's room. Or maybe that hand-me-down bureau had a few knobs missing to begin with. Not to worry. If it's a standard-issue child's dresser in white, off-white, or a primary color, you can use golf balls as replacement knobs. You might even want to replace all the knobs, so they'll match. Drill a small hole in each ball just big enough so that you can insert the tip of a screw into it. If the drawer already has a screw that fits and has a sharp point, simply screw the golf ball on in place of the original drawer knob. Otherwise, replace the existing hardware with a sharp-pointed screw and attach the ball.

❏ Not a golfer? Not a problem. Instead of golf balls, use wooden blocks for fanciful but functional dresser drawer handles.

A Different Twist

This Is Your Life, Cowboy Dan

For a bedcover that any youngster will love, piece together squares or strips from the child's outgrown blue jeans into a quilt that's uniquely his own. Back the whole thing with an old sheet in a dark color. Then, whenever it's time to do the laundry, just toss Junior's rough-and-ready quilt in with the rest of the dark wash.

Let Sleeping Teddies Lie

❏ Who needs a fancy doll or teddy bear bed? A child will be just as enchanted with a drawer from a small dresser. Make a pillow from single socks rolled into balls, a mattress from a padded mailing envelope, and covers from scraps of material. (Old flannel shirts are particularly good for this.) If you like, paint the drawer or cover it with scraps of wallpaper. Or cut out pictures of teddy bears and dolls from magazines and glue them on the sides.

The Bedroom

❏ Alternatively, for the mattress use a down pillow that your allergies won't tolerate, or the ancient seat cushion that's been mashed down until it's unfit for human derrieres. Put an old pillowcase on it and fold the edges down about two inches from the top, so that dolly or teddy can slip right in, sleeping bag style.

STORAGE SOLUTIONS

Drop Your Drawers

❏ If you're like most folks, you're trying to take advantage of every last inch of storage space in your home. So is the space under your bed being underused? Try organizing it by attaching wheels to the bottom of an old dresser drawer. The wheels from an old roll-along luggage carrier work well, or you can use the ones from Junior's outgrown in-line skates. Place items in the drawer that you need to get at only occasionally, such as sweaters and heavy pants in the summer or shorts in the winter. The drawer will slide out and away with ease.

Bring Those Coat Hangers out of the Closet

❏ Create extra storage space with a decorative flair by mounting an old wooden shutter on the bedroom wall or back of the door. Then hang shirts, a light jacket, and

---

7 Things You Can Stash in a Plastic Shoe Bag

Store all kinds of things in an old plastic shoe bag—the type that hangs on the back of a closet door, with separate pockets for each shoe. A shoe bag with clear pockets is best because you can see every item. Here are a few ideas for storage items.

1. Socks
2. Panty hose
3. Undies
4. Silk scarves
5. Rolled-up belts
6. Rolled-up neckties
7. Small toys (in a child's bedroom)

Storage Solutions

other items from wire hangers tucked between the slats of the shutter.

Tool Around

❏ Want to add more storage space to your bedroom decor and give it a masculine touch as well? Haul that old wooden toolbox out of the basement or garage, clean it up, and put it in the bedroom. Now you can use it to organize all kinds of things, from collar stays to the TV remote control.

The Bedroom

CLOSETS

Hang Two

❏ Double the hanger space in your bedroom closet by hanging a shower curtain ring from the neck of each hanger. Then you can hang one item on the original hanger and another on a second hanger hooked onto the ring.

Cut the Creases

❏ Ordinary wire coat hangers were a great invention, but they're less than ideal for storing certain items—say, a pair of silky trousers, which will end up with a nasty crease if you drape them over a hanger. The answer is as close as the recycling bin and all those cardboard tubes from paper towels. Grab one of the tubes and slit it lengthwise, then place it over the bottom wire of the hanger. Now gently lay your clothing over the top of the cardboard. The tube will keep your clothing from getting creased.

Jug for Yourself

❏ Increase your closet shelf capacity with plastic milk or laundry detergent jugs. Wash out an empty jug, cut the top off, place the bottom half on your closet shelf, and pitch in socks, panty hose, shoulder pads, hair accessories, whatever. If you use a different type of jug for each type of item, you'll be able to identify the contents more readily.

ODORS IN CLOSED SPACES

Have a Glass of Soda

❏ To reduce closet odors, fill a small jar with baking soda and punch holes in the lid. Place the jar on the closet shelf or floor. Change the baking soda every three months.

Get Fresh

❏ Keep your dresser drawers—and their contents—smelling fresh by taping a fabric softener sheet to the inside back of each drawer.

Sachet Around

❏ Freshen your closet with a potpourri sachet. Cut off the foot of an old nylon stocking, fill it with potpourri, and tie off the opening. Hang your sachet from a hook in the closet or from the neck of a clothes hanger.

Hose Off

❏ You can use a similar technique to keep mothballs from rolling around the area where you store your off-season clothes. Cut one foot off an old pair of panty hose, insert several mothballs, and tie off the open end of the nylon.

CLOTHING

Give It Up for Lint

❏ You don't need to buy a lint remover to get lint off your clothes. Instead, get out the masking tape. Hang your garment from a hanger over the back of a door or from a hook and unroll a length of tape. Holding the tape taut with two hands, gently pat the surface of the garment—and watch the lint disappear.

Here's the Rub

❏ Want to get rid of those annoying little pills that crop up on wool sweaters, blazers, and slacks? Don't shave them, which could ruin the fabric. Instead, head to the medicine cabinet for the pumice stone you keep on hand to smooth calluses on feet and elbows. Gently rub the stone over the surface of the garment to pluck those pills for good.

The Bedroom

FOOTWEAR AND LEATHER GOODS

You Don't Need to Do Windows

❏ It's tough to keep white leather sneakers looking new, but there is a way. Spray them with window cleaner, then wipe them with a damp cloth. Window cleaner works more quickly than products made especially for cleaning sneakers, which often involve soaking your shoes and letting them dry for a day or more. With this approach, you can spray, wipe, and be on your way.

❏ Alternatively, scrub your leather sneakers with a paste of baking soda and water. Wipe them clean with a damp cloth.

Get the Patent on Cleaning Leather

❏ You can polish patent leather purses and shoes easily by wiping them down with vinegar on a clean rag. Follow up by wiping the surface dry with another clean cloth.

---

6 Fun Things to Wear in Place of Belts

There's no need to rush out and buy a new belt to spruce up an outfit. Instead, give your outfit a new look with an unusual belt made from one of these items. If a single scarf or necktie won't quite reach, simply tie two similar items together to create a sash of a more appropriate length.

1. Necktie
2. Silk scarf
3. Pair of cotton bandannas
4. Cotton napkins
5. Length of rope
6. Long leather bootlace

The Bedroom

This Is Patently True

❑ Make patent leather shoes and purses shine by rubbing petroleum jelly on the surface and buffing with a soft cloth.

Keep Boots Standing Tall

❑ You don't need to buy expensive wooden boot trees to keep your tall leather boots in shape. Instead, insert an empty plastic soda bottle—the one- or two-liter size, depending on the size of the boots—into each boot.

Duct This Responsibility

❑ If the soles of your leather moccasin slippers are looking a little the worse for wear, don't pitch them— tape them. Cut several strips of duct tape and lay them side by side, sticky side up, until the combined strips are wide enough and long enough to cover the bottom of each slipper. It's best to do this on a workbench, a piece of plywood, or another surface that you don't mind cutting on with a knife. Press the base of each slipper onto the tape and trim away any excess tape from the outline of the slipper with an X-Acto knife. Smooth the tape against the sole of each slipper with your hands, paying special attention to the edges. Then don your slippers and shuffle off to Buffalo!

JEWELRY

Lend Me an Ear(ring)

❑ Organize pairs of earrings in an old plastic ice cube tray. Make sure it's clean, then place the tray in your top bureau drawer and fill it with

---

Pass It On

Dress for the Occasion

Many charitable organizations welcome donations of old clothing, but here's a way to do something a little different with your castoffs. Call your local kindergarten or nursery school and ask if they would like donations of used clothing for a classroom "dress-up" box. (Sports or work uniforms, rain gear, theater or dance costumes, and accessories such as shoes or boots, purses, and costume jewelry are particularly desirable.) Clothes should be small adult size or large child size. Classrooms often have corners or "centers" where children can put on grown-up clothing to act out plays, stories from children's books, or career roles, and they're likely to welcome such gifts. (Make sure you launder all items thoroughly before dropping them off at school.)

---

your favorite pieces. When you open the drawer, you'll be able to see at a glance which earrings you want to wear.

❑ Alternatively, use an old egg carton to keep your earrings separated in a dresser drawer. The compartments are just the right size.

Don't Let Stray Earrings Bedevil You

❑ When, exactly, did you ever use that platter that has the 12 oval indents for deviled eggs? Or when was the *last* time you used it? Could it be time to move it to your dresser to hold earrings? It will add a touch of class to your room and keep your jewelry organized at the same time.

Celebrate a Silver Anniversary

❑ Need a jewelry box? Dust off an old wooden silverware box that's been languishing in the attic. Most silverware boxes have velvet linings and various drawers and compartments that are perfect for jewelry.

Turn Earrings into Wall Decorations

❑ Here's an interesting way to store and display your fishhook-style earrings and at the same time reuse some stuff you might otherwise toss out. Find that old picture frame you've been saving. It doesn't need to be very large unless your earring collection is. If you've saved the glass with the frame, remove it and save the glass for another project. Pull out any nails or points that held the glass in place. Measure the inside (rabbet) edge of the frame from the back. Cut a clean piece of scrap chicken wire to fit. (You can spray-paint it to match or contrast with the frame if you choose.) Attach the chicken wire by stapling it in place. Now hang the whole thing on the wall as you would any other picture. Hang your earrings from the chicken wire, and they'll be easy to get to when you decide to wear a pair.

Keep Your Jewelry in Suspense

❑ Another way to store costume jewelry necklaces and bracelets is to snap a dozen plastic shower curtain hooks onto the horizontal wire of a coat hanger, then hang several necklaces from each ring. Hang your new jewelry rack from a hook on a closet wall, and you'll be able to access the pieces you need easily.

The Bedroom

Enter a Bake-Off

❏ Clean silver jewelry by sprinkling some baking soda on a soft cloth and gently rubbing it into the silver piece. As the baking soda disappears, buff with the cloth.

A Little Dab Will Do

❏ Polish silver jewelry with a dab of toothpaste (not the gel type). Rub the paste gently into the piece, then wipe clean with a cloth.

Have They Ever Tried This at Fort Knox?

❏ Gold jewelry that's been sitting around a while may need a good cleaning. To get it sparkling again, soak it for several minutes in a solution of 1 cup dishwashing liquid and 1 teaspoon ammonia. Then scrub it gently with an old toothbrush, rinse, and pat dry.

It's Crystal Clear

❏ Remove minor surface scratches from your watch crystal and polish it at the same time by rubbing toothpaste (not the gel type) on it, then wiping the crystal clean with a cloth.

Brush Often

❏ Clean tiny grooves in jewelry with an old toothbrush. Just dip the brush in your jewelry cleaner and apply it directly to your pendant, bracelet, earrings, or other jewelry. Brush gently, then rinse with water and buff dry with a soft cloth.

Let the Chain Be Unbroken— And Untangled

❏ Untangle a snarled gold or silver chain by sprinkling a little talcum powder or baby powder on the knot. The powder is smooth and slippery and will allow the knotted chain links to separate.

Back Your Watch

❏ Some folks have such sensitive skin that the metal of a watch causes them to break out. If that describes you, protect yourself by painting the back of your watch with clear nail polish. (Do the same thing to the band if it's metal.) Be sure to repeat the process whenever the polish starts to wear off, and you'll have a clear case of protection.

The Bedroom

NECKTIES

Don't Lose That Tie

❏ Want to hang up your neckties but don't need a full-size tie rack? Take a toilet paper holder and mount it on a wall inside your closet or on the back of the closet door. Then drape your neckties over the holder.

Spring into Action

❏ Make a tie rack for your closet with a spare spring-loaded curtain rod. Mount the curtain rod between the front and back walls of a narrow closet. Then loop your neckties over the rod.

Earl's Favorites

It's a Tie

I don't wear a lot of ties, but when I do wear one, I like it to be neat and well-pressed. Here's a great idea I got from a veteran tie wearer. Mount a towel rack on the wall at the back of your closet and drape your ties over it. The towel rack is thick enough to prevent creases from forming in your ties, and they won't bunch up, so you can easily select the one you want.

Neckties

The Bedroom

OTHER FASHION ACCESSORIES

Play Ringtoss

❏ Keep silk or cotton scarves organized in your dresser drawer by threading each one through an old napkin ring. Be sure the napkin rings have a smooth surface on the inside so they won't snag your scarves.

Take a Shine to Heavy Metal

❏ Bring back the shine on metal belt buckles with three or four coats of clear nail polish. Allow each coat to dry before applying the next one.

SLEEPING PROBLEMS

Cure Snoring—With a Tennis Ball

❏ Tired of sleeping (or not sleeping) with a snorer? If you or your bed partner is also a tennis player, you may have a cure close at hand, in the form of an old tennis ball. On the back of the snorer's pajamas, somewhere around the middle of the top, stitch a patch pocket just large enough to hold the ball. Then pop the ball in the pocket before turning in for the night. The ball will make it uncomfortable for the snorer to sleep on his back—and as long as he stays on his side, he'll be less likely to snore.

And Next Spring, Use It to Plant Catnip

❏ Trying to get a cat to stop sleeping on your bed? Give her an added incentive—a bed of her own that's kitty size and comfy. Dig around in the gardening shed for an extra-large clay bowl (the kind you use as a planter) or the type of clay dish that catches water under plants. You'll want one that's about 20 inches in diameter. Scrub it with warm, soapy water and let it dry completely. Then place it in a tantalizing spot—say, the top of a dresser from which the cat can look down on the world—and wait for kitty to make herself at home.

❏ If you're trying to make the transition in the cold, harsh winter, add an irresistible touch: heat. Warm the clay planter in a 250°F oven for 10 minutes, then place it on a heat-proof mat on the dresser. What cat could resist such a cozy retreat?

THE BEDROOM AS SICKROOM

Who Says It's No Fun Being Sick?

❏ When you must care for a child who's bedridden, you know that quiet, clean activities are the order of the day. To help out on that front, scrounge around for the box from an old board game that no one ever uses anymore. Now hunt up a couple of empty canisters that

A pair of old oatmeal canisters combine with the box from an abandoned board game to make the perfect bed table.

once held oatmeal or cornmeal. Large ones are best, but the important thing is that the two canisters are the same size. Place the first one on its side and hot-glue it to the bottom of one end of the box. Repeat the process, hot-gluing the side of the other canister to the other end of the box to create an instant bed table. Be sure the two canisters are far enough apart that there's plenty of space for the child's legs to fit in between them.

❏ Still have the tops to those canisters? When you glue the containers into position, place them so that the part where the lid fits extends slightly in front of the box. Then the child can hide all sorts of treasures inside—crayons, markers, perhaps a half-used roll of toilet paper for a runny nose.

The Bedroom as Sickroom

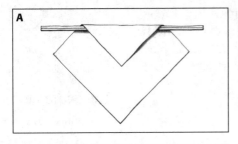

Does Teddy need a hankie, too? Glue a small diamond of fabric over a twist tie (A), then wrap it around the wrist of a sick child's stuffed-up friend (B).

Of Course, Anything Is Amusing When You're Running a Fever

❑ Trying to cheer up a bedridden child who's strongly attached to a stuffed animal or doll collection? Provide handkerchiefs for the whole crew. You'll need one twist tie (the kind that comes with garbage bags) for each animal or doll, along with a few old rags—any scrap will do. Cut two- by two-inch diamonds of fabric and position each diamond over the center of a twist tie. Then fold enough of the top corner over the twist tie that you can staple it, stitch it, or hot-glue it to the bottom of the fabric. Wrap the twist tie around the doll's or animal's arm so that Teddy can take care of his sniffles, too.

Sickbed Activities: Keep Them Puzzled

❑ So what exactly can this quietly resting child do without getting agitated by a blaring television or smearing clay and paint all over the bedclothes? How about a jigsaw puzzle? If you don't have one on hand, let the child help you make one from the front of an old cereal box. Just choose a box with a good illustration, then cut it into interlocking pieces.

❑ If all you have are boring adult cereal boxes, consider gluing a magazine photo, a pretty piece of stationery, or a child's simple, colorful drawing to the front before you cut the panel into pieces.

The Workshop
and Garage

When you stop to think about it, the garage and the home workshop are two of the most practical and inspirational rooms in the house. With their stocks of tools and machines, they can become minilaboratories for turning creative ideas into realities. Sound ridiculous in the suburbs? Not when you realize where some industrial giants got their start.

William R. Hewlett and David Packard produced their first electronics products in 1938—inside a garage. The first Apple computer came together in a garage owned by the family of Steve Jobs. And where else would Henry Ford have worked out the kinks in the forerunner of the Model T but in a garage?

You may not invent the next laser in your basement, but tinkering with the tools and materials at hand can result in using common items in some pretty uncommon ways. Here are some ideas to get you started.

The Workshop and Garage

GETTING ORGANIZED

Contain Yourself

❏ Sure you could make a trip to the home superstore and buy a fancy workshop organization system. But that's a waste of gas, time, and money, especially if you have a collection of empty milk jugs lying around the garage. Cut the tops off near the handles, and you have your own thrifty tool organization system. Place the jugs under your workbench and use them to store small tools and equipment such as screwdrivers, files, and nails. If the jugs tend to tip over, just place a stone in the bottom of each one to anchor it.

Try Gutter Talk

❏ In any workshop, it's always a challenge to store small pieces of hardware in a way that lets you put your hands on the piece you need quickly. You can meet that challenge by taking a short length of half-round metal gutter, capping it on the ends with stock caps, and dividing it into compartments with home-cut semicircles of wood, secured with panhead sheet metal screws. Now you have a durable and convenient set of bins for nails, screws, or other hardware.

To store all those odds and ends of small hardware, bolt one end of an old muffin tin to the underside of your work table (A). Use a washer so the tin can swing out when you need it (B).

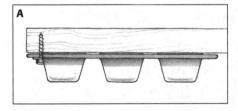

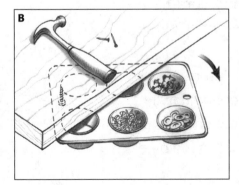

Cook Up a Great Workbench Organizer

❏ An old muffin tin makes a great small hardware organizer for your workbench. Attach it to the underside of the table with a bolt and washer so it can rotate out when needed and disappear when you're done.

Take Up a Collection

❏ Another way to separate all those odds and ends of hardware is to contain them in a series of ice cube trays. The old metal type with a removable divider is especially good

Tired of Fishing around the Junk Box? Get Hooked

Almost every toolbox and workshop has a box, can, or drawer filled with unsorted nuts and washers. Although everyone saves these things, few people can actually find what they need without dumping the contents out on the workbench and pawing through the pile. You could go to the hardware store and buy one of those little chests with two dozen tiny drawers. But a less expensive solution is to string the nuts and washers on old-fashioned metal shower curtain hooks.

Sort your nuts and washers by size and assign one (or more) shower curtain hooks to each size. If you are a linear type of person, hang each hook from a nail or pegboard. If you're a more creative type, you can make a daisy chain of hooks that looks something like a garlic braid made of steel.

I've found a number of advantages to the hook system over the small drawers.

● You can add or subtract hooks as needed. (You can't do that with drawers. Once you fill the chest, you have to buy another.)
● You can tell at a glance whether you have what you need to do the job.
● The hooks don't take up space on the bench.

To me, however, the most important advantage is portability. If I have a job in the house, in the garage, or on the other side of town, I simply grab the hooks holding the nuts and washers I think I will need and toss them into my tool bucket. Try doing that with those little plastic drawers.

–Lee Michaelides
Norwich, Vermont

for this. Or use the plastic kind and sort washers, nuts, and so on into the individual compartments.

❏ If your collection of hardware is a little larger, consider storing it in one of those kidney-shaped bedpans. At the very least, it will be a conversation starter whenever anyone visits your workshop.

Baby Your Odds and Ends

❏ Old baby food jars make excellent containers for screws, nails, and other small hardware. They do have

a few drawbacks, though. Since they're made of glass, they can break if they're knocked off your work area. And they have to be opened with two hands, which usually means having to put down a tool. A way to solve both of these problems is to attach the lids directly to the underside of a wooden shelf over your worktable, with a screw through the center of each. Be careful not to bend the lids out of shape, so the jars will still close. Now you have a batch of clear storage compartments that are fixed in place out of the way and that you can open and close with one hand.

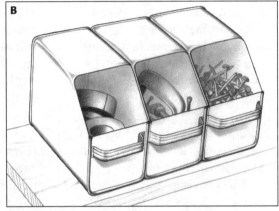

Store the small stuff in glass jars, with the jar lids screwed into the base of a workshop shelf (A). Leftover paint thinner containers hold slightly larger items (B).

Get a Handle on Better Storage

❑ Looking for an organized way to store your workshop supplies? Take another look at those leftover one-gallon containers that paint thinner or mineral spirits come in. Whether plastic or metal, they make great storage bins. Simply cut half the top off at an angle, being sure to leave the handle intact. After you've eliminated any sharp edges with a file or sandpaper, place the container on its short side, handle out, and fill with your chosen hardware or supplies. When you have a shelf full of these containers lined up side by side, you can pull the one you want like a drawer by grabbing the handle.

Do Fence Me In

❑ Basements, garages, and workshops of all ilks are usually minimally finished spaces—not always having interior walls and ceilings, for example. And no matter how much storage space they offer, it's never enough. Exposed floor joists overhead can be a storage blessing in disguise. A quick way to use this valuable space is to attach light-duty garden fencing—leftover wire poultry netting is easy to handle—across the bottom with heavy staples. The "hammocks" so created in each of the joist bays can hold lightweight items such as life preservers or lawn furniture cushions.

The Workshop and Garage

Be a Lumber Wrangler

❏ Don't throw out those worn-out blue jeans. Use them to organize and store lumber scraps. Sew the leg bottoms closed and hang the jeans on a nail from one of the belt loops. They make a great repository for leftover molding and light lumber.

Lumber Storage: Try This, Old Sport

❏ Next time you're looking for a way to organize spare bits of long lumber, molding, or anything else that can be stored vertically, head for that pile of old sporting equipment that's stashed in the attic. If you find an old golf bag, place those awkward odds and ends in the bag, and they'll be out of your way but handy when needed.

SUBSTITUTIONS

Short-Circuit the Problem

❏ Handy folks take note: Here's a great way to give a second life to those old blue jean shorts. Just take them apart at the side seams and inseams, discarding the back section but keeping the front and sides as well as the front belt loops. Run an old belt or a length of clothesline through the belt loops, then around your

The Inside Story

Nails: Getting a Grip

Virtually all of the 10,000 different types of nails on the market today fall into one of two categories: They are either cut nails or wire nails.

Cut nails are literally cut from a plate of steel, aluminum, stainless steel, or bronze. Wire nails are formed by machines from coils of steel wire. The sharp edges of cut nails offer superior gripping power, but their high prices put them out of reach of the typical home builder. As a result, the primary use for cut nails today is in special projects such as boatbuilding, where a tight fit is essential, and historic building renovations such as Shakespeare's Globe Theatre in London.

That means that home builders (and fixers) generally use wire nails—some 70,000 of them in the average new American home. Mindful that wire nails have less grip than cut nails, lumber mills and nail makers have invented new products such as "sinkers" to counter this deficiency. Sinkers are basically common wire nails with a resin coating. When the nails are pounded (or shot into wood with an air gun), the resin heats up and acts as a lubricant, making it easier to drive the nail. When the resin cools, it glues the nail to the wood. Before pounding sinkers into your next project, remember—if you goof, you're glued!

waist. With their sturdy pockets, even worn-out shorts make a serviceable carpenter's apron.

Don't Fiddle with That Filter

❏ Almost everyone who changes her own automobile engine oil at one time or another has been stuck trying to remove the oil filter. When the filter is on too tight to unscrew by hand, the auto parts store can sell you a hooplike tool that slips over the filter to give you more leverage. But suppose you don't have that option. Don't despair. A large, slip-jawed pipe wrench will usually do the trick.

❑ If you don't have a wrench or there isn't room to fit it around the filter, your last resort is a screwdriver. Carefully puncture the thin metal of the filter on two sides so that you can slide the screwdriver through it like a shish kebab skewer. (Don't worry about the filter itself—you're going to dispose of it anyway—but be prepared for the cup or so of oil that will leak out.) Then use the screwdriver to turn the filter like a capstan until you can spin it by hand.

Rip Off This Idea

❑ Demolition of building parts, such as removing plaster walls or old roofing, is not exacting work, but the appropriate tools help. An automotive tire iron—the kind that looks vaguely like a golf club and is part of a bumper-style jack—makes an effective wrecking bar. It's designed to be a lever, and it even has a chisel tip for prying.

That's the Spirit!

❑ When you don't have a spirit level handy, you can still find level the way the ancient Egyptians did, with a framing square and a plumb bob. Attach the plumb line to one leg of the square and hold the new tool up to the work. When the vertical leg of the framing square lines up with the plumb line, the other leg is dead level.

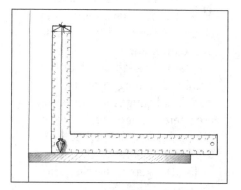

One framing square plus one plumb bob equals one instant spirit level.

Make a (String) Cut-Up

❑ Why is it that you can never find those scissors when you need them? Here's how to make a handy string cutter for your workbench. Rescue that broken hacksaw blade and nail it securely to the side of a leg of your workbench. Attach it so that the teeth of the blade protrude about one-sixteenth inch in front of the surface of the leg, and you'll have a perfect string cutter. (This setup is good for trimming sandpaper to size, too.) Be sure to mount it on a side where no one will brush up against it.

MEASURING ACCURATELY

Circumnavigate with a Hacksaw Blade

❑ Suppose you need to draw a circle, but there's no compass in your tool kit. Grab a hacksaw blade. Anchor one end of the blade at the center of the circle by tacking a nail through the hole. Next, place a pencil on the toothed side of the blade at the desired radius. Then rotate the blade to draw the circle. The teeth will keep the pencil dead on the radius.

A Different Twist

Try the Nickel-and-Dime Approach

When hanging entry doors, you must have the proper clearance between the outside of the door and the inside of the frame to keep the door from binding or letting in drafts. The traditional gauges for carpenters are spare change. When the door is closed, the gap at the top should be the thickness of a nickel; the gap at the side, the thickness of a dime.

Close Your Jaws around That Pipe

❑ If you're going to alter your plumbing—adding a branch line, for example—you'll need to know the outside diameter of the existing pipes to buy fittings. But did you ever try to measure the diameter of a water pipe in a wall without a machinist's caliper? It's not easy—unless you have an adjustable wrench handy. Simply take your monkey wrench or Crescent wrench and close the jaws around the pipe until you have a fit that's snug but not tight. Carefully remove the wrench from the pipe without disturbing the jaws. Measure the distance between the jaws to get the outside diameter of the pipe.

HOMEMADE TOOLS

You Saw It Here First

❑ A flooring saw comes in handy for making the necessary blind cuts when you're repairing strip flooring or wall paneling, but why buy one when you can make your own? Start with a fine-tooth 7¼-inch circular saw blade. Then take a 1- by 6- by 14-inch board, cut the

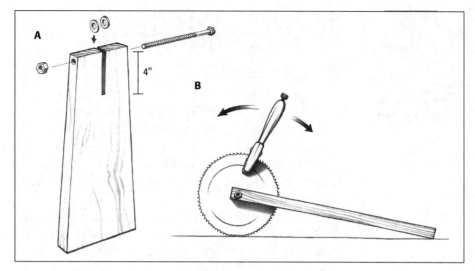

sides to make a keystone shape, and slot it 4 inches deep at the narrow end to accept the circular saw blade. Bore a hole through this end for a ½-inch-diameter bolt to make an axle for the blade. Then assemble the saw with a nut and washers. To use the saw, grasp the blade with locking pliers and move it back and forth. The board will stabilize the saw and keep it vertical. The pliers will give you precise control over your cuts.

Make a slot in the end of the board (A). Insert a circular saw blade and secure it with a nut, a bolt, and washers. When you grip the blade with pliers (B), the board will keep it perpendicular to the surface.

Punch Up Your Act

❏ You need a sturdy punch to make holes in leather or canvas, and you can't find anything in your tool kit that fits the bill. Maybe you're looking in the wrong place. Any metal tube, such as a gun shell casing or a part from an old lamp, can be turned into a punch for this purpose. Just file one end of the tube flat, then carefully sharpen the tube by filing the outside circumference to produce a knife edge. Don't worry about getting it razor sharp, but do be careful about the direction in which you file. It's important to start at the edge of the tube and file into its length, not the other way around.

File away from the end of the metal tube to make a punch.

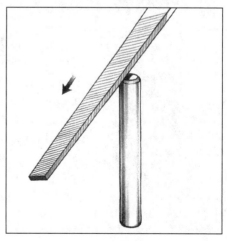

The Workshop and Garage

STORING AND PROTECTING TOOLS

Do Your Level Best

❏ Large carpenter's and mason's levels are expensive precision tools that, when made of wood, are things of beauty. However, they're useless if they get so scratched they can't be read, or banged until they become inaccurate. To guard a four-foot or six-foot level when it's not in use, try making a protective sleeve from a scrap of vinyl downspout. Adapt standard gutter parts to make removable end caps. For added cushioning, at each end glue foam rubber around the inside of the tube. Old seat cushions and pillows are good sources of scrap foam rubber.

❏ To protect a two-foot level, encase it in an old woolen hiking sock.

When It Comes to Level Protection, Pipe Up

❏ You can make a protective container for a level from a length of leftover polyvinyl chloride (PVC) pipe. Glue a standard cap on one end of the pipe. Place the level inside. On the other end, screw through the side of another cap and into the PVC to make a removable cover.

Earl's Favorites

You Can Hack It

In my experience, there are few tools handier than a hacksaw blade wrapped with electrical tape at one end to make a handle. This slim saw is ideal for cutting nails in tight spaces—say, when you're removing moldings that you'll use later—or freeing up windows that are painted shut. And it sure doesn't take a lot of storage space.

Storing and Protecting Tools

Keep Your Saw from Baring Its Teeth

❑ Dovetail saws and other small handsaws for fine woodworking have to be sharp for quality results. Yet they can get dull just lying in a toolbox, especially when traveling in a car. To keep their teeth sharp, raid your desk drawers for a plastic binder sleeve—the kind made to bind a bunch of papers into a report. Slip it over the teeth of the saw, and they'll stay sharp longer.

❑ Alternatively, if you have an old garden hose lying around, you have a perfect protector for your saw. Cut a piece of the hose the length of your saw and slice it down the middle. Place the hose over the teeth of the saw and hold it in place with a couple of rubber bands.

One Size Fits All Mauls

❑ Heavy outdoor hand tools such as axes, wood-splitting mauls, sledge-hammers, and picks often suffer a lot of wear at the neck of the handle— the part just below the head. This section takes most of the impact from missed blows, eating up the wood (or fiberglass) at a critical point. To protect the neck, cut a section of an old bicycle inner tube about six inches long and wrap it around the handle to make a rubber guard. Secure the ends with duct tape.

Offer (an) Instant Retraction

❑ The last thing you need is a retractable tape measure that won't retract. To keep it in good working order, use a drop of auto polish on a soft cloth to lubricate the metal tape. That'll keep it gliding smoothly.

A Different Twist

Keep Your Snakes Captive

Snakes for clearing plumbing lines, or fish wires used to run electrical cables inside walls, can be ornery tools to store. These long lengths of stiff metal don't coil neatly like rope, and they tangle easily if you try to tie them with cord like a garden hose. The near-perfect way to store snakes is inside an old bicycle tire. As you lay the snake inside the tire one foot at a time, the metal's natural stiffness will keep the snake captive inside the circumference of the tire. The walls of the tire will close over it like a cover, and the diameter is ideal—large enough not to put kinks in the snake, yet small enough to hang conveniently on a hook somewhere in the basement.

SIMPLE
HOUSEHOLD REPAIRS

The Workshop and Garage

Drive Faster

❏ Driving wood screws can be tiring, especially when they're large and you're using a lot of them in a cabinet or furniture project. For this reason, you should always keep an old bar of beeswax within reach. An old candle stub is also a good alternative, as is a wax gasket ring (the kind used for installing a toilet). Before you start a screw, simply drag the threads once across the bar. The wax you pick up will lubricate the screw so that it will go in more easily, without staining or swelling the wood.

Conquer Rust on Tough Nuts and Bolts

❏ The usual approach to removing a rusted nut or bolt is to soak it in penetrating oil, then work it loose. But if you don't have any oil available, you may have a great substitute right in your fridge. Just soak a cloth in any cola drink and leave the wet cloth on the hardware for about an hour before you try loosening the nut or bolt again. Repeat the process if necessary.

Out of the Golf Bag and into the Door

❏ When the screw holes for door hinges—or any screwed-on hardware—have become so worn that the screw doesn't grab anymore, try this trick. Take wooden golf tees, dip them in carpenter's glue, and tap them into the offending holes until they're snug. When the glue is dry, cut the tees off flush with the rest of the door or frame. The restored holes can now be rebored as if they were virgin wood.

Pass It On

Catch the Flue

If you've recently dismantled an old chimney and can't figure out what to do with the flue tiles, share them with friends who garden. Flue tiles make great containers for all sorts of garden uses. They work well to hold an unwieldy mess of garden stakes. They also make a great catchall for short-handled garden tools stored in the garage or shed. Or a friend might want to set one in a corner near the door to the house and plunk work gloves and knee pads there when coming in from a session of weeding. Then she'll know right where everything is when she's ready to start again.

A Close Shave

Years ago, I was working with a friend who was installing some drywall in his house. I noticed that he had an old electric razor in his tool kit, so of course I ribbed him about it.

"What are you going to do," I asked, "shave the walls down?"

He laughed, but I have to admit, he had a good comeback. "I use it to find studs."

He explained that he turns the razor on, holds it up, and runs it along the wall. The razor buzzes the whole time, but the sound it makes is noticeably different when it moves over a stud. He showed me, and sure enough it worked.

Of course, that's all the expensive stud finders do—bounce sound into the wall—but his solution was much less expensive, and a good conversation starter, too.

Door Hardware:
Mask before You Polish

❑ When you're polishing brass door hardware, you run the risk of soiling or harming the finish on the wood surrounding the lock plate or knocker—especially if the metal is very oxidized or you're using steel wool. Old manila file folders can get you out of this door dilemma. Make a reusable mask to protect the wood by tracing the outline of the hardware on the folder, then cutting it away to leave a border you can move from door to door as a mask.

Unstick That Window

❑ Window sash can be hard to raise because of friction in the channels on either side. When you have this condition, resist the temptation to oil or spray the channels; it will only swell the wood and make things worse. Instead, grab a candle stub from your last dinner party. If

Simple Household Repairs

The Workshop and Garage

you lightly wax the sash with the candle, they'll slide better.

Stubborn Window Putty: Blow It Away

❑ One of the most difficult parts of replacing a broken windowpane is removing the hardened glazing putty that inevitably remains in some, if not all, of the sash. Not only is it tedious digging out this stonelike material with a screwdriver or chisel, but any slip risks damaging the wood or puncturing your hand. Next time your pane is a pain, try softening the putty first with a blow dryer. As you heat the putty, it will become more pliable, making it easy to remove with a putty knife.

Use a Splinter Hinderer

❑ A clean cut is a sign of an expert carpenter, but what if the wood won't cooperate? When you cut wood by hand, the surface of the lumber often splinters as you saw, leaving a ragged edge. To lessen the chances of that happening, secure a length of masking tape to the underside of the wood, along the cutting line. This will support the surface and reduce the damage to the edge.

PAINTERS' HELPERS

Try Your Hand at Painting Radiators

❑ To paint hard-to-reach areas such as the inside edges of pipes and radiators, a brush just doesn't do the trick. You need a painting mitt. Make one from an old sock—preferably one without holes in it. Orphaned sweat socks work best. First slip your hand into an old rubber glove, as a precaution in case the paint soaks through. Then pop the sock on top of that. (Depending on the thickness of the paint and the socks you use, you may want to double the socks.) With the sock on, dip your hand into the paint, then grab the pipe or radiator and slide your hand along the inside edge.

Fresh Paint: Add a Dash of Vanilla

❑ The guest room would look a lot better with a fresh coat of latex, but you don't look forward to inhaling the

Pick-Your-Own Wood Scraps

A truism of modern construction is that it is impossible to buy the small amount of wood needed to make, say, a birdhouse. Another truism is that it is faster, cheaper, and more profitable not to recycle anything from a remodeling job. Each day, truckloads of used building materials are hauled to landfills. Which means that a scavenger in search of wood and hardware for anything from a child's tree house to the aforementioned birdhouse is likely to discover an infinite source of materials in the construction debris section of the local dump.

What will you find? Windows, doors, dimensional lumber, pallets, and plywood scraps both large and small. In many small towns, it is all there for the taking, as long as you bring some common sense along with your bargain hunter's instinct. (The free wood won't look so great if it's next to the bill for an emergency room visit.) If you decide to pick the wood dump, always follow these rules.

- Leave the children and the dog at home. A construction dump is no place for playing.
- Speak with the caretaker first. It's unlikely that you'll be turned down, and you might be directed to what you need without delay. And while the rule is likely to be "poke at your own risk," it's common sense to be sure that someone knows you're there.
- Wear thick-soled, steel-toed boots and heavy work gloves.
- Pay careful attention to where you step. Watch for nails, broken glass, and sharp pieces of metal.
- Don't pull from the bottom of the pile. You don't want to end up at the bottom of a *new* pile.
- Don't climb on piles of debris. Assume they are unstable.
- Stay clear of dump trucks and loaders. The operators are not expecting to see anyone poking around.

To find your own source of free wood, ask a local builder where he hauls his scraps. Most towns have residency requirements for people wanting to bring stuff *into* the dump. Few, if any, are concerned about nonresidents hauling stuff *out.*

fumes from the wet paint. Not to worry. Add a tablespoon of vanilla extract to each pint of paint you use. Stir it in thoroughly, then apply the paint as usual. The vanilla won't affect the other qualities of the paint, but it will get rid of that awful odor.

The Workshop and Garage

❏ Alternatively, absorb the odor by placing large chunks of raw onion in a pan of cold water, then setting the pan in the middle of the room being painted.

Bag a Lamp

❏ When you're painting a room—especially a ceiling—you'll want to protect the nonpainted surfaces from drips and spatters. A drop cloth is fine for floors and furniture, but what about the chandelier? The answer is at your cleaner's. Take one of those dry-cleaning bags used to protect freshly cleaned suits and dresses and recycle it as a ceiling fixture cover. It's large enough to cover most chandeliers and light enough to be held to the base with tape. And you can just throw it away when the painting's done.

CARS AND OTHER VEHICLES

Wipe That Tar off the Car

❏ Looking for a way to get road tar off your vehicle? Just dip a clean rag in mayonnaise and spread the mayonnaise over the tar. Let it sit for a few minutes, then wipe with a clean rag.

Make a Colorful Repair

❏ When your car gets a major scrape, you need to get it touched up before rust sets in. But you can cover a minor scratch yourself, with a little help from the kids' arts and crafts supplies. Select an ordinary wax crayon of an appropriate shade and just color in the scratch, then buff it with a soft cloth to blend in the color.

Don't Let a Dirty Windshield Bug You

❏ It's easy to remove dead bugs from a car windshield if you have the right equipment. And what's the right equipment? How about a couple of old mesh onion bags? The mesh gives you enough of an edge to scrape off the bugs, but it won't damage the windshield. Just apply a mixture of dishwashing liquid and water to the windshield to soften things up, scrub a bit with the

Unmentionables?
Now That You Mention Them . . .

Some folks would never spend a single day in slightly worn underwear—their fear being that, should they wind up in a hospital emergency room, every doctor in town would discover the weakest point in their wardrobes. Personal demons aside, there's no reason to discard underclothes that are past their prime. These specialized textiles can find new life before they're ready for their final reward.

Boxer shorts. If you're interested in wall glazing—that is, the decorative paint effect in which subtle abstract motifs are applied like stencils over a base color—an old pair of boxer shorts may become one of your favorite tools. When crumpled in your hand and dabbed on the wall, the fly seams and elastic waistband can produce some of the most intriguing patterns you'll find.

Brassieres. When you're working on your knees on a hard-wood floor, the cups from old padded bras may be the perfect cushion to keep your kneecaps from crying. Or if you're stuck for a simple dust mask, try getting creative with a single cup. Believe it or not, the foundation material is often the same stuff used in those disposable filters found in hardware stores.

Diapers. Soft and absorbent to begin with, old cotton diapers are the softest materials available for polishing furniture and automotive finishes.

Nylons. Ordinary panty hose have a remarkably fine and porous weave—making them nearly ideal for straining impurities from paints and varnishes. Just stretch a leg across a new container, then pour. If you still have a few worn-out pairs left, you'll find there are few options better than nylons for polishing shellac finishes.

onion bags, and then wipe dry with clean rags. Now you'll be able to see the road again.

Unstick Those Bumper Stickers

❏ Bumper stickers have their place, but if yours are still showing your support for a candidate who lost in 1988, it might be time for a change. The trouble is, sometimes those stickers have more staying power than the politicians. To remove an outdated sticker, coat it liberally

Play the Circle Game

Those worm screw, stainless steel hose clamps made for cinching the connections on rubber automotive hoses, plastic sump pump hoses, and laundry discharges can have many other uses beyond flexible plumbing. For example, because they are strong and rustproof, they are excellent for lashing together pipes of all sorts—say, attaching a garden umbrella to a fence post. They undo easily, so they make great fasteners for temporary connections—such as when you need to bind up a failing planter barrel. They come in diameters from one inch to more than one foot, but you can make any size clamp you need by joining the "female" end of one clamp with the "male" end of another in a limitless daisy chain.

with vinegar, let it sit until the vinegar has thoroughly penetrated the paper, and then scrape it off. The vinegar will loosen the glue and make the rest of the job much easier.

Return to Sander

❏ If you find yourself doing auto body repair work on your vehicle, you may also find that it's tricky to sand the body filler evenly into some of the concave features around fender wells and front grilles. A piece of old radiator hose—or any large-diameter rubber hose—will make an ideal curved (and flexible) sanding block. Just wrap the sandpaper around it in any way that's practical and convenient.

Oily in the Morning

❏ If you change your own engine oil, you probably already know that, when washed clean, one-gallon liquid laundry detergent containers are good for collecting the used oil and transporting it to the recycling station. However, did you also know that other containers make good disposable funnels for transferring the oil? One-gallon bleach bottles are ideal, but any good-size container with a small mouth (that fits into the mouth of the laundry detergent container) will work. Simply cut off the bottom with a sharp knife, invert the container to take advantage of the handy spout, and pour carefully.

Give Spills a Litter Help

❏ The next time you change your car's oil and have a spill on the garage floor, clean it up quickly by pulling out a bag of clay kitty litter. Throw enough litter onto the puddle to cover it, then sweep it up, absorbed oil and all.

Cars and Other Vehicles

A ten-pound bag of kitty litter will absorb more than a gallon of liquid; gauge your proportions accordingly.

Mirror, Mirror on the Manifold

❏ Inspecting a modern car or truck engine for leaks, electrical connections, or just general condition is not always easy. The engine compartment is typically covered with hoses and wires, and the engine/transmission assembly may have more nooks and crannies than a Thomas' English Muffin. To help you find what you're looking for, you need an old compact with a mirror (the kind used for applying makeup). Tape it to a stick, and you can examine the engine as a dentist examines teeth.

Radiator Leaking? Add Seasoning

❏ As they age, automobile radiators are prone to pinhole leaks. These tiny holes usually weep only a fine stream of coolant and are barely noticeable—that is, until the radiator is half-empty and the engine starts to overheat. The ideal fix for pinholes is metal repair at a radiator shop. There are also stop-leak products you can buy at auto parts stores and add to the coolant. But suppose it's a holiday and you're out of luck on both options. Try shaking a couple of tablespoons of ground pepper into the radiator. The flakes will act just like a stop-leak product by seeking the pinhole and plugging the leak until you can get the radiator repaired.

Stock Your Garage with Olive Oil

❏ When you're working on an automobile engine—or just about any mechanical part of the undercarriage—you're bound to wind up with dirty, greasy hands. A splash of any cooking oil—especially olive oil—worked over your hands will loosen most of the grease so that you can wipe it off with a paper towel, then wash as usual. The oil is a good emollient for your skin, too.

Outside the House

Sowing new grass. Maintaining the lawn mower. Keeping driveways and walkways free of weeds in summer and ice in winter. Storing all that equipment. Could it be time to open the wallet and bring in the heavy lawn care artillery?

Not hardly. The space may be larger once you cross the threshold to the great outdoors, but it's no less tamable by ordinary household items that you've pulled out of the recycling bin. In these pages, you'll find ideas you can use to hold the clothespins for that outdoor line, clean the terminals of your lawn mower battery, and carry sand to provide winter traction for walkways. We'll tell you how to use old spools to keep squirrels out of the bird feeder, worn-out panty hose to deter raccoons, and unwanted perfume to get rid of skunks.

And now that you no longer have as much garbage to fill that old metal trash can, we'll even suggest another way you can put *it* to good use.

LAWN CARE

See What You Sow

❏ It's not always easy to determine whether you've ad-equately reseeded an area of your lawn, since grass seed is too small to be easily seen. A simple solution to the problem is to add a handful of sawdust from your last woodworking project to each cup or so of grass seed. When you scatter the mixture, you'll be able to see the sawdust and make sure you're covering the entire area you want to reseed.

Outside the House

Give That Grass Seed a Special Welcome

❏ Need a quick way to work new grass seed into your prepared soil? Drag a woven or plastic doormat over the ground where you've sprin-kled the seed, and you'll work it into the ground much more quickly.

Make Your Grass a Binge Drinker

❏ Grass roots grow deeper into the soil if you water your lawn deeply but infrequently. Give your lawn a heavy drink—one inch of water—about once a week during the growing season. And how do you make sure you're watering heavily enough? Grab those old coffee cans you were about to toss out, place several of them in the path of your sprinkler, and measure the amount of water that collects in them. This simple measurement system also will tell you whether you're getting the same amount of water to different parts of your lawn.

A Different Twist

Lawn Mowing: Get out of a Sticky Situation

Your mower's not so efficient when grass clippings stick to its rotary blade. And clumps of clippings can create a rust problem on the bottom of the mower. Here's a way to keep the grass from sticking. Before you start your mower, spray the underside with nonstick cooking spray. It works on your pots and pans, and it can work on your lawn mower blades, too.

Pass the Jug around the Yard

❏ Next time you need to broadcast a little bit of lime, dry fertilizer, or grass seed over a small section of your yard, try this technique. Start with a clean, dry milk

The Long-Distance Watering Can

In the world of business, there are visionaries and there are salesmen. A revolutionary new product needs one of each. Charles Goodyear was the man who in 1839 first discovered a way to keep rubber pliant after it dried by adding sulfur to it. He knew it would be useful for something, maybe a lot of things. Unfortunately, he went into great debt and died before he could cash in on his genius.

A few years later, Benjamin Franklin Goodrich, who had worked as a surgeon in the Civil War and a businessman afterward, envisioned the commercial possibilities for rubber. His first project: rubber hoses. Goodrich reasoned that more flexible hoses would be a great improvement over the leather hoses of the day, which were prone to stretching, cracking, and splitting. In 1870, the BF Goodrich company introduced a smaller counterpart to the fire hose, marketing it as a garden hose. Instead of carrying huge watering cans back and forth across the yard to keep the grass growing, a home owner could just turn on the outdoor faucet. Although it didn't take all the effort out of yard work, it certainly did shorten our steps.

jug—the gallon size made of plastic—and use an awl to poke holes in the bottom. Now funnel your grass seed or lime into the top and shake the jug over the area you want to plant or fertilize. It's a great way to spread seed or fertilizer over a small area without a lot of fuss.

Get the Drop on Fallen Leaves

❏ To ease the chore of raking leaves or grass cuttings, save your old drop cloths or plastic tarps—the ones you use to cover the floor or furniture while painting—and bring them outside. Just spread the canvas or plastic sheet on the ground next to the leaves and rake the leaves onto it. When you have a good mound of leaves on the tarp or drop cloth, gather its four edges together and pull the bundle to your desired location—a trash can, a compost pile, or the garden.

❏ Alternatively, rake your leaves onto a discarded shower curtain or old vinyl tablecloth and follow the same procedure.

Outside the House

LAWN MOWER MAINTENANCE

Maintain Your Balance

❏ If you're sharpening your own rotary mower blade, you should make sure it's balanced. A blade heavier on one side will cause the mower to vibrate, making the mower hard to handle and wearing down the engine bearings. Although you can find a simple balancing fulcrum in a lawn and garden shop, a fine low-tech solution is to balance the blade on a pencil or on a nail stuck in a wall. Place the center of the blade on the fulcrum, and if it doesn't balance, file or grind off metal on the heavy side until the blade remains horizontal.

Keep That Current Coming

❏ It's important to clean your power mower's battery terminals to maintain the best possible electrical connection, but what cleaner do you use for this? A tablespoon of baking soda mixed with a cup of water will clean off dirt and corrosion. Just be sure to keep the cell caps on so that you don't splash the mixture into the cells.

Prevent Carburetor Decay

❏ The carburetor is the only part of a two-cycle lawn mower engine that is designed to let in the outside world. So it pays to clean the outside of the carburetor every time you remove and clean the air filter. (Air filters on two-cycle engines should be cleaned after every eight hours of use.) First, to prevent debris from falling in, close the choke. Then dip an old toothbrush in a solvent such as gasoline to wipe away the dust, dirt, and grease that collect on the outside of the carburetor and

can sneak past the air filter into the crankcase. Be careful not to disturb the settings of the mixture adjustment screws as you brush.

OUTDOOR CLOTHESLINES

The Plant May Be Gone, but the Planter Lives On

❏ Anybody who has an outdoor clothesline needs a way to keep clothespins handy. One good way is to clean up an old plastic hanging planter, then hang it from the clothesline. The pins will be ready when you are, and you can leave the container in place all the time. When it rains, the water will just drain out onto the ground.

Transform That T-Shirt into a Clothespin Holder

❏ Another way to make a convenient clothespin holder is to stitch closed the arms and bottom of an old T-shirt. Put the holder on a coat hanger, then hang the whole thing on your clothesline so it's always handy.

Fill That Jug with . . . Clothespins

❏ You can make a good clothespin holder from an old plastic milk jug. Cut a larger-than-fist-size hole in the side of the jug opposite the handle and drop your clothespins in there. Then cut off the bottom inch of the handle. Use the remainder of the handle to hang the jug from the clothesline. If you poke a few holes in the bottom of the jug to allow rainwater to drain out, you can leave your clothespins on the line all the time instead of having to cart them out there every time you hang up a load of laundry.

A Different Twist

Put Clothespins on Hold

For a simple clothespin container, sew closed the legs of those old blue jean shorts that won't take another patch. Run a spare bit of clothesline through the belt loops, then tie the ends of the line together around the neck of a coat hanger. Fill the improvised container with clothespins, and you'll have a nifty hanging holder.

Then Hang Up
Those Beach Towels to Dry

❏ A child's old plastic sand pail makes a good clothespin holder, too. Just poke a few holes in the bottom to let rainwater escape, hang the handle of the pail over the clothesline, and pop the clothespins in. Now they're ready whenever you are.

Outside the House

ANIMAL PESTS

Don't Let Your Bird Feeder
Be a Squirrel Feeder

❏ To keep squirrels from raiding your bird feeder, hang the feeder from the center of a length of heavy wire. String empty spools of thread on the wire on both sides of the feeder, then hang the wire between two trees. Squirrels will not be able to pass the spinning spools without falling off the wire.

Ban the Bandits

❏ Do you awaken at night to the clanking of raccoons opening up your trash cans? If your cans come with lids that have open handles on the sides and lid, rummage through your drawers for a pair of worn-out panty hose. Use them, bungee cord style, to tie the lid down and deter those masked raiders.

Use an Eau de Odor

❏ Has a skunk decided to make its home under yours? Or in your garage? You can discourage such an unwelcome neighbor and also get rid of some old perfume. Skunks, oddly enough, generally avoid perfume— and you can use that bit of trivia to keep them out of your woodshed, your garage, or anyplace else they've

---

A Different Twist

How to "Antique" Your Weather Vane

Your farmer neighbors have a copper weather vane that looks as if it's been on top of the barn for decades, but you know they just bought it last month. How did they get that green weathered look so quickly, and how can you get the same effect on your own weather vane? Easy. Bury it in a manure pile for a couple of weeks. When you unearth it and clean it off, your new copper will be thoroughly antiqued.

**Outside the
House**

been visiting. Cut the foot and ankle off an old nylon stocking. Then douse a handful of scrap yarn in the perfume and tuck it inside your improvised pouch. Close the top, tie it in a knot, and leave it anyplace you want to discourage skunks.

❏ Alternatively, take that solid bathroom deodorizer that turned out to be a little too strong for such a small room. Open it up so that it releases as much of its scent as possible in the space you want the skunk to leave.

Skunks: Feed the Problem

❏ When skunks become a nuisance in your yard, you can get rid of them without a close encounter of the smelly kind. Just leave a few pieces of a chewable laxative in spots where the skunk is likely to find them (and neighborhood children and pets won't). That will send Mr. Skunk on the run.

Try This Cheesy (Cloth) Idea

❏ Whether you're camping in the woods, barbecuing in the backyard, or doing some late-afternoon gardening, blackflies and mosquitoes can be quite a nuisance. Somehow, they always seem to be in your face. One way to keep them at bay is with a homemade mosquito net. Break out the leftover cheesecloth that you saved from your last painting or kitchen project. Cut a two-foot-square piece, then drape it over your head. Put on a baseball cap or other hat to keep it in place, then tuck the bottom edge of the cheesecloth into your collar. It will keep the bugs at bay.

Blackflies: Give Them Plain Vanilla

❏ If blackflies are turning your yard time into their own movable feast, smear undiluted vanilla extract over any exposed skin before you head outdoors. The flies will look elsewhere for a meal.

❏ Alternatively, fend off blackflies by rubbing apple cider vinegar on your skin. Flies are surprisingly fussy eaters, and although they may still annoy you by circling your head, they won't actually zoom in for a bite.

A Tale of a Tub

The usual by-product of a bathroom renovation is an old, stained bathtub muscled from the house and left outside on the lawn until it is hauled away by the junk man. With a bit of creative recycling (a fancy name for forgetting to call the junk man), the old tub can find a new life as a bathtub for the dog, for window screens, or for anything else that is too large or too dirty to haul inside for soaking and cleaning.

True, an old tub plunked in the middle of the lawn doesn't do much for the landscape. So take a cue from Hollywood: If movie stars can have sunken tubs in their homes, there is no reason you can't have a sunken tub in your yard (as long as you take appropriate safety precautions). Simply dig a hole somewhat larger than the tub—something more easily said than done in rocky New England soil—and slide the tub into the hole. You'll want to dig the hole at a slant, or shim the tub so it lists toward the drain; otherwise the water won't run out. Fill in the area around the tub with gravel or rocks to improve the drainage.

But wait! An open, sunken tub in the yard could be a hazard if left as is. Instead, gather fieldstones and build a knee-high ring around the perimeter. That way a person or animal won't accidentally fall in. The final touch? If you plan to wash a dog in the tub, line the bottom with chestnut-size pebbles a few inches deep so that the dog won't slip. Then grab the garden hose, the pet shampoo, a rubber stopper for the drain, and Rover—who will soon be one clean pup.

Make a Homemade Swatter

❑ Flies giving you a hard time? Swat 'em with an oversize homemade flyswatter. Collapse a wire clothes hanger so that it forms a long oval with the hook on one end. Widen the oval to the size of your fist. Wrap duct tape around the handle end and across the swatter end. Now you have a fly swatter, complete with a hook from which to hang it when it's not in use. You may not get *all* the flies, but your new contraption will certainly give you and the kids something to do on the back porch on a slow summer day.

Tender Is the Bite

❑ Stop the pain of an insect bite with meat tenderizer. The active ingredient in many meat tenderizers is an enzyme called papain, which tenderizes meat by breaking down protein. As it happens, the toxin in insect bites is protein-based. To relieve the pain of a bite, combine some tenderizer and water to make a thick paste and spread it on the bite. It will stop the hurt in no time.

Take the Bite out of Mosquitoes

❑ Mosquito bite got you down? Or at least itchy? Dab it with a teeny bit of ammonia (it's the same stuff you'll find in commercial anti-itch products). That will kill the itch right away. Just avoid scratching the bite before you try this. If the ammonia hits broken skin, it'll sting like crazy.

Stick 'Em Up (and Off)

❑ Next time you come in from a walk to find a tick or chigger on your skin and no tweezers at home, grab some duct tape. Put the sticky part over the tick, making sure the tape is in contact with the tick. Give the tape a quick yank, and the tick should come off right along with it.

❑ You don't have any duct tape on hand? Shame on you! In a pinch, try using the sticky part of a Band-Aid in the same way.

DRIVEWAYS AND WALKWAYS

Give Moss the Slip

❑ Shady areas of your walkways or driveway may be prone to grow moss, and since wet moss is extremely slippery, that can be a safety hazard. To get rid of the moss, scrape it off with an old putty or kitchen knife.

❑ To make sure moss doesn't return, soak the area with a solution of equal parts water and household bleach and allow the solution to dry. Repeat the treatment as needed, being careful to keep the bleach solution away from the lawn and tender plants.

Brew Up a Weed Killer

❏ Plagued by weeds in your brick or stone walkway? The next time you have a cup of tea, heat a little extra water. Then bring your teakettle outside and pour the boiling water over the weeds. Immediately cover the treated area with an old blanket or other cloth to hold in the heat. Keep the covering in place as long as it is still warm to the touch. The heat will finish off the weeds.

Outside the House

Don't Let This Fall between the Cracks

❏ A relatively simple way to strip weeds from between the cracks in paving stones or bricks is to use a letter opener, a broken hacksaw blade, or an old metal knitting needle to dig up the weeds by their roots.

Bring the Beach to the Driveway

❏ Sanding an icy driveway is a good way to get better traction, but lugging pails of sand around is no day at the beach. A better way is to salvage a child's discarded plastic or metal snow coaster. Dump a pile of sand in the middle of the coaster, then use the pull rope to lug the sand where you want it.

Earl's Favorites

Feed the Birds for Less

I enjoy feeding the birds, but I hate to spend hard-earned money on fancy feeding stations. So I was tickled to hear this idea. Take a clean gallon-size milk jug that still has its cap. Cut a large hole in the side of the jug to remove the handle and give the birds a place to perch. Fill the jug up to the opening with birdseed. Poke a hole in the middle of the cap with an ice pick. Thread a sturdy piece of string through the hole and knot the string to hold it in place, then hang the feeder by the other end of the string.

Outside the House

Avoid Slipups

❏ After the milk has been spilled—er, drunk—save that gallon milk jug to help improve winter traction on your front walkway. Cut off the narrow top of the jug, but leave the handle intact. Fill the base with sand and keep it by the front door during the winter months. It's ideal for spreading sand, and it won't be mistaken for an ashtray or garbage can either.

ROOFS

Hit the Roof

❏ Excessive moss on roofing shingles can work the shingles loose and cause serious problems. To avoid such potential disasters, you need to get rid of the moss early. Just pour two capfuls of household bleach into a gallon of water, dip a sponge in the mixture, and thoroughly douse the shingles. Repeat every three to four years if the moss problem is a serious one.

A Different Twist

Roofing: We Have Liftoff

A good way to remove old roofing is with a coal shovel. The straight, flat blade makes it useful for literally shoveling off shingles.

Try This on-the-House Tool

❏ When you're removing old asphalt shingles or roll roofing in preparation for installing a new roof, there's no better tool for the job than a garden implement. That's right, the long tines of a garden pitchfork are almost perfect for sliding under the shingles and around the nails that attach them to the building, then prying up whole sections of shingles at a time, nails and all.

OUTDOOR STORAGE SHEDS

Make Your Trash Can Last Forever

❏ Plastic trash cans that are used outdoors will occasionally crack from exposure to extreme temperatures, not to mention rough handling by garbage collectors. If the crack isn't that bad, repair it with duct tape. Tape over the inside and outside surfaces of the crack. For added strength, tape around the circumference of the pail as well.

Have Garbage Can, Will Garden

❏ Try storing your rakes, hoes, and other long-handled tools in a metal garbage can. (Plastic cans may not be heavy enough to keep from tipping over.) You may want to place a few rocks in the bottom for ballast. Attach S hooks to the rim for hanging small tools that would get lost if placed inside. If you want to bring all your tools into the garden with you and the path to the garden is not too bumpy, use a garbage can with wheels.

Keep Out Kids and Critters

❏ If you use an old five-gallon drywall joint compound bucket to store lawn and garden supplies such as fertilizer or lime, you'll want to make sure kids and pets can't get into it—and a lid alone may not be enough. For added protection, seal it securely with duct tape. Wrap the tape a few times around the edge of the bucket where the top overlaps the sides. Then, when you need to get into it, just cut through the tape with the point of your garden shears or pocketknife.

Protect That Padlock with a Pirate's Patch

❏ To keep the latch and padlock on your garden shed from rusting or corroding, try this "pirate's patch." Cut a flap from an old inner tube big enough to cover the lock and still leave several inches on each side.
Leave enough space beyond the patch so that you can open and close the door easily. Secure the flap to the door just above the lock by hammering in a row of small galvanized nails. Lift the "patch" to get to the lock and open the door.

Outside the House

My Way

An Old Yarn about Locks

I have several padlocks that all look alike, and I have trouble remembering which key belongs to which lock. My solution is to tie a piece of scrap yarn around the lock and another piece of the same color around the matching key.

–Carmela Cavalieri
Long Beach, New York

Outside the House

Buck(et) Up That Hose

❏ Your garden hose will last much longer if you roll it up after every use. Not having a store-bought hose reel is no excuse for leaving a hose lying in the sun, where ultraviolet rays will break down its fibers, or in the path of vehicles. To protect this vital piece of lawn care equipment, just nail an old metal bucket to your shed wall through the bucket's bottom. Wrap the hose around the bucket and store nozzles and sprinklers inside.

Hang Your Hose Here

❏ Alternatively, try this simple solution. Get a sturdy wooden coat hanger from your closet and wrap the hose around it. Then just hang the whole thing from a nail in your garden shed.

OTHER PROJECTS

Post It

❏ Old fence posts, lampposts, and other similar buried poles are either a snap or murder to pull up. When they won't budge, enlist the aid of an automobile bumper jack. Take a chain or heavy rope and wrap it several times around the post, leaving a couple of looser loops that can be grabbed by the jack tongue—the part that meets the car bumper. When you support the jack on planks (so it doesn't sink into the earth), you should be able to jack the post right out of its hole.

Stop Blister Disease in Walls

❏ As houses get repainted every eight years or so, the buildup of paint makes it harder for moisture vapor inside the house to escape through the siding. Sometimes the moisture buildup inside the walls causes shingles or clapboards to peel paint down to the wood, no matter how many times you recoat them. The solution is to introduce air passages in the siding. There are little louvered vents made specifically for this purpose, but you have to bore holes in the siding to install them. An oldtimer's trick is to take tenpenny cut nails—the kind, made for masonry, that look like triangular spikes—and drive them up in between the laps of clapboards or shingles every two to three feet. The nails will wedge open the siding about a quarter of an inch—enough to vent the wall, but not enough to be obvious or to expose new surfaces to the weather. And since the nails themselves are protected from the elements, they won't rust and stain the siding.

❏ A modern variation on the nail trick is to use plastic swizzle sticks. Just drive them in a few inches, then break off the excess.

Swab the Decks

❏ Got a spot that's too tight to reach with a paintbrush, or one that's difficult to paint accurately, such as a groove in the trim around a window? Head for the medicine cabinet. Dip a cotton swab in paint, and you'll be able to reach the tight spot *and* paint it without making smudges or stray brush marks.

Hidden Treasures

Ask Your Carpet Dealer for Some Support(s)

When you're pouring cement to support a porch or deck, the standard approach is to use Sonotubes, special forms that hold the cement until it's hardened and can then be peeled off. But you don't have to buy the tubes that are designed specifically for this purpose. Instead, ask your local carpet dealer if you can have a few of the leftover cardboard cores on which rugs are wound. Oil the insides before you pour in the cement, and it will be easier to remove the cores after the material hardens.

–Jim Collins
Canaan, New Hampshire

Just Be Sure You Label the Bottle

❏ Getting bar and chain oil into that filler hole on a chain saw can be a challenging exercise, to say the least. To make the job easier, transfer the oil to a clean container that once held dishwashing liquid. The pop-up top lets you aim the oil where you want it, so you can get on with clearing those fallen trees.

Gardening
Indoors and Out

Entire television talk shows have been de-
voted to the penchant many folks have for
gadgets—those bright, shiny gewgaws that
look so appealing in the catalog. But you don't
need fancy equipment. With just a little effort, you
can make your own equivalents from the knitting
needles, milk jugs, egg cartons, and old window
screens that are already lying around your house.

In this chapter, we'll tell you how to save time
and money in your gardens (both indoor and out)
by outfitting houseplants with old shower caps,
turning a panama hat into a hanging planter,
starting your seedlings in egg cartons, and converting a downspout into a strawberry planter.
We'll suggest ways to grow vegetables in limited
space and to find plant pots in unexpected places.
We'll even tell you how to handle those special
arrangements of cut flowers.

Now grab those recyclables and head for your
plants!

INDOOR GARDENING

**Gardening
Indoors and Out**

Dip In

❏ It's not always easy to know whether your potted plants need watering. One way is to stick any long pointed object, such as a knitting needle, a pencil (eraser end first), or a chopstick, into the soil. If the object comes up dry, add water.

Give Them a Drink before You Leave

❏ If you are going away for a week and no one is available to water your small houseplants, fear not. They'll be fine if you give them a little help from the bathroom. Water the plants before you leave, then put a plastic shower cap over each one. (The disposable shower caps that hotels give away are fine for this. You knew there was a reason you were saving those, didn't you?) The elastic on the caps will keep them in place, and the plastic will help your plants retain moisture while you're gone.

Let Them Sip through String "Straws"

❏ Here's another method for watering your indoor plants when you're away for a week or so. Put a big bucket of water in your bathtub and set your plants around the bucket. Cut ordinary household string in lengths long enough that you can put one end in the soil and one end on the bottom of the bucket of water. Your plants will drink enough water through these "straws" to survive your temporary absence.

Keep Your Plants Bottled Up— And Thriving

❏ If you have a terrarium in a bottle, you might think about buying special tools to maintain it. Well, that's what you'd do if you were an everyday sort of person, but not if you're a frugal Yankee. Make a pair of extra-long gardening tongs from last year's thin wire garden stakes or a wooden dowel left over from your last woodworking project. Each stick should be long enough to reach into the soil in the terrarium. Use the tongs, chopsticks style, to reach down through the neck of the

Gardening Indoors and Out

bottle and arrange plants or dig holes. If you don't already know how to use chopsticks, ask a waiter for a lesson the next time you have dinner at a Chinese restaurant.

❏ While you're at that restaurant, grab some extra chopsticks. They work well as terrarium tools, too. If they're not long enough, take four and tape two together to form longer sticks.

Knit One, Spear Two

❏ In a pinch, a pair of knitting needles will work as terrarium tools. And a single one makes a great spear for retrieving dead leaves from inside the bottle.

My Way

Why Fish Owners Make Great Indoor Gardeners

Aquarium owners know the routine: Every two weeks, you're supposed to vacuum debris from the tank bottom and replace 20 percent of the tank's water. The water you siphon out contains visible gunk and invisible forms of nitrogen that, if left unattended, will eventually prove fatal to fish. As it happens, those same chemicals make houseplants happy.

A number of years ago, I started watering my indoor plants with the wastewater from the fish tank, and they went on an unprecedented growth spurt. The wandering Jew hanging from our second-story loft not only flowers, but we regularly cut it back so that it won't creep across the kitchen floor 15 feet below. Our spider plants constantly sprout babies. And the jade tree and palm tree have never been greener or taller. This all happened without the use of any commercial fertilizers.

I'm not a chemist, botanist, or biologist, but the booklet that came with my daughter's fish tank went into great detail explaining the so-called nitrogen cycle of the aquarium. Simply put, fish excrete nitrogen. It stands to reason that if waste from other animals is good for garden plants, waste from fish could be good for houseplants. But there *is* a difference: I would never have tried this experiment in my home with cow manure.

–Marga Rahmann
Norwich, Vermont

DISPLAYING HOUSEPLANTS

Gardening Indoors and Out

A Planter, Just off the Top of Your Head

❏ Your daughter-in-law just walked through the door with a geranium, but you're fresh out of hanging pots. Now what? Well, if the brim on that old panama or straw hat still seems firmly attached to the crown (and you're sure you're not going to wear it anymore), you can turn it into a hanging basket. Use an awl to poke four holes through the brim—at the front, back, and on each side. Cut two 6-foot lengths of heavy-duty jute cord. Thread one end of one cord down through one of the holes, under the brim, and back up through the next hole. Repeat this on the opposite side with the other cord. Tie the top ends together, then hang the hat from the resulting knot. With the weight of a potted plant, over the seasons the hat will come to look more and more basketlike.

If that old straw hat has seen sunnier days, turn it into a holder for a hanging plant.

Break the Ice

❏ For a distinctive indoor garden, empty an old ice bucket—wooden, brass, pewter, or the like—and plant flowers in it. Or poke drainage holes in the bottom of an old metal coffeepot, teapot, or watering can and use that container as an original holder for your indoor garden.

Create a Movable Garden

❏ You can give your potted plants an attractive mobile home by placing them together in an old child's wagon with wheels.

Reflect on This

❏ Plants and flowers look beautiful in any room, but sometimes they can be a hazard when you water them

and the water accidentally drips onto the table or floor below. If you have an old mirror, framed or not, place it under the plants. The glass will protect the table below, and the reflective surface will double your enjoyment of the plants or flowers. If you are feeling really creative, paint a design on the mirror. When it's dry, cover it with varnish. Wait until the paint and varnish are completely dry before placing anything on top.

Take Out Rings on the Table

❑ Terra-cotta pots are great for most houseplants because they absorb and retain moisture. Unfortunately, for the same reason, they can be murder on polished wood surfaces. To keep houseplants in clay pots from marring your furniture's finish, place each pot inside the shallow plastic top of a take-out food container.

Have a Seat

❑ Here's a perfect plant stand for the corner of your living room or family room: an old commode chair. Just choose a ceramic pot (one without a drainage hole) that fits in the hole in the chair seat. Plant your greenery in the pot and slide the pot into place.

STARTING OUTDOOR PLANTS

Treat Plants as Individuals

❑ If you're starting plants indoors before planting them in the garden, you know that it's helpful to put them in individual containers instead of flats. The roots of one plant won't become entangled with the roots of others, and they'll be easier to transplant. Where can you find appropriate containers? Before you look elsewhere, try raiding your trash. Cutoff milk jugs work well for starting tomato and pepper plants, while Styrofoam cups, Dixie cups, or individual yogurt containers are just the right size for smaller plants. (Be sure to punch holes in the bottom for drainage.) Until you're ready to transplant, place the individual containers on top of a layer of small rocks or gravel inside one of those deep trays from the deli or from your last take-out meal. (Plastic or Styrofoam containers are best for this because they won't rust.) The tray will collect any water that seeps through the drainage holes of your containers. It also will act as a humidifier for the last dry days before spring appears.

We'll Start the Garden Right after Breakfast

❏ Styrofoam egg cartons also work well as starter planters. Rip off the top of each carton and set it aside. Poke holes in the bottom of each egg holder and place the top of the carton underneath as a water collection pan.

Planting Humpty-Dumpty

❏ You can also plant your seeds directly in eggshell halves, then plant the shells directly in your garden. The protein and calcium will degrade in the soil and give added nourishment to seeds. Of course, you may want to keep the delicate eggshell-guarded plants in egg cartons until they're ready to go into the garden.

The Eyes Have It

❏ After cutting potato eyes for planting, put each piece of tuber in one compartment of an old egg carton. Keep the carton warm but out of the sun for a few days to encourage sprouting. Once the eyes have sprouted, plant them in soil.

Hidden Treasures

Flower Bulbs for Free

Every spring, especially after Memorial Day, many cemeteries clean up old flowerpots. Typically, they simply discard them, even though some of the pots have perfectly good bulbs in them. You may be able to get tulip, hyacinth, daffodil, and other bulbs for free merely by asking if you can take some of the discarded flowerpots, or by offering to collect the pots from the graves, thereby saving the cemetery that labor. Or offer to plant some of the bulbs in a park or other public place—with permission, of course.

Go for the Greenhouse Effect

❏ Give your new seedlings a window on the world— and a healthy start. When you're replacing old windows, hold on to the windowpanes. Place the panes

Gardening Indoors and Out

over seed flats after you've put plants in them to keep the humidity high and reduce the need to water. The couple of inches between the soil and the window will create a perfect hothouse environment for those critical first days.

Now *That's* Iceberg Lettuce

❏ If you're gardening in a small space or just eager for the first salad of the year, try planting your salad mix in the individual compartments of old ice cube trays filled with potting soil. Plant no more than four to six seeds per compartment. Amazingly, many lettuce and salad varieties can get to harvestable size in the trays. The trick is to maintain proper moisture levels and to infuse the plants with extra nutrients.

PLANTING OUTDOORS

Small Seeds: Card 'Em

❏ Small seeds bedevil the gardener, especially at planting time. It can be excruciatingly hard to see how many you're planting and where they're actually ending up. Would you believe that a three- by five-inch file card can solve this problem? Just fold the card into a V shape, pour the seeds into the crease, and place the seeds on or into the soil as required. The light color of the file card will help you see the seeds more clearly, and the V shape will give you better planting aim.

Shake It

❏ Here's another trick for scattering tiny seeds. Mix the fine seeds with unflavored gelatin (which also adds extra protein) or flour and scatter the mixture from a saltshaker. The shaker will give you good distribution control, and the gelatin or flour will let you see where your seeds have landed.

Soft and Absorbent

❏ Alternatively, place those hard-to-see seeds in the garden on top of a single layer of toilet paper. Cover the seeds with another layer of toilet paper and moisten both layers. Add a thin layer of soil over the whole business. The moistened toilet paper will give your seeds a head start on germination and quickly decompose underground.

Get Cagey

❏ If animals just won't leave your bulbs alone, try caging them—the bulbs, that is. Before planting the bulbs in the ground, place them in an old metal mesh container. (The kind that many folks hang from the ceiling to store onions is perfect.) Or use a bunch of plastic baskets from strawberries. The bulbs will still have plenty of room to grow, but the varmints will no longer be able to reach them by burrowing underground.

Hatch Some Fine Fertilizer

❏ Is it guests and eggs that smell after five days? Not if they're boiled eggs. But that doesn't mean you can eat

**Gardening
Indoors and Out**

them. After a week or so in the refrigerator, you should leave them alone. You can, however, keep your hard-boiled Easter eggs in the refrigerator after the holiday until it's time to plant summer squash, zucchini, or cucumbers, then use the eggs for fertilizer. Plant an egg six to eight inches deep in the center of each hill, then plant three pairs of seeds in a circle around it. As the egg decomposes, it will provide nutrition for the squash plants.

RAISED BEDS

Restrain Those Herbs

❏ If you're using a raised bed to raise herbs, you need to watch that they don't overtake the bed. (Tarragon and mint are particularly notorious space offenders.) Try burying a section of old stovepipe a couple of inches below the plants when you first put them in the bed. Place it vertically, so that the roots can extend down into the opening in the pipe. When the roots are confined to the pipe, they won't be able to hog your limited space.

Play Rungs and Ladders

❏ To give definition to a raised garden bed, especially if you're growing herbs or other plants that don't need a lot of space, try planting in the spaces between rungs in an old ladder placed flat on the ground, or in the openings of an old small-paned window (without the glass, of course). Either of these devices will create small, easily tended spaces.

GARDENING IN LIMITED SPACE

Itsy-Bitsy Plants, in the Waterspout

❏ To grow strawberries or other short-rooted plants when you don't have a lot of gardening space, create a vertical garden with an old downspout. Fill the spout with soil, poke holes in it, and plant your strawberries

or herbs in the holes. Attach the spout to a fence post
to give the plants a good dose of sun.

❏ Alternatively, you can use an old gutter in a similar
way. Just fill it with dirt, insert the plants, and mount it
horizontally along the top of the fence. You'll have a conversation piece, a space saver, and a garden all in one.

Think Vertical

❏ If you're short of growing room, think vertical instead
of horizontal when it comes to planning your garden.
Create a simple and easily reusable vertical support for
vegetables such as peas, beans, and cucumbers by
starting with leftover wire mesh fencing approximately
four feet high. Drive five-foot stakes into the ground four

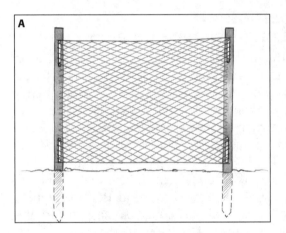

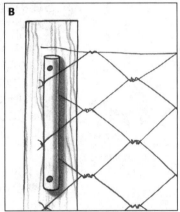

to five feet apart. Lace thin dowels through the mesh at
the top and bottom. Nail the dowels to the stakes, or
drive in a nail at the end of each stake, rest the dowel
on it, and lash the dowel to the stake. At the end of the
season, remove the dowels and roll up the wire to use
next year.

*To make a quick
vertical support for
vegetable vines, drive
a pair of stakes into
the ground and link
them with wire mesh
fencing (A). Secure the
fencing with dowels
(B), and you're ready
to grow.*

Help Melons Hang Out

❏ Even melons and squash can be grown vertically
with wire mesh fencing for support. As these plants
ripen, you'll need to provide some extra support to keep
the weight of the fruit from pulling the vines back onto
the ground. That's where your collection of old panty
hose comes in. Slip a midsize melon into each toe of

each pair of hose. Then hang the stockings on the fencing. The melons and squash will ripen more evenly, and you'll have more space for other crops.

Offer Some Help to Those Baby Vegetables

❏ Need a trellis for growing veggies? Take a baby crib that's outlived its original purpose and remove two sides of the same length. Prop them against each other to form an inverted V and tie them together at the top. You now have a trellis for cucumbers, peas, beans, or spaghetti squash.

CONTAINER GARDENING

Strawberries: Deter Long-Distance Runners

❏ Most strawberry varieties send out runners. This is their means of propagation, so healthy runners will lead to the next producing plants. But in the meantime, you need to keep them under control. To do that, dig a few holes in the soil near the parent plant and place in each hole a starter pot (or a Dixie cup or single-serving yogurt container) filled with dirt. Then route the runners from the parent into the starter pots. This is where your refusal to throw anything away comes in. Hold the runners lightly in place with old-fashioned clothespins (not the spring-loaded kind) until the roots are established. Then cut off the tip of each runner beyond the starter pot.

Pipe In Your Own Water

❏ Potted plants dry out more easily than plants in the ground, so special watering systems can make your life easier and help your plants, too. Before placing plants in large containers such as strawberry jars, grab a length of polyvinyl chloride (PVC) pipe with holes and stand it upright in the jar. (If you have some PVC pipe lying around but it doesn't have holes in it, it's easy to drill holes two inches apart.) When you water the plants, pour water into the pipe to refresh the whole jar at once.

Air Out Containers

❏ You don't want your plants becoming waterlogged because water can't flow through their containers. To prevent this, make sure your containers have drainage holes in the bottoms. Then place them over pairs of leftover bricks or pieces of scrap wood to aid the circulation of air and give water a place to drain.

Don't Send Good Money down the Drain

❏ To further encourage good drainage, try putting any of these items in the bottom of your container before you pot your plant: broken pieces of clay pots, broken dishes, walnut shells, seashells, marbles, or stones. To keep fragile roots from getting cut on these drainage pieces, add a layer or two of discarded panty hose over the pieces.

Hidden Treasures

Restaurant Take-Out for Your Garden

The large food containers used by restaurants, school cafeterias, and other institutions are perfect for container gardening. Placing your soil and plants in them lets you maintain a garden in a small (and portable) space. It also lets you contain the roots of notoriously invasive plants such as mint and violets, preventing them from taking over the entire lawn. Stop by your favorite restaurant or any other institution that serves food in large quantities and see if the staff will let you take a few empty containers off their hands.

WATERING PLANTS

Water on Time

❏ Before you go away from your garden for the weekend, set up this simple irrigation system. Poke several small holes in the bottoms of a couple of plastic one-gallon milk jugs and place them next to your thirstiest plants, such as tomatoes or newly planted trees. Fill the jugs with water from your garden hose right before you leave. The water will slowly leak out of the jugs, gently watering the plants in your absence.

Juice Up Your Irrigation System

❏ Who needs an expensive garden irrigation system, or even a system of soaker hoses, when you can build in

Earl's Favorites

A Darned Good Watering Can

You don't need a store-bought watering can to sprinkle your plants with water. All you need is an empty one-gallon milk or water jug. Use an ice pick or nut pick to poke about 10 tiny holes around the lower edge of the jug opening. Fill the jug with water and put the lid or cap back on to create some suction and keep the water from pouring out all at once. Then sprinkle away.

a juice can irrigation system? When you're planting your garden, add foot-deep holes about a foot from each plant. In the holes, "plant" 32-ounce juice cans with the bottoms and tops removed. (Position them so that the open tops are level with the top of the soil.) When you water your plants, fill the juice cans with water as well. They'll draw water down to the soil below the plants and encourage healthy root growth.

Keep Them Swingin' in the Rain

❑ If you'd rather not have water dripping from the drainage holes in your hanging plants, try fitting them with plastic shower caps. They'll catch the light drips, though not a heavy downpour. Just remove the caps after the shower is over.

TOOLS

Dibble in the Dirt

❑ A dibble is a handy tool to have at the beginning of the gardening season, when you're planting a lot of seedlings. You typically poke a dibble in the ground to create a seedling-size hole. Although you can buy a dibble at your lawn and garden store, you have many options for making one at home. The wooden handle from a no-longer-useful shovel makes an excellent dibble. Just cut the handle down so that it measures about eight inches from the grip, which you keep in place. Then sand off the rough edges. Or you can make a dibble without a grip by cutting down an old broom or mop handle.

Fork It Over

❏ It's simple but effective: A long-handled kitchen fork makes an excellent weeding tool. Bend the tines, if you like, to create a "hoe" effect.

OTHER GARDEN HELPERS

Now Showing on the Big (Old) Screen

❏ Try this down-to-earth way to break up clods of soil before you plant. Set an old aluminum or steel window screen on blocks or buckets, then sift the soil through the screen. Your back and your hands will appreciate it!

And Now It's Time for the Garden Report

❏ Need a bunch of instant (and cheap) markers to help you remember what you planted where?

> ## My Way
> ### Yankees Are Made, Not Born
>
> My grandfather—Italian by birth, Yankee by choice—saved all his old hoses. He took the ones that had holes in them and made them into a long, snaking drip irrigation system. He spent his days managing a garden supply store but always made do at home. I've learned to do the same with my old hoses.
>
> **–Laura Simoes**
> *Hillsborough, New Hampshire*

Turn to your teenager for help—not with the work, but with the materials. The plastic binder strips that held last year's term papers are perfect for marking your plants. Just remove them from the papers, label each with magic marker, and insert it in the ground next to the appropriate plants. You'll have no more excuses for forgetting what's planted where.

Mark Those Plants

❏ Why pay for fancy plant markers when you have a ready supply of weather-resistant markers in your laundry room? Cut strips from the sides of white plastic bleach bottles and write on them with an indelible marker. You can use clear plastic bottles, too, but they won't be as easy to spot in the garden.

Scrunch Now, Munch Later

❏ When it comes to securing tender plant stems to their supports, you need something that's strong but flexible, something that won't cut into the stems. How about discarded hair scrunchies? Just loop them around stem and stake, and you're all set.

Stake 'Em Up

❏ It's hard to find something that will hold your plants to their stakes without cutting or otherwise harming them. If your newspaper comes in a long, thin plastic bag, you have a great option for a soft and supple stake tie. It's not as harsh as twine or wire, but it will hold a knot around a stake.

Cushion Your Knees

❏ Do you find that gardening is tough on your knees? Here's a way to save your pants and your knees at the same time. Put on an old pair of work pants, then fasten a spare cellulose kitchen sponge to each knee with duct tape. (Donning the pants first lets you see where the sponge will be most effective.) If a hole has worn through one knee, turn the pants leg inside out and line the hole with a strip of duct tape, sticky side down. Then step into the pants and apply the sponge patch to the outside. Be sure to remove the sponge and tape before laundering the pants, then reapply them before taking up the weeding again.

My Way

Adventure in the Garden

I'm both an avid gardener and an outdoorswoman, which of course means that in the summer I am torn between working in my garden and going hiking or sailboarding. One advantage I have to my conflicting passions is a ready supply of unusual (but functional) contraptions for my garden. For example, I stick old ski poles in the ground for my peas to climb up. And an old sailboard boom is the only pole sturdy enough to handle my aggressive raspberry plants. It's a nice way to combine these two important parts of my life.

–Cath Carine
Seattle, Washington

❏ Alternatively, take the cups from an old padded bra and tape them over those work pants in exactly the same way. Hey, if you apply the tape carefully, no one has to know just what that padding used to be!

Weed in Comfort

❏ Another way to cushion your knees in the garden is to bring along a couple of old mouse pads from your computer and kneel on those. Or attach them directly to your pant legs with strips of duct tape. (Don't overdo the duct tape. You want to be able to remove the pads later so you can wash the pants.) To double the cushioning effect, fold each pad in half before taping it to your pants.

Peg Those Pots

❏ How can you store clay pots after the gardening season is over? You can stack them on top of each other, but if they tip over, they are likely to break or chip. A simple solution is to create a wooden peg "home" for the pots. Measure the diameter of your pots, then nail together several boards of scrap wood to create a sturdy, square base of roughly the same size or slightly larger. (If the pots are 10 inches in diameter, the base should measure about 10 inches by 10 inches and be 2 inches thick.) Then drill halfway through the middle of the base and glue a 2- or 3-foot dowel into the hole. A cut-down broom or mop handle will make a fine dowel, although the size of your dowel will be dictated by the size of the drainage holes in the bottom of your pots. Once the glue is dry, slide the pots onto the peg, where they'll be ready for the next gardening season.

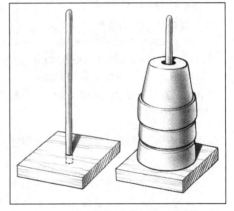

A dowel secured to a base of scrap wood makes a handy winter home for clay pots.

Add Personality to Your Garden

❏ Scarecrows may no longer be considered useful as bird and animal deterrents, but they still mean "garden"

Gardening Indoors and Out

to many people. They also mean recycling—you certainly wouldn't go out and *buy* one! Start your scarecrow with the handle from an old broom or mop. Use a gallon milk jug for a head. Let the lopped-off mop become the scarecrow's hair, then cut old aluminum pie plates into fingers or feet. Wherever it suits your fancy, add glittery items that move, which are more likely to scare off birds or deer. This contraption may or may not deter pests, but it definitely will add interest to your garden.

Mail In Your Garden Tools

❑ If you'd like to avoid carting small garden tools back and forth every time you want to work with them, try planting an old rural delivery mailbox at the edge of your garden. Slip your spades, trowels, and gardening gloves in there, and they'll be handy when you need them.

A Different Twist

Who Needs a Whetstone?

You can sharpen a pruning knife or shears without leaving the garden if you have a clay flowerpot handy. Just use the edge of the pot as a sharpening stone.

Cleanup: Put the Hose Next to the Hose

❑ Sometimes it would be nice to have an outdoor shower just so you could scrub yourself off after working in the garden. You can have the next best thing if you simply drop a bar of soap in a leg cut from an old pair of panty hose and hang up your improvised scrubber next to the garden hose. After you finish gardening for the day, you can wash up without even taking the soap out of the nylon.

Leave the Mud Bath to the Spa

❑ It's hard to avoid mud when you weed your garden, especially early in the season and after a heavy rain. To help win this mud wrestling match, try rolling out the carpet—strips of an old one, that is—between your garden rows. Or set out a row of carpet remnants for an elegant but practical path above the mud.

COMPOSTING

Give It Air

❏ A normal compost pile stands between four and six feet high. To keep the pile from overheating or developing a strong odor, it helps to aerate it—to get air into the middle of the heap. That doesn't require any fancy equipment. Just save a few of the cardboard tubes from wrapping paper or paper towels. Insert them vertically into the pile as you're building it up, so the pile grows around your homemade aerators. Continue adding new tubes occasionally, always being careful to keep the

The Inside Story

It's a Growth Industry

Back around the turn of the nineteenth century, the Shakers of the New Lebanon and Watervliet, New York, communities first began packaging and selling seeds in envelopes they filled themselves. This changed not only the seed industry but also the Shakers' place in it. The convenient packages were easy to store and inexpensive to send through the mail. By 1836, the Shakers of these two communities had become a kind of clearinghouse for seeds of every variety. They grew some seeds and accepted others from outside sources, then packaged them all and sold them. Eventually, they were sending out about 150,000 packets a year.

Ever practical, the Shakers did a lot of controlled testing on their seeds in different conditions. Out of concern for their customers, they wrote a manual that listed all the varieties they sold, where each plant grew best, when to plant different seeds, and other cautionary advice. They were hoping to steer customers to the varieties of plants with which the growers might have the best luck. This *Gardener's Manual* is considered the first modern seed catalog. These days, most gardeners can't think of getting through February without a few seed catalogs to help them fantasize about the spring to come.

Nutrition Boosters You Were About to Pour down the Drain

Some of the best sources of nutrients for your plants, both indoor and out, are the leftovers from your own meals. From breakfast through dinner, here are just a few of the possibilities.

1. The leaves from leftover tea bags or loose tea. These contain nitrogen, which is just what your plants need. Spread them over the soil and work them in a bit for the best effect.
2. Club soda. Didn't finish that bottle you opened, and now it's gone flat? Don't pour what's left down the drain. Instead, pour it over your plants.

The minerals in the soda will be good for them.
3. Cooking water from pasta or potatoes. It has nutrients your plants can use, and the starches will give them an extra boost.

If you use all these and your plants are still thirsty, go back to the kitchen sink. One pleasure of doing dishes by hand is being able to use the rinse water in your garden or on your houseplants (except African violets). Soap in the water kills a number of pests, and you'll be doing your bit to conserve water as well, especially in times of drought.

tops above the surface and open to the air. As older tubes are covered up or decompose, the more recent additions will carry on the aerating task.

Go Nuts for Compost

❑ Looking to boost the nitrogen content of your compost to make it even more beneficial for your plants? Save the shells from all the peanuts your family consumes and work them into the compost pile. The shells will decompose easily and are a terrific source of nitrogen.

Breakfast Makes the Best Compost

❑ Coffee grounds offer another way to add nitrogen to compost, and their ability to retain moisture also helps keep the pile from drying out. Just dump the grounds on top of the pile.

❑ Alternatively, bolster the quality of your compost by tossing onto it an occasional handful of grapefruit, orange, or lemon rinds. In addition to nitrogen, these will provide the phosphorus and potassium that healthy plants need.

PESTS

Kids Will Want to Help with This Chore

❏ It's a sad fact: To grow beautiful flowers or plants, gardeners are forced to kill the bugs and pests that feed on them. Here's a way to make an onerous task a little less so—maybe even (dare we say it?) fun. Along with your weeding tools, carry into the garden a squirt gun filled with soapy water. Spray flying insects, such as aphids, with the squirt gun. Even if the water spray doesn't kill them, the soapy coating on their wings may, and it will definitely make it harder for them to reach their destination—which was, of course, your precious plants.

'Ear This

❏ The European earwig is known for feeding at night on tender plant parts. To deter these pests, place tubes of rolled-up newspaper or the cardboard cores from gift wrap horizontally on the ground near affected or vulnerable plants. Earwigs will collect in the cylinders. You can then gather up the tubes and dispose of them.

Their Mothers Never Told Them about the Evils of Alcohol

❏ You can also attract earwigs with containers that you've partly filled with a mixture of equal parts vegetable oil and beer. Empty the containers daily.

Host a Beer Bash for Slugs

❏ Slugs like their liquor, too. A time-honored and consistently effective way to trap slugs is to create a drinking hazard for them. Fill a bowl with beer and plant the bowl in the garden so that the lip of the bowl is raised ever so slightly above the ground. The slugs will seek out the beer bash and drown in the bowl.

Pests

Gardening Indoors and Out

Fight Slugs with Seashells

❏ If you have a problem with slugs and you live near the ocean, try this fun and low-cost way to keep the pests away from your plants. Collect all the seashells you can find (this is a great assignment for kids), then crush them and spread the crushed shells around your plants. The slugs won't like crawling over the sharp edges, so they'll look for more comfortable dining quarters.

Collar Those Cutworms

❏ There are more than 3,000 species of cutworms in North America, so it's the rare gardener who doesn't

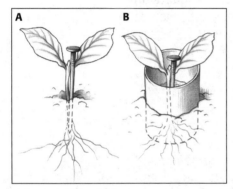

Poke a nail into the soil next to each plant's stem (A), then tuck a "collar" into the ground around the young plant (B). That will prevent larvae from making the cut.

have to contend with these voracious caterpillars. One way to battle them is to create "cutworm collars" around plants you want to protect. You can make collars out of cutoff milk cartons, short lengths of PVC pipe, metal cans, or sections of cardboard tubes. Lengths of three to four inches work best. The goal is to create a barrier between the plant stem and the soil. Slit the collar material lengthwise to fit it around the stem, then press the outer edge of the collar one to two inches into the soil around each plant. Cutworms won't go over your barricade. As an extra precaution, try inserting a nail or stick into the soil directly next to the stem of the plant you want to protect. It will deter cutworms because the larvae can't wrap around the plant stem to fell it.

Mealybugs: Rub Them Out

❏ Mealybugs are small, white, wingless insects that prefer ferns, ficus, chrysanthemums, and African violets. If you have a single infected plant, remove the mealybugs using cotton swabs moistened with a solution of equal parts rubbing alcohol and water.

Don't Coddle This Moth

❏ The codling moth is considered the most destructive insect affecting apples and pears in the United States.

Its larva is *the* worm in a wormy apple. Two or three generations can appear each year, with the second generation, in high summer, typically the most damaging to fruit trees. You can spot the larvae by looking for telltale crumbly brown excrement on the outside of fruit. To trap adult moths, and thus eliminate the larvae they'll generate, create traps baited with equal parts molasses and water or molasses and beer. Hang this fermenting mixture in cutout milk jugs on tree limbs. Clean out the jugs every couple of days.

Gardening Indoors and Out

How Sweet It Is

❏ Another sweet but deadly bait for fruit pests is 1 cup water, ½ cup apple cider vinegar, ¼ cup sugar, and 1 tablespoon molasses. Pour about an inch of this mixture into soup cans with the lids removed or into individual yogurt containers. Hang two or three traps on each fruit tree. Clean and refill the traps as necessary.

Cabbage Maggots: Lay Out the Carpet

❏ Cabbage maggots feed on broccoli, cauliflower, and cabbage and lay their eggs in the soil beneath plants. Creating a "maggot mat" can disrupt this cycle and save your plants. Get a one-foot-square carpet remnant or piece of tar paper and make a hole in the middle for the plant stem. Cut the mat so that you can slide it around the plant on top of the soil, then tape the slit shut with waterproof tape. The maggot mat will create an effective barrier to keep the pests away from the soil around delicate young plants.

My Way

Guess They Couldn't Handle the Chopsticks

We had a terrific problem with the neighborhood cats coming into our newly planted vegetable garden, destroying our dreams of arugula salad and corn on the cob. We tried many methods before hitting on one that kept them away long enough for the plants to take hold. We put lengths of chicken wire down on the ground and secured it by poking old chopsticks through the wire into the ground. The chicken wire "carpet" deterred even the most avid feline diggers, and we got our salad and corn after all.

–Rebecca Todd
Seattle, Washington

Bet They Can't Eat Just One

❏ If you think your potted plant may have a problem with root-damaging worms, set a slice of raw potato on

A garden of milk jugs? Why not, if they'll protect your melons?

the soil's surface. The worms will come to the surface to get at the tasty treat. Then you can get at—and get rid of—them.

Keep the Mice from Those Melons

❏ Protect melons such as cantaloupes from mice and chipmunks by placing each still-growing melon in half a plastic one-gallon milk jug. Cut the jug vertically, from the top to the bottom, then turn each half on its side so that the melon lies along the length of it. Leave or make holes so that rainwater can drain out.

Light Up the Night

❏ Have the neighborhood raccoons been hanging out in your backyard and garden? Here's a way to discourage the little darlings. Next time you're doing spring-cleaning and run across the blinking Christmas tree lights, don't put them in the attic. If your garden is close to the house, string up the lights on old broomsticks or mop handles or whatever you use to stake up your vegetables. The blinking lights will deter the animals (and give your neighbors something to talk about) at night. Just be sure to disconnect the power when you water the plants.

Keep Your Garden from Being Habit-Forming

❏ Deer are creatures of habit. They repeatedly follow familiar paths until they sense or encounter danger. If the path to your garden has become a habit you'd like the neighborhood deer to break, try this behavior modification technique. String heavy-duty monofilament fishing line two to three feet above the ground directly in the deer's regular path. Tie each end of the line to flexible tree branches. Add lightweight, noise-causing objects. The deer will back away from the distraction you've created and are likely to deviate just far enough from their regular path to stay away from your garden.

Pests

Hair Here, No Deer

❏ Deer don't care for the smell of human hair, which can work to the gardener's advantage. Create small sachets of human hair in lengths of nylon stocking or cheesecloth. (You can get the hair from family hairbrushes or from local hairdressers.) Hang them on four-foot stakes, placed four feet apart, all around the garden. Replace the sachets every four days to keep the human smell fresh.

Gardening Indoors and Out

ARRANGING CUT FLOWERS

Not Quite Mr. Potato Head

❏ Don't have florist's foam for arranging flowers? No problem, as long as you have some potatoes. Cut a large raw potato in half and place it flat side down for a base. Poke holes in the potato large enough for your stems. Insert the stems in the holes. If you wish, cover the edges of the potato with cloth.

Give Tulips Some Posture Pointers

❏ If your tulips, mums, or other ornamental flowers have drooping heads, try sticking a straight pin just below the bottom of each flower to keep it upright on its stem. Sharp-ended toothpicks also work well.

A Different Twist

We Think This Is Called Pickling

Some swear by this alcoholic floral preservative. Add a teaspoon of gin or vodka to the water in a vase. Nobody's saying what they do with the *rest* of the bottle . . .

PRESERVING CUT FLOWERS

Put Stems through a Searing Experience

❏ Flowers with hollow stems, such as poppies and dahlias, secrete a milky substance when cut. The stems of these flowers need to be seared after cutting to make them last longer. And how exactly do you sear the stem? Hold it against a hot chafing dish or in the flame of a candle. The flowers will last even longer if you set the stems in warm—not cold—water after searing.

Gardening Indoors and Out

Even Flowers Like Soft Drinks

❑ Cut flowers can be rejuvenated by adding a mixture of equal parts water and a citrus-flavored carbonated soft drink with sugar. The flowers should perk up after drinking this mixture.

Offer Them a Sip of Vinegar

❑ Another refreshing drink for cut flowers is a mixture of 2 tablespoons vinegar, 1 teaspoon sugar, and 1 quart water.

Don't Quite Bleach Their Roots

❑ To keep cut flowers fresh a little longer, add a solution of 2 drops household bleach, 1 teaspoon sugar, and 1 quart water to the vase.

PRESERVING VEGETABLES

Baby Your Produce

❑ Looking for a way to clean freshly picked produce and keep it crisp? When you head out to the garden, bring along a baby bathtub that's no longer needed for its original purpose. Use the hose to fill it with clean, cool water, then drop the vegetables in the water as you pick them. They'll stay crisp longer, and you'll also have a chance to wash them before bringing them into the kitchen.

Find Your Roots

❑ Most people don't have dirt floors in their cellars anymore, much less an actual root cellar. So how can you store your root vegetables over the winter? A fine backyard alternative is to dig a hole before the ground freezes and place a clean plastic garbage can in the hole. Layer your root vegetables in the can, put the lid on it, and mulch thickly over the top. (For mulch, use something that is easily removed and replaced, such as evergreen branches, since you'll want access to the "cellar" during the winter.) Be sure to mark your backyard root cellar so that you can find it once the snow falls.

Getting Rid of Zucchini? We Have Our Ways

You've used them in every stew, soup, and stir-fry you can think of. You've given so many to neighbors and friends that they've started walking the other way when they see you coming. And you haven't the heart to start leaving them anonymously on people's doorsteps or in their mailboxes (although you've thought of it). It's time to try these ideas for using up that most infamous of garden successes, the zucchini.

● Add a little flair to your giveaway. It's devious, we know, but one gardener of our acquaintance dressed up the first zucchini of the season with a big red bow and gave it to an elderly friend on her birthday. And the friend actually *liked* it!

● Give in bulk. Donate your garden's bounty (not just your summer squash) to the local food pantry or soup kitchen. Both often need food during the summer, when other donors are vacationing. If you're not sure how to contact a food pantry or soup kitchen, try calling your town or city hall. The folks there are sure to know.

● Add some elbow grease. For a little extra effort, you can create gifts that many people will appreciate and want. Bake up a quadruple batch (or more) of zucchini bread, freeze the loaves, and give generously over the next several weeks.

● Think of the children. Try offering a basket of zucchini to your local day care center for the children to play "Mrs. Zucchini Head" with or to use in art projects.

● Make it a game. Ask neighborhood kids over for some vegetable batting practice, with zucchini for the bats and no-good cherry tomatoes for the balls. They'll have some fun, and the troublesome zucchini will be gone. Of course, this option works only if your yard or neighborhood contains some space that can absorb the mayhem. An unmowed field, for example, would be perfect.

Get a Leg Up on Onion Storage

❏ To make your harvested onions last much longer, store them in a leg from an old pair of panty hose. Put one onion in the leg and tie a knot above it. Then slide another onion into the leg and tie it off. Each time you need an onion, simply cut the lowest-hanging onion,

Gardening Indoors and Out

leaving the knot above it intact. The knots will keep all the onions from cascading down when you remove the first one, and they'll also keep them separated, allowing air to circulate between them and thus preventing them from rotting.

PRESERVING HERBS

Get Into Cubist Art

❏ A lovely way to keep herbs is to chop them up, then place them in ice cube trays, fill the trays with water, and freeze them. An average cube holds about a tablespoon of chopped herb and a tablespoon of water, which means you can simply add the herbed ice cubes to many recipes. And ice cubes made of mint are refreshing additions to drinks at any time of year.

4 Alternative Uses for Herbs

Every good cook knows that adding a little basil to the spaghetti sauce or a bit of sage to the turkey stuffing can add a world of flavor. But have you tried using herbs as breath fresheners or hair conditioners? If you have more plants than you know what to do with in your herb garden, consider using them in any of the following ways.

1. Scented clothing rinse. In a covered pan, simmer 2 tablespoons dried rosemary and 2 tablespoons dried lavender with 2 cups water for 15 minutes. Strain. Discard the herbs, then add the liquid to the washing machine's final rinse cycle to give a lovely scent to your wardrobe.

2. Hair conditioner. Combine ½ cup dried chamomile leaves, ¼ cup dried rosemary leaves, and 1 cup safflower oil. Heat the mixture for 30 minutes, let it stand for a week, and then strain it. Warm the mixture slightly before working it into your hair. Shampoo to remove the conditioner.

3. Tooth cleanser. Rub a sage leaf over your teeth and gums for a fresh taste and feel.

4. Breath freshener. Chew on pulverized nettle leaves or on fresh watercress or parsley to sweeten your breath naturally.

SAVING SEEDS

Harvest Sunflower Seeds with a Toothbrush

❏ When the backs of the heads on sunflower plants turn brown, it's time to harvest the seeds to plant next year. An easy way to do that is to brush the tops of the plants with an old toothbrush. The brushing will release the seeds from the heads.

Gardening Indoors and Out

Just Add Milk

❏ One of the keys to developing your own seed stock is keeping the seeds completely dry over the winter. When you first put saved seeds in a glass jar, close the jar tightly. Check each day for the first two or three days to be sure moisture hasn't developed. If it has, the seeds need more drying time. To keep humidity down during the rest of the winter, place 2 heaping tablespoons of powdered milk in a stack of 4 facial tissues. Fold and roll the tissues to make a small pouch and secure it with tape or a rubber band. Place the pouch in the jar with the seeds. Replace the powdered milk with a fresh batch every six months or so.

FROST PROTECTION

Give Tender Plants Proper Toppers

❏ For early frost protection for tender seedlings, cut off the bottoms of plastic milk jugs, but keep the tops on. Place one bottomless jug over each plant as a "hot cap."

Plants Are Fragile, Too

❏ Save the plastic bubble wrap from your packing boxes and use it to protect the container plants you don't move inside for the winter from frost damage. Wrap each container so that the bubble wrap extends a couple of inches above the lip of the container. Hold the wrap in place with string or duct tape. With this extra insulation, the soil in the container will be as warm and protected as if it were under several feet of snow.

**Gardening
Indoors and Out**

THE GARDEN IN WINTER

Remember Your Garden Faucets

❏ If you don't have a frost-free faucet for your garden, you need to spend some time winterizing your outdoor faucets when the weather starts to get nippy. Before the ground freezes, shut off the flow to those faucets, then drain each spigot and cover it with newspaper. Wrap the newspaper in a plastic bag and secure the bag with rubber bands or tape. The newspaper will insulate the faucet, and the plastic will keep it dry.

Bough Down

❏ You worked hard preparing your garden for the winter, and now the winter winds have flung aside your ground cover or the sun has melted the insulating snow. Let your discarded Christmas tree give you good cheer! Trim some of the branches and use the boughs as a mulch for those areas where wind or sun have removed an insulating layer of snow from garden or flower beds.

Don't Open a Mouse Hotel

❏ Mice and other rodents will be tempted to set up winter quarters in any shelters you create for your plants or trees. To keep them away, place mothballs around the base of the wrapped or covered plants. Mothballs are poisonous if eaten, however, so use them only if you're sure that children and pets will not get at them.

Recreation, Sports, and Hobbies

When did hobbies stop being simple ways to relax and start becoming major investments? Whether you're into boating, skiing, or handicrafts, these days you could pour your life savings into a new hobby before you make it through your first mail-order catalog.

You could, that is, unless you read this chapter first. Here we'll tell you our favorite techniques for transporting a canoe without destroying your car roof, creating an instant pincushion, and cleaning tree sap off your tent. And, of course, we'll suggest plenty of frugal substitutes for everything from a golf bag to a knitter's stitch holder to a replacement piece for a board game.

So, are you looking to get the most mileage out of your sporting equipment without buying more? Wondering what to do with that old croquet set? If one of your hobbies is being thrifty, you'll love the answers to these and other questions that appear in this chapter. Let the games begin!

CAMPING

Claim Your Stake

❏ Don't have and don't want to buy tent stakes? There are probably plenty of handy items around the house that will make good substitutes. Try heavy-gauge knitting needles (number eight or higher), old cutlery, paintbrushes, clothespins, or an old wooden dowel cut into six-inch lengths. Of course, if you're already in the woods and don't have stakes, just scout around for some sticks. And lacking sticks, tie each nylon line to a large rock, then pull the line taut. Unless a real storm blows, this shelter will keep you dry from late spring to early fall.

Put a Little Lump in Your Tarp

❏ You say there are no grommets in your tarp? Find some small round stones, some acorns, or even a couple of hard clumps of dirt, each about the size of a marble. Place one under the tarp edge, fold the tarp down around it, and then twist some line around that so the whole thing resembles a head and neck. This is called "choking the chicken." Now tie the cord around this neck and tie the end to your stake.

Get Well-Grounded

❏ If you've ever rolled over on a sharp rock or a stick in the middle of the night, you know what a pain in the back, neck, or butt it can be. And when that point tears a hole in the floor of your tent, that's adding insult to injury. Keep those nasties from poking through your tent by using a ground cloth. One of the best and most durable ground cloths available is an old shower curtain liner made of heavy plastic. (Another great thing about using a waterproof ground cloth is that it will keep ground moisture from soaking your tent floor, so you won't be sleeping in a puddle.)

Be an Ultralightweight

❏ If your tent didn't come with a rain fly, or if you want to backpack ultralight and skip the tent altogether, try using Tyvek house wrap as a shelter. Anyone who's recently built an addition to a home is likely to be familiar with the material. It's typically used on exterior walls as a protective waterproof barrier while construction is in progress and before installing shingles or siding. Now your leftover pieces have another use. Save scraps of this extremely lightweight and durable sheeting for use as a temporary rain cover or tent replacement. Stretch some nylon cord between two trees and fold the Tyvek so that it straddles this ridgeline. Tie nylon cord to each corner and anchor the pieces of cord to tent stakes. Or, lacking stakes and cord, place a heavy rock on each corner. This shelter won't hold in a full gale, but it will keep you dry in light to moderately heavy rain.

Recreation, Sports, and Hobbies

Tell Me Again
Why We Go Winter Camping

❑ Picking up a cold fuel bottle in the winter can smart like heck. And to make matters worse, cold fuel doesn't work as efficiently as warmer fuel. You can solve those problems and have some emergency mending tape along on any trip by wrapping some duct tape around the outside of your stove's gas bottle. The tape will provide a little insulation for the fuel, keep you from freezing your bare fingers in the winter, and provide a handy source of duct tape for all those in-the-field mending jobs.

Tape Me Along
in Emergencies

❑ If your sleeping bag, tent, rain fly, jacket, or almost any other piece of camping equipment develops a tear or hole, you can do a quick repair with duct tape (the same duct tape you wrapped around your fuel bottle). A word of warning, though: This patch might be permanent. The glue from the tape will be difficult to

A Different Twist

Spaghetti Comes
to the Big Screen

A colander comes in handy for certain campground meals (spaghetti comes to mind), but it's a pretty bulky addition to your camping equipment. Instead, pack a square of clean window screen that's big enough to cover the top of your largest pot. Cover the edges with duct tape. When the spaghetti is cooked, place the screen over the pot, hold it in place while you pour off the water, and your pasta will be ready for the sauce.

Recreation, Sports, and Hobbies

remove, so consider this tactic only if you don't have the proper repair kit along.

I Can't Believe It's Not . . .

❏ Pitched your tent under a tree and came home with a little sticky sap on it? Gently rub the stain with a dab of margarine until the sap is worked out, then wash the spot with a wet, soapy cloth. This combination is gentle enough not to harm the tent's waterproof finish but tough enough to get the sap out.

Borrow from Kitty to Help Your Tent

❏ Residual moisture can cause mold to grow inside your tent when it's packed away. One way to eliminate the moisture and potential mold problems is to use desiccant sachets. You know, something like those little packs included with new electronic equipment or in jars of vitamins. They contain silica gel that absorbs mois-

---

Hidden Treasures

Where to Find Used Sporting Equipment for Next to Nothing

I manage a sporting goods store that rents equipment, and I've learned that most stores like ours typically sell off the old rentals when new models are purchased. After all, one of the main reasons stores rent equipment is to interest you enough to buy it. We rent only equipment that we also carry in stock. Whenever a manufacturer changes a model's style, we keep the current model as a rental for about one more season, then it goes on sale. By buying used gear, you can often save from 50 to 70 percent off the price of a new item.

It is important to recognize that not all rental equipment is the same. Don't buy a used one-, two-, or three-season tent, especially from a store near a popular campsite. Everybody has used it, and like folks driving rented cars, they weren't thinking of the maintenance. Do buy a used four-season or expedition tent, though. Most stores have one around, and it hardly ever gets rented. How many winter campers do you know?

–Trent Harrison
New York, New York

---

ture. Unfortunately, they are not reusable, but you can create your own version with some clay kitty litter and an old sock. Place a handful of litter in the sock and knot the sock so that the litter won't spill out. Place the "sachet" in a bag along with your loosely stuffed tent and fly.

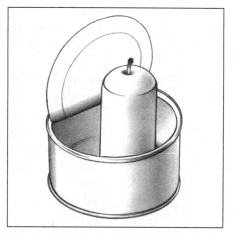

Pump It Up—And Out

❏ A camper's water-filtering system works only as long as the filter itself is clean, and buying a new filter cartridge before every trip is an expensive proposition. To clean your filter at home (unless the manufacturer recommends otherwise), you can make your own bleaching solution by adding 1 tablespoon household bleach per quart of water. Pump the solution through the filter at the end of your next camping trip, then follow up by pumping a quart of fresh cold water through the system. Dismantle the filter and rinse it under cold running water, then allow it to air dry before putting it back together. If you store the filter in a stuff sack during your camping trips, wash the inside of the sack with a mild bleach solution before placing the filter back inside. Repeat this procedure after each outing.

Don't Curse the Darkness

❏ If you're planning a vacation in which you'll be outside in the evening enjoying the stars, try this neat trick for shedding some light on the situation. Next time you have canned salmon or tuna, cut the lid not quite all the way off. Get the food out, then carefully wash and dry the can. Take it with you on your vacation, along with a plumber's candle or the stub of any old candle. When night falls, open the can, lifting the lid so it stands straight up. Place the candle in the can and light it. The can becomes a candleholder, catching the wax. The lid reflects the light and, if you place it carefully, keeps the wind from blowing out the candle.

An old tuna can makes a great candleholder for camping. Just be careful not to cut the lid all the way off.

Recreation, Sports, and Hobbies

Light a Candle in the Wind

❏ You're sitting at a picnic table at night, enjoying the evening, but your candle keeps going out. If you've recently emptied a plastic one- or two-liter soda bottle, you're in luck. Cut off the bottom (make sure it's level) and the top of the bottle with your Swiss Army Knife, leaving a cylinder a little taller than the candle. Light the candle and place the bottle over it, being careful to avoid letting the flame come in contact with the plastic. The bottle will protect the candle from the wind but provide enough oxygen to keep it lit.

Pot Too Hot to Handle?

❏ Camp cookware is designed to transfer heat efficiently. This often means that pot handles get hot, too. A few layers of duct tape wrapped around the handles will provide enough insulation to allow you to pick up a pot without burning yourself. Make sure the tape isn't directly exposed to the camping stove's flame, though, or it will burn.

HIKING AND BACKPACKING

Keep Stops Stopping

❏ The stop on a nylon carrying strap is the folded-over end that keeps the strap from slipping out of the buckle. One of the most frustrating mishaps that can occur on a hiking trip is for the stop to come loose—leaving you to watch your sleeping bag, pots and pans, or sneakers tumble into a stream. If your nylon strap starts to fray, take a butane lighter to the end. This will melt the nylon, which will bubble up and make a serviceable stop on the end.

Ring In the New

❏ Carabiners are those metal rings that mountain climbers use to manage their ropes. They serve multiple purposes, but they also cost a fortune. That's because they need to be able to hold a lot of weight. If you usually use them to lash your sleeping bag, sneakers, or water bottle to your pack, you'll probably get along just

Velcro: From Seedpods to Launchpads

One day in 1941, a Swiss engineer named George de Mestral took his dog for a walk in the woods. Afterward, he noticed that his wool socks and jacket, as well as his dog's coat, were covered with cockleburs (the seedpods of the cocklebur bush). These bushes produce hundreds of football-shaped burrs, each about one inch long and covered with stiff, hooked spines. Removing these tenacious little plants fascinated de Mestral, and he wondered, Could the cockleburs be a model for a product that would be an alternative to or a replacement for zippers?

Initially, de Mestral had difficulty convincing anyone to manufacture his manmade burrs, but he finally found a weaver in Lyons, France, who was willing to try. The first version they produced comprised two strips of cotton fabric—one with tiny hooks, the other with tiny eyes. When pressed together, the two sides held and stayed together. De Mestral called this sample "locking tape."

It was a beginning, but the invention was not yet ready to take over the world of rough-and-ready fashion. Although the fabric strips worked initially, the delicate cotton thread wore out after repeated use. With further research, de Mestral discovered that nylon, woven under infrared light, created a nearly indestructible hook and loop. With that modification, the invention was ready for mass production. To christen his work, de Mestral combined parts of the words *velours,* the French word for "velvet," which the fuzzy loop side resembles, and *crochet,* the French word for "hook."

Today Velcro is everywhere—on clothing and car bumpers, heart valves and the space shuttle. All because one man stopped to look at what was stuck on his socks.

fine with a lightweight, cheap alternative. A metal shower curtain ring, for example, opens and closes with a squeeze and is just about the right size for toting your gloves. A heavy-duty key ring will hold the weight of a full canteen. A brass curtain rod ring won't hold a lot of

Recreation, Sports, and Hobbies

weight, but it will suffice for carrying a cap on the outside of your pack.

Pacify Your Thirst

❏ Sure, you could fork over the cash for a brand-new, high-tech water bottle for hiking. But you're smarter than that, right? After all, baby bottles make perfectly good trail bottles. They're designed to be sterilized by boiling. They don't leak, especially if you have the cover for the nipple. And they're plenty tough: Just think what the average baby puts them through.

BOATING

Look for a Mooring That Meets the Eye

❏ You know that the mooring line is there somewhere, but the marker disappeared with the last tide. Once you locate the line, replace the marker with an empty one-gallon plastic bottle after sealing the bottle cap permanently in place with some silicone adhesive. Tie the bottle to the mooring with some nylon cord.

Play Bleach Bottle Bailout

❏ Getting your feet wet while you are out for a row can be annoying and uncomfortable. Here's a lightweight way to deal with the problem. Wash out an old one-gallon plastic bleach bottle, then cut off the bottom, being sure to keep the handle in place. Replace the screw cap and keep the bottle in your boat for use as a bailer.

Put Your Boat on a Magic Carpet Ride

❏ Transporting your wooden canoe on top of your car doesn't have to be a problem. If you have some scrap carpet or an old rug, place this on the roof before you put the canoe on top. This will provide a more slip-resistant surface, not to mention protecting the roof of your car and the gunnels of the boat.

5 Uses for Old Sporting Equipment

Bat broken? Dinghy dinged up? Golf club gone kaput? Don't throw them away. Instead, put those worn-out pieces of sporting equipment to good use.

1. Once you decide to retire that old wooden dinghy, prop it up in your yard and use it as a decorative planter. Filled with soil and flowers, it will brighten up any outdoor space.

2. If your golf club head has lost its zing, flip it upside down and and put it to use as a walking stick or cane.

3. After you've replaced the old dartboard in your game room, carry it up to your dining room and use it as a colorful trivet. It's considerably larger than ordinary trivets, so it's perfect for large, informal gatherings.

4. Once the kids have grown and the Little League bats are languishing in the garage, use them (the bats, that is) to pound stakes in your garden.

5. When that old tennis racket is ready to be hung up, use it instead to beat your carpets during spring-cleaning.

Insulate, Separate, Appreciate

❏ Another way to protect your boat's gunnels (and your car roof) while in transit is to cover the gunnels with leftover pieces of the stuff you wrap around the pipes in your home's crawl space: foam pipe insulation. All you have to do is cut it to the right length and slide it over the boat's gunnels. One side of the sleeve is already sliced open, making this an easy task. When you're ready to put the boat in the water, the insulation will come off quickly and store easily.

FISHING

The Fish May Get Away, but the Gear Won't

❏ If you don't have a tackle box but still want to keep your fishing gear organized without spending any money, try this. Store your hooks, lead weights, and any other small items in old film canisters. They're water-

tight, and the lids pop on and off easily. Then you can keep all those containers in that big old lunch box you don't use anymore. Sorry, fish.

Tackle Accidents before They Happen

❑ When you're fishing with a young friend, it's important to keep your tackle box safe from small hands. Try storing your extra hooks in old childproof aspirin and prescription medicine bottles.

A Different Twist

Now If You'll Just Polish Those Fish Stories . . .

When the fins on a prize stuffed fish start to crack, haul out the clear nail polish. A quick coat of polish will hold those damaged fins in place.

Is There an Electrician on Board?

❑ You know how it feels to open your tackle box and realize that spool of monofilament has unraveled. Kind of a pain, huh? Well, you can prevent an unwanted tangle by holding the loose end of the line in place with a piece of rubber electrical tape. The tape is waterproof, and the glue on it will remain tacky with repeated liftings, such as when you need more line.

Let's All Band Together

❑ Had broccoli or lobster for dinner lately? Those fat rubber bands that keep the bunches together and the claws from pinching will also keep a spool of monofilament from unraveling.

Keep Those Worms Lively

❑ The only good worm is a live worm. You can keep your bait worms lively longer if you add coffee grounds to the dirt you carry the worms in. We're not really sure why, but the worms seem to stay alive longer in soil with coffee grounds. Maybe they like the caffeine?

Put a Cork in It

❑ It's the night before your fishing trip, and you look through your tackle box only to discover. . . no bobber.

Don't worry. Grab that cork you saved the last time you had wine with dinner and drive a staple into the top. Pry the staple up just a bit with a letter opener, leaving enough space to run your fishing line through. If you're using light test line, use half a cork.

BIKING

Powder That Tire

❏ Need a way to help a repaired inner tube fit back into the bicycle tire smoothly when you're ready to reinflate it? Sprinkle the inner tube with some talcum powder. The powder will act as a lubricant, allowing the tire to slip into place as it reinflates.

GOLF

Slip a Sock on It

❏ Even an inexpensive set of golf clubs deserves to be kept dry and clean with head covers. So here's your chance to use all those orphaned wool socks, gloves, and mittens you've been saving. Slip them over the heads of your clubs. They may not have the chic of store-bought club covers, but they certainly have more charm. Plus, they make terrific conversation starters!

Become a Well-Oiled Putting Machine

❏ Carbon steel putter heads can dry out and go "dead," but you can keep yours feeling lively. Take an empty sample-size shampoo bottle and fill it with baby oil. Put a few drops on your putter's head and wipe it off with a paper towel. This will help your putter retain its feel. Make sure to wipe your hands so that you don't get oil on your other clubs' rubber grips. Otherwise, on your next drive, the club may travel farther than the ball.

A Different Twist

Hatch a Great Way to Store Golf Balls

Need a handy way to store all those golf balls—and to bring them along to the golf course? An old egg carton is perfect for the task.

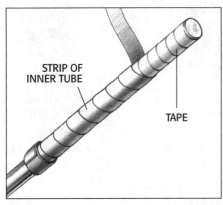

STRIP OF
INNER TUBE

TAPE

After removing the old grip from a golf club, as well as the tape that held it in place, wrap the club with fresh tape and then with a strip from an old inner tube.

Re-Cycle Your Golf Game

❑ Too . . . er . . . thrifty to buy a new rubber grip for that golf club? An old bicycle inner tube, cut into a strip approximately 1 inch wide and 36 inches long, will do the job in a pinch. Remove the old grip. Underneath you'll find a layer of double-sided tape that was holding the grip in place. Getting rid of this would be a problem for an unresourceful person, but not for you. You can just rub it with lighter fluid or nail polish remover that contains acetone. Replace the tape with a new strip, winding it along the same distance up the shaft. Then cover the tape with the inner tube strip. Wind it up the shaft, too, making sure the edges just meet. Finish the job by trimming off the excess and sealing the ends with electrical tape.

Be a Fair-Leather Friend

❑ Your old leather grips will last longer if you keep them soft and supple. But you don't need any fancy leather conditioners for the job. Whenever they feel too dry, apply a little petroleum jelly to the grips and rub it in well. (Be conservative; all you need is a scant one-eighth teaspoon.) This is especially helpful after you've played a round in the rain. In that case, just give the grips a chance to dry before applying the treatment. The petroleum jelly will soften the leather and prevent it from absorbing moisture.

Mind Your Tees

❑ Lots of folks keep their golf tees in plastic bags. Pretty thrifty, right? Well, not really, because the pointy ends of the tees poke holes in the bags, then the tees fall out and scatter. Here's a better idea. Use the plastic bags for something else and keep all those tees in an old change purse that has a clasp. That way, you'll know where they are for a change.

Don't Throw In the Towel; Hang It

❑ While you're golfing, it's always a good idea to have a small towel handy to wipe your hands or your golf clubs. But you don't want to carry it; it's unwieldy. Here's a better answer. Keep the towel attached to your golf bag with an old metal shower curtain hook. The ring opens and closes easily, but once it is closed, it will stay that way, securely.

Recreation, Sports, and Hobbies

Dress Casually for the Course

❑ Sure, you have that big, expensive bag for all your clubs. But what if you're just going to the driving range or the pitch and putt and need only a few clubs? You can leave that big old bag in the closet if you make a day bag for your golf clubs out of an old pair of jeans. Sew the bottom of each leg closed, then pop two or three clubs into each stitched-up leg. That still leaves you with plenty of room for spare tees, your scorecard, and pencils in the pockets. To finish off the contraption, run an old belt through the belt loops for a shoulder strap.

Earl's Favorites

Be a Cut-Up off the Course

Anyone who knows me can tell you how much I love golf. So I'm always happy to get—and to pass along—tips about golf. One I especially like has to do with practicing golf indoors. One way to avoid a catastrophe when you're doing that is to practice your swing with a club that you've cut down. Start with a club from a set you don't use anymore. Use a hacksaw to cut through the shaft about eight inches below the grip. Remove the grip, then reinstall it on the section with the head. Now you can practice your swing as usual. You won't reach the ground with your club, but you won't reach that vase either.

Brighten Your Game

❏ After knocking a couple of hundred balls into the cup, the "sight" on your putter may be worn away. Here's how to make it visible again. If the sight marks are indented, touch them up with brightly colored nail polish. Wipe off any excess and let it dry.

❏ Similarly, if you and your golfing buddy bought the same brand of golf balls and often grab the same-numbered ball, you might not know whose is whose when you're fishing them out of the same patch of rough. To avoid confusion, mark yours before the game with brightly colored nail polish.

3 Pieces of Exercise Equipment You Never Knew You Owned

A regular exercise program can help keep you in shape and relieve stress. And you don't have to put any additional stress on your wallet, because you probably have everything you need. Most of these routines are not terribly strenuous, but check with your doctor before beginning any exercise program.

1. If you buy bags of dried beans or peas, you can use a full bag as a foot weight. Rest the bag on top of your instep and, sitting in a chair, raise your lower leg slowly, unbending your knee until your leg is straight out in front of you. Then let it down. Repeat with the other leg. Start off by doing three lifts, resting, and doing three more.

2. Grab a pair of old plastic soda bottles—any size will do—and fill them with water until they're a comfortable weight. Put the caps on securely. Make sure you have a good grip, then use your improvised dumbbells to perform arm lifts. Starting with your arms at your sides, slowly raise the bottles, then bend your arms to bring the bottles up to your shoulders. Try it again, this time slowly raising and lowering your arms while they're extended out to your sides.

3. An old dog leash makes a good jump rope if it's long enough. Find one that's about double your height. Wrap the ends around your hands and start jumping.

It Was a Clothes Score

❑ Now where did you put that scorecard? One way to make sure you don't put it down and forget it again is to keep it clipped to the outside of your golf bag with a clothespin.

Place Your Chips Here

❑ What happens when you want to practice your chipping in the backyard but don't want to put a divot in the lawn? Well, if you have a spare piece of indoor-outdoor low-pile carpeting around, your problem is solved, because it will make a terrific chipping tee. You'll need a scrap approximately 18 inches square. Make sure the piece is large enough that you don't hit the back edge with your downstroke. If the carpet lifts every time you take a swing, you can nail it into the lawn with some long galvanized nails or, if you have them around, old croquet wickets. To practice your tee shots, punch a small hole in the center of the carpet with a nail, then insert a tee.

Swing with Me, or I'll Belt You

❑ An important part of a good golf swing is moving both arms as a single unit. A good way to train yourself to do this is to use your belt. Cinch the belt around both arms at the biceps—you may need a friend to help get you started with this—and practice your swing, with or without a club. You'll be forced to move both arms in unison.

Recreation, Sports, and Hobbies

HORSESHOES

Set Cheap Stakes for Horseshoes

❑ What's the point of throwing horseshoes if you have nothing to throw them at? If you're missing the stakes from your set, grab some of that iron pipe left over from your last plumbing project. Each pipe should be ½ inch in diameter and about 2½ feet long. Drive the pipes about 10 inches into the ground and start pitching those shoes.

Toss This Game Off

❑ Here's an instant game of horseshoes anyone can play during a backyard barbecue. Grab an old plastic fork (or a skewer or stick) and three of those foil plates that take-out food comes in. Push the fork, tine side down, into the ground about five paces away from you. Toss the plate with a flick of the wrist, Frisbee style, toward the "post." Use standard horseshoe rules or make up your own.

CROQUET

That's Not Wicket

❑ Lost a wicket? Not to worry. You can easily replace it with an old wire coat hanger. Bend it to match an existing wicket, then paint it white so that it shows up.

Wicket Good Ideas

H as your croquet set seen better days—and little use since the Carter administration? Take heart! Even if you no longer have every ball or wicket, there are plenty of ways you can use the remaining pieces.

PIECES	USE
Wickets	Line them up side by side and create a border for your garden or yard.
Stakes	Use them to prop up your smaller tomato plants, or as a target for your kid's (or grandkid's) plastic horseshoe game. Or use them to poke holes in the soil when you're getting ready to plant seeds.
Mallets	These cute little hammers are handy when it comes to pounding in plant stakes. If you find that the long handle makes the mallet unwieldy, saw it off to a comfortable length.
Balls	You can use these wonderful wooden balls to mark the edge of a walkway. Or give them a light sanding, drill holes in them, and use them as finials in your game room. Or use them to hold the tarp down over your firewood pile.

Handle a Croquet Emergency

❏ A lost stake or mallet handle is a problem that's a bit trickier but by no means insurmountable. Replace either with a broom handle, cut down to size.

BASEBALL

Shoe Me the Athletic Tape

❏ Break a lace on the field? No problem. Wrap the entire shoe with cloth athletic tape. (If it's not in your gear bag, it should be.) Make sure to tape between (not over) the spikes on the bottom of the shoe. And wrap it just tightly enough that it fits the way your shoe normally does. After the game, the tape will peel easily off the shoe's leather or vinyl. If it sticks to the laces, cut them; you're going to have to replace them anyway.

Look Out for the Brushback

❏ If you take a look at the back of a major league pitcher's mound, you'll see a brush on the ground that the pitcher uses to clean his spikes when they get filled with mud. You can treat yourself like a big leaguer by bringing an old bristle scrub brush with you to the game. You may not have a mound to hide it behind, but you can keep it next to the bench and run it over your cleats between innings.

Need a Sweatband? No Sweat!

❏ Make sweatbands from an old terry cloth towel. Cut a three- or four-inch-wide strip that's just long

---

My Way

A True (G)love Story

I had an old baseball glove that got soaked when a pipe burst in the basement one winter. After I dried it out thoroughly, the glove needed to be re-treated. Unfortunately, the local sporting goods store didn't have any glove oil, as it was out of season. And I'd just used the last of my neat's-foot oil on my hiking boots. Fortunately, I did have some olive oil.

Working with just a few drops at a time, and rubbing the oil all over the glove, inside and out, I was able to restore the leather to its former suppleness. I packed a ball into the pocket of the glove and tied the whole thing up with some twine. By the time spring rolled around, the glove was as ready for a workout as I was.

—**Tom Cavalieri**
Long Island City, New York

Spring-Cleaning

Here's an idea for cleaning out the treads of your muddy sneakers that I discovered quite by accident.

I was at our summer cottage in Maine, a house on a cove. It was low tide, and I decided to go exploring on the mudflats in my sneakers. That was a mistake. When I finished, my sneakers were a muddy mess.

Just as I got back to the house, it started to drizzle. I didn't want to leave my shoes out in the rain, but they were too muddy to bring into the house, so I needed to clean them off. I absentmindedly put my hand in my pocket and realized I had a bread bag closer—one of those little square plastic tabs with a notch cut out of it—in my pocket from lunch. I used that to clean off my sneakers, and it worked like a charm. I scraped the mud off the sides of the sneakers and used the tab's corner to get into the treads. Now I keep one or two tabs in our mudroom, and I always have one in my golf bag to clean off my spikes.

—Susan Gagnon
Hopkinton, New Hampshire

enough to fit tightly around your wrist. Instead of sewing the ends together, use a wide piece of elastic from an old pair of men's undershorts to act as a bridge between the two ends and to provide some give. Repeat for the other wrist.

Stick to It

❏ You don't need baseball equipment to play an impromptu ball game. If you have a broom handle and an old tennis ball, you can play stickball, a time-honored amusement. First, tape one end of the broomstick with electrical tape to get a better grip. Then make up game rules. One way to play is with two people. The batter stands in front of a wall on which a strike zone has been drawn in chalk. The pitcher stands an agreed-upon distance away and throws to the strike zone. Before play begins, you'll want to decide on the number of balls, strikes, and outs allowed, as well as what constitutes a single, double, triple, and home run.

FOOTBALL

Tackle That Torn Lace

❏ You're playing with a genuine leather football, the kind closed with real lacing (not the molded rubber kind), and the lacing breaks with nary a piece of string or an old shoelace in sight. Run for the duct tape. Without removing the old laces, place a strip of tape over them. Press it down well so that it conforms to the shape of the laces. This still leaves you with an obvious place to get a grip on the ball, and it will hold the ball together until the last touchdown.

Screw It Up

❏ Don't give up on a game of touch football just because the ball is punctured or is leaking air from the valve. First, make sure there's only one leak and it's not big. Next, carefully screw a round-headed screw into the puncture, then reinflate the ball. (Install the screw after inflating if the leak is in the valve.) As long as the screw stays in place, your patched-up ball should stay inflated. And you'll be able to finish that game.

TENNIS

You'll Love This Hat Trick

❏ If you wear a hat while you play tennis, you know that while it provides some sun protection, it also can really make you sweat. Here's yet another chance to show off your ingenuity. Using an old, clean terry cloth towel, facecloth, or bathrobe, cut a strip that will fit inside your hat. Either sew or glue it directly to the hat. Or if you're really creative, attach it with Velcro from an old jacket so that it can be removed and washed from time to time.

A Penny Saved Is a Tennis Ball Earned

Spare change been piling up on your bureau or in your car? One of your old tennis ball cans will make a great bank. Using a sharp knife or razor blade, slice an X into the plastic lid, making it large enough to push a quarter through. When the can is filled, pop the top off and buy yourself a treat—like a new can of balls.

---

5 Uses for Old Tennis Balls

Old tennis balls never die; they just turn into packing material. Here are a few uses for tennis balls that are past their prime.

1. **Pet toys.** Dogs love to chase them, and cats can really get their claws into the fuzz on the outside.
2. **Jar openers.** Cut a tennis ball in half to make a handy gripper for all those hard-to-open bottles and jars.
3. **Light bulb changers.** One half of a tennis ball that's been cut in two is a terrific device for grabbing a hot light bulb when it needs to be changed.
4. **Hand exercisers.** Hold a tennis ball in the palm of your hand and gently squeeze it to exercise your fingers and wrist.
5. **Packing material,** to protect a delicate, odd-shaped item stored in a box. Put some tennis balls on the bottom of the box, add the object, and then pack more balls on top to create a snug fit before closing the box.

Bounce Higher and Dryer

❏ Tennis balls are sold in pressurized containers. Once you open a fresh can, they start to lose their bounce. But don't worry if your tennis balls are dead. You can rejuvenate them by putting them in a hot clothes dryer for a few minutes. The heat will expand the air inside the balls and give them new bounce—temporarily anyway.

Keep Your Can Cool

❏ It gets awfully hot sitting in the sun waiting for your match, but you're too resourceful to put up with that discomfort. Thoroughly clean an old plastic tennis ball can, then fill it nearly to the top with water and put it in the freezer the night before a match. This makes a great ice pack.

SKIING

Spray First, Then Ski

❏ Cross-country skiing on a warm winter day can be a delight, but not if sticky snow stops you in your tracks.

If you don't want to go to the time and trouble of applying the perfect wax, stop by the workshop on your way out of the house. Grab a can of light lubricating oil such as WD-40 and spray a light coating on the base of your skis just before you hit the trails. Now you can really enjoy the expedition.

Go Fog-Free and Low Cholesterol, Too

❏ Having your ski goggles fog up when you're careening down the slopes can certainly add to the adventure, but most of us aren't looking for that kind of excitement. Here's an old remedy to keep your goggles clear and fog-free. Before leaving the chalet, rub the lenses with a piece of raw potato, then polish them with a soft, dry cloth. (This works for sunglasses, too.)

See through the Fog

❏ There are lots of products on the market to keep your goggles fog-free as you fly down the slopes. The trouble is, most of them come in a bottle or can. Although the label usually implies that one application will last most of your run, in practice you may need to reapply the stuff before you make it all the way down the mountain. One solution is to carry a fog cloth. Any scrap of soft, lint-free cloth such as chamois or flannel will do. Impregnate it with rubbing alcohol diluted with a little water, and keep it in a resealable plastic bag. Besides being less cumbersome, a fog cloth is a lot softer to land on than a plastic bottle.

Whip Up a Batch of Homemade Gaiter-Aid

❏ Need a pair of gaiters for your next cross-country ski trip but don't want to buy them? Cut the sleeves from an old nylon windbreaker or rain jacket. With a seam ripper, open the seam of each sleeve. Finish the open seam edges, as well as what used to be the top of the sleeve, with seam tape. Then salvage the Velcro from the front of the jacket and sew it in vertical strips in appropriate spots on the sleeves. Wrap your new gaiters

around your calves and secure them with the Velcro. If the fabric is not already waterproof, treat it with silicone spray—the same stuff you use to lubricate that squeaky garage door.

SKATING

Polish Your Act

❏ If your leather ice skates are looking a little the worse for wear, anyone knows you can touch them up with shoe polish. But what if you have plastic, ski-boot-style hockey skates? No problem. Polish them with some car polish, such as Turtle Wax, and a soft cloth. This works well for in-line skates, too, but be sure not to get any on the wheels or blades.

The Hose Knows
How to Protect Your Blades

❏ A sharp blade is a good blade. But the blades on skates that are tossed into the back of the closet don't stay sharp for long. Here's a better idea than buying those special skate guards. Cut two pieces of old garden hose long enough to cover your blades. Split the hose open, place one piece over the bottom of each skate blade, and use heavy-duty rubber bands to keep the hose attached. This inexpensive approach will protect your blades just as well as store-bought guards.

OTHER OUTDOOR FUN

Play Jug-Ball

❏ The next time you're searching for something fun to do outdoors and are tired of all your other games, try this one. You'll need one plastic milk jug (gallon size) for each person and some kind of ball. An old tennis ball works well. Cut the bottom two to three inches off each milk jug, leaving a kind of scoop. Give one jug to each player. Instruct each person to hold the jug upside down by the handle, using the jug to catch the ball and toss it to another player. You can make up other rules as you go, depending on the ages of the participants. It doesn't really matter whether you keep score—the fun part comes when everyone scrambles to catch and throw the ball using only the milk jugs.

Try This Meshy Solution

❑ Smash! Right through the net. What do you do if you've lined up a hot badminton date and your net has more than the normal number of holes? How about making a patch with a mesh onion bag? Or if you've just finished a painting project, you may have some leftover cheesecloth. Cut either material to cover the problem spot, then hold it in place with duct tape. It won't win

5 Great Tools for the Sand Castle Architect

Before your next trip to the beach, take a minute to scour the kitchen for odds and ends like these, which any builder of great castles can put to good use.

1. Yogurt containers, large and small. They're perfect for making miniature sand castles or turrets on larger ones.

2. Popsicle sticks. When your kids have finished with their frozen treats, wash the sticks and toss them in your beach bag to use as flagpoles for your sand fort. Foil gum wrappers make eye-catching flags.

3. Food coloring. Take along a few vials from the kitchen cupboard, along with some large plastic ketchup bottles (the kind that you can squirt). Make sure the bottles are clean. Scoop up some sand in each bottle, then add some

ocean water and a few drops of food coloring (which is non-toxic). Shake the whole thing up, then squirt the sand out of the bottle to decorate your sand castle or write your name on the beach. Mother Nature will take care of the cleanup.

4. Anything that holds or sifts food and is unbreakable. Strainers, colanders, empty cardboard berry baskets, decorative Bundt pans, old Styrofoam egg cartons, and past-their-prime ice cube trays can all be used to mold and decorate sand.

5. Other kitchen stuff. Ice cream scoops shape sand perfectly. The tines of a fork will make interesting patterns, and so will old cookie cutters. (Be careful not to leave these things lying in the sand, where someone might step on them.)

Pies in the Skies

In the early 1950s, inventor Fred Morrison had a mild obsession with UFOs. He invented a toy called the Pluto Platter that he thought kids would like. It looked something like the flying saucers that science fiction had introduced into popular culture. A kid could fling the platter out, and it would sail through the air.

In the late 1950s, Morrison sold his product to Wham-O, a company that appropriately renamed it the Flyin' Saucer. Wham-O had high hopes for the product, but sales were slow. Some kids in California liked the saucers as beach toys to toss back and forth, but that was about it. Wham-O wanted to find a way to give the product national appeal, so it sent representatives to playgrounds and college campuses on the East Coast to give away free samples and stir up some interest.

One marketing rep who ended up on the Yale campus was startled to find students there playing with pie tins. In those days, the Frisbie Pie Company, one of the top bakeries in New England, was located near the campus. It turned out tens of thousands of pies every day. The kids at Yale loved to eat the pies and then take the used tins outside and toss them back and forth. They called their game frisbie, probably because the company name was stamped on the bottom of each tin.

The marketing team at Wham-O knew what to do. They quickly took out a trademark on the word Frisbee—a slight variation on the spelling of the pie company name. In 1959, the company unveiled a little plastic disk that has been a fixture on college campuses ever since. These days, the Frisbee is as American as, well, apple pie.

any awards for aesthetics, but at least you'll be able to keep playing.

Have a Ball with Duct Tape

❑ You're all set for a quick game of catch, but the ball's missing. Break out the duct tape. Wrap some tape around a sponge (or just wad some up into a ball shape), and you're ready for a game of catch or hackey sack, or even a modified game of baseball, using your hand as a bat.

Bat? Who Needs a Bat?

❑ Now the kids want to practice hitting the Wiffle ball, but the bat is nowhere to be found. Not to worry, there are plenty of items you can use instead. Try a length of polyvinyl chloride (PVC) tubing wrapped with some electrical tape for a grip; a broom handle; a one-inch dowel; a vacuum cleaner tube, again with an electrical tape grip; or even an old table leg. Batter up!

Recreation, Sports, and Hobbies

BILLIARDS

Fresh from the Oven Rack

❑ You head down to the game room to practice your billiard shots, but you can't find the rack. Don't give up. Run upstairs to the kitchen and grab a nine-inch cake pan. Invert it over the balls, then gently lift it off so the balls stay in formation. Of course, this isn't regulation, but it will do in a pinch.

PARLOR AND BOARD GAMES

It's the Cuff Link's Turn

❑ Lost one of the game pieces for your Monopoly or other board game? Replace it with a cuff link, a button, a small interesting stone, or even a thimble. Then let the games go on.

Put a New Spin on It

❑ In some games, you determine how many spaces a player can move by rotating a "spinner." But if you lose or break this essential item, how will you know how far to go? You can make a new spinner from materials in your desk drawer. You'll need a manila file folder and a brass paper fastener. Cut a six-inch square from the folder. Then, with a marker, draw lines from the center

At a big party that involves a lot of different age-groups, bingo is the ideal game. Almost everyone can understand it, different folks can take turns hamming it up as the announcer, and it's gently competitive without being cutthroat. Dig out your game, and if you need extra cards, cut some out of empty cereal boxes. Then all you need are chips, which seem to disappear like socks in a clothes dryer. For substitutions, try any of the following:

1. Large dried beans, such as pintos or kidney beans
2. Pennies
3. Buttons
4. Paper clips
5. Safety pins (closed, of course)
6. Pieces of cereal, such as Cheerios
7. Pieces of candy, such as M&M's or Sweetarts
8. Pieces of elbow macaroni

to the edges to divide the card into eight pie-shaped spaces of equal width. Cut an "arrow" from the remaining manila folder, making it about one-half inch wide and four inches long. Punch a hole in the middle of the arrow and in the center of the card and insert the brass paper fastener through the arrow and the card. Make sure the arrow can turn freely. Number the spaces on the card from one to eight. If you are using the spinner as a substitute for a die, which has only six sides, you may want to label two of the spaces "Spin Again."

Slice and Dice

❏ Lost a die from a parlor game? With a razor blade, carefully cut an art gum eraser in half, making two cubes. Draw spots on them with a magic marker. They may bounce around a little more than regular dice, but they'll work.

❏ In a pinch, you can draw spots on sugar cubes with a felt-tipped marker. But don't expect them to last long.

Tape Me on Board

❏ Some folks get together to play the same game on a regular basis—a nice custom, but one that can be tough on any game board that's involved. If your game board is falling apart, cover it with a sheet of clear contact paper. If the board is breaking at the spine or where it folds for storage, repair it from behind with fabric tape or cloth athletic tape.

CHILDREN'S GAMES AND TOYS

Try Pint-Size (or Quart-Size) Bowling

❏ Are the kids getting a little bored with store-bought toys? Make your own instant bowling alley. Cut the tops off half-gallon-, quart-, or pint-size cardboard milk and juice containers. Wash them out well and let them dry. Take two cartons of the same size and fit them together by sliding one inside the other. You may have to squeeze one to make it fit, but it will. Set up some of these lightweight "pins" at the end of the hall, add a tennis ball, and you have indoor bowling for kids or adults.

Be a Beanie Baby

❏ Here's a toy kids can make for themselves. Before you pitch those jeans they've outgrown, cut the front pocket linings off and save them. Have the youngsters fill each one with about a handful (his hand, not yours) of small beans, peas, or rice. Twist each open side together and tie it closed with a piece of string. There are lots of things kids can do with this basic beanbag: practice soccer-style juggling and passing with the homemade hackey sack or make several and try traditional juggling. A note to parents: Check the kids' work before they start to play with their beanbags, or you'll be playing the "vacuum up the rice" game.

Be a Dollhouse Decorator

❏ You can make all sorts of dollhouse furniture just by raiding your junk drawers. The little plastic gizmo that pizza parlors place on top of the pizza to keep the box top off the cheese makes a great table. With the addi-

tion of some scrap fabric, a spool of thread becomes a table or chair. Matchboxes also can be transformed into tables with a little imagination. Toothpicks and string become rattan blinds. Material scraps make attractive drapery and upholstery.

Cope With Fluffy's Delicate Constitution

❏ Some plush toys are too delicate to get wet. If your bear (or rabbit or raccoon) can't stand the water, don't despair. Somewhere under your sink or in your closet there is hope. Clean your little buddy with carpet cleaner, the kind that you apply dry and then brush or vacuum off. Teddy will thank you.

SCALE MODELS

Curse You, Red-Hot Needle

❏ If you're interested in building model military aircraft, occasionally you may want to depict one of the losers. Here's a way to make realistic-looking bullet holes in the fuselage. Grasp an ordinary sewing needle with a pair of needle-nosed pliers, then heat the needle in the tip of a butane lighter flame. Carefully poke the hot point several times into the side of the model, so that it makes little indentations. If you do this before assembling the rest of the fuselage, you can pull a bit of cotton through the holes to simulate smoke.

Sail the HMS Pin-afore

❏ Here's a way to add a special touch to your next model ship. Using a pair of needle-nosed pliers, hold a common pin in the tip of a butane lighter flame. Use the hot pin to poke out the portholes in the bulkhead. Cut a small hole in the bottom or in the side that won't be displayed, and work a few miniature Christmas lights through that hole and into the interior of the model. (Uncolored lights work best for this.) When the string of bulbs is plugged in, the ship will look as if its cabin lights are on.

He Put His Stamp on Collecting

When stamp collecting first caught on in the nineteenth century, it was only for the very rich. The standard that great collectors aimed for was a stamp from every country. These people paid a fortune for rare sheets of stamps and traded only with other very wealthy collectors. They hunted for a few special stamps for years. This rarefied approach prohibited most people from starting their own collections, because the very idea of obtaining a stamp from every nation was overwhelming.

Then in the late 1940s, Jerome Husak, a teenager in Wisconsin, had an idea. What if you could make a stamp collection based only on how the stamps looked? People could have fun collecting only stamps that featured birds, airplanes, or maps—or any subject that caught their fancy.

Husak, reasoning that stamps collected for their subject matter would be easier to obtain and keep track of than traditional collections, started a club for topical stamp collectors. People never looked at their mail the same way again. Suddenly, ordinary kids could collect the stamps all around them. They begged friends to send postcards when they went on vacation. They showed up in mail rooms of international companies to sift through discarded envelopes. They even bought stamps from the post office.

Nowadays, when it comes to collections that cost relatively little *and* take only a small amount of storage space, these simple bits of paper merit any parent's stamp of approval.

Keep Cool; Build a Model

❏ While you're working on your models, you may have several small parts scattered about your worktable. One way to keep them organized is to keep an old ice cube tray handy. Place small parts in the compartments until you're ready to use them, and you'll be able to locate the right pieces at a glance.

Recreation, Sports, and Hobbies

PAINTING

Meet an Old Pal-ette

❑ Need a palette in a pinch? Stretch a sheet of waxed paper over a piece of Masonite that you've painted white, then fix it in place with a few clothespins. This makes a good disposable palette for oil and acrylic paints, as well as watercolor paints from tubes. When you finish a painting session, remove the clothespins and peel the paper away. Then start fresh the next time.

Try This Scrappy Idea

❑ If you paint pictures, models, or anything else that requires a clean brush between colors, you need something to dry the brush on after dipping it in water or turpentine. That's where those small scraps of leftover carpeting—the ones that have been lying around the garage—come in. Pick out a clean piece of an appropriate size and anchor it in place on your palette or workbench with a piece of double-sided tape. If you have a choice, use a scrap with a low pile. Your no-cost paintbrush dryer will be ready when you are.

Stick to the Long and Narrow

❑ Looking for a cheap and easy way to organize your long-handled watercolor paintbrushes? Hold on to those cylindrical boxes that some liquors come in. They're perfect for the job. You can even spruce them up by gluing some paper or fabric scraps onto them.

❑ Alternatively, save your old oatmeal cartons and use them for the same purpose.

SEWING

Go on a Tear

❑ Why is it that pattern companies manufacture their patterns out of the most fragile paper available? Is it because they think that when a pattern tears, we'll run out and replace it? Ha! Next time one of your favorite patterns tears, head to the closet and grab some of the tissue paper from inside an old gift box. Cut out a scrap of the tissue and tape it lightly in place so that it covers the tear in the original pattern. Now you're ready to start that sewing project.

Use a Poky Eraser

❑ Anytime you construct an item that has corners (such as a pillow), there comes a time when you need to turn the article right side out. After you've done that, you need to poke the corners a bit to make them square. You don't want to use a pair of scissors or a seam ripper, because those might tear the seam. But if you're something of a pack rat, you just might have the perfect tool. Check in your junk drawer for one of those old pen erasers that look like pencils (the eraser is the point; you sharpen it to expose more of the eraser). You can easily get the pointed tip into the corner, but it's flexible enough that it won't poke through.

❑ Alternatively, use a knitting needle to push out those pesky corners.

Sweet Schemes Are Finished with This

❑ To finish off the edges of a decorative homemade pillow, carefully stitch a length of spare macramé cord into place along the outside seams.

Spin Yourself a (Button) Yarn

❑ How does one organize spare buttons so that all buttons of the same size or color are always together and easy to find? Funny you should ask.

Sew There!

Folks who sew like to have a smooth, padded surface to work on when they're cutting, pinning, and pressing. But you don't have to spend wads of money to have one. In fact, if you have an old hollow-core door and a spare blanket or two, you can make one.

First, make sure the blanket is clean. Next, wrap the blanket over the door so that it completely covers the top and extends over the back at least four inches on each side. Staple the edges in place from the back. You may have to use more than one blanket, but be sure the surface is smooth.

Finally, cover the blanket with a clean cotton sheet or some muslin. Pull it taut and staple it to the back the same way you anchored the blanket. Place this new work surface on a pair of sawhorses, and you have a worktable.

Sort your buttons by size, color, or material—or in any other way that strikes your fancy. Then thread the buttons onto separate pieces of that scrap yarn you've been saving. Tie the ends of the yarn together in a bow so that you can undo them easily. If you want to get clever, match the color of the buttons and the color of the yarn so that you can easily find the color you want in your sewing kit.

❏ If you don't have many buttons but you do have an old kilt pin lying around, simply place your buttons on that.

O-Pin Sesame

❏ Keep extra pins, buttons, and small pieces of dressmaker's chalk organized in plastic film canisters. The canisters won't take up much room in your sewing box, and they're easy to open.

My Way

These Are Clean Figurines

Hummel figurines usually have a matte finish, so they don't need to be polished. However, they do get dirty, especially if they're displayed near a kitchen or in a household with smokers. To clean my Hummels, I use a spray-foam bathroom cleaner, the kind meant for bathroom tile surfaces. I lightly dampen the figurine with a soft cloth, being careful not to submerge it and trying not to get water into the piece's vent hole (the small hole, usually hidden under a figure's arm, that allows steam to escape during the manufacturing process). I spray a small amount of bathroom cleaner onto a cloth or a soft sponge and apply it to the figurine. Then I wipe the bathroom cleaner off with a clean, damp cloth and set the figurine on a dry cloth to air dry for a day. Don't stand the figurine on a wooden surface, because the unglazed base will make a ring. If you're in more of a hurry, run a warm blow dryer over the unglazed surface to speed things up.

–Bob Dous
Yardley, Pennsylvania

Sew, Don't Get Hurt

❏ If you have children around and you sew, you don't want to organize supplies in containers that are easy to open, because someone could accidentally swallow a button or get poked by a pin. Keep all those tiny hazards (your pins and buttons, not the kids) safely put away by storing them in childproof prescription medicine or aspirin containers. With a permanent marker, write the size of the needle or the type of button on the outside of each bottle. Since the lids lock, you won't need to worry about the needles or small odds and ends falling out. And if you want to take your projects with you, just toss the containers into your sewing bag.

Recreation, Sports, and Hobbies

Lay Down Some Rubber

❏ If your sewing machine has a foot pedal (as most do these days) and you sew in a room with a hardwood or tile floor, you have probably had the experience of placing your foot on the pedal only to have it skitter away, sliding on the floor. Here's how to fix that problem. Remember the rubber matting you bought last year to keep the area rug from slipping? Cut a scrap from that and place it under your foot pedal. It works on the same principle, keeping the pedal in place.

❏ Alternatively, place the rubber seal from an old canning jar, or a piece from an old bicycle or car inner tube, under that foot pedal. Any of these will hold the pedal firmly in place.

Steel This Needle

❏ Sometimes even stainless steel needles and pins rust if they're left in fabric that can absorb moisture. If this happens to you, poke your pins through a ball of steel wool before you put them away, and they'll be as shiny as new. Then all you have to do is deal with your rusty fabric.

Attract More Than Attention

❏ There may not be a sadder sight in sewing than that of a box of dressmaker's pins cascading off a worktable.

Trying to pick up all those pins without picking up a lot of dust can be a real challenge—unless you pick them up in a hurry with an old refrigerator magnet. Keep one in your sewing kit, where it will be handy for just such an occasion.

Make That a Pincushion to Go

❏ If you are hemming a dress or a skirt and are working around a mannequin, you want to have your pins handy at all times. You could place a few between your lips, but that's not the safest technique in the world. What you need is a portable pincushion, one that moves around with you. To make one, you need about a cup of beach sand and an orphaned cotton sock that's still in good shape. Make sure there are no holes in the sock, then fill the toe with the sand. Knot the sock as close to the sand as possible. Tuck the longer section of the sock into your belt or waistband, and tote that pincushion with you as you work.

Get Stuffed

❏ Another great stuffing for pincushions is the contents of your pencil sharpener. The graphite in the shavings will even help to keep your straight pins sharp.

Make Your Mark with Soap

❏ If you love making your own clothes but hate buying expensive chalk markers to trace out the pattern on the fabric, start saving those little slivers of bar soap. Their sharp edges give a much truer line than any piece of chalk, and once the fabric has been cut, the soap will wash or dry-clean out of most fabrics.

KNITTING

Twist and Shout

❏ Keeping your knitting needles organized in an old oatmeal carton or a tall box from a liquor bottle is a terrific idea. But if you have lots and lots of needles, it can be a pain in the neck finding two of the same size. One way to keep the needles together is with those extra

A Nine-Letter Word for Puzzle Craze

Like many little boys in the late nineteenth century, Arthur Wynne loved word games. He worked over the acrostics and anagrams published in popular magazines. And his grandfather encouraged Arthur's love of words by challenging him with another game. He would give Arthur a list of five words, each five letters long, then draw a box that was five spaces across and five lines long. Arthur's task was to arrange the words in the box so that they could be read across on one line and down another.

It's no surprise that Wynne grew up to be a writer of puzzles. In 1913, he was working for the *New York World,* looking for something new for the Christmas edition. Wynne decided to include his favorite type of childhood puzzle, but with a twist. Instead of giving a list of words, he gave only clues to words that should be written either across or down the squares.

Almost the day after the puzzle appeared, Wynne received letters from readers begging for more. Other readers compiled their own crosswords and sent them in.

Within a few years, most other newspapers had copied the game. In 1924, Simon and Schuster published the first book of crossword puzzles—an instant best-seller. Dictionary sales went through the roof. Puzzles appeared in wedding announcements and on the backs of menus. People carried them everywhere.

Far from being a fad, the word game only grew in popularity over the years. Today millions of Americans start each morning with the *New York Times* crossword puzzle in one hand and a pencil in the other.

twist ties that come with your trash bags. Wrap one twist tie around each pair of needles, near the tops. When you need a set, you can easily see and grab just what you need.

❏ Alternatively, use scraps of yarn to tie pairs of needles together for storage.

Knitting Yarn: Tame the Tangles

❏ Some of the prettiest homemade sweaters are those made from several different colors, but it can be a hassle keeping the balls of yarn from getting tangled. To get them under control, thoroughly clean an old potato bag (the kind with holes in the sides). Plunk the yarn inside and thread a strand of a different color through each hole. No more tangles!

Slip Your Stitches to a Handy Holder

❏ When you're knitting a garment from a pattern, you'll often read something like this: "Transfer stitches to holder." Well, if you've priced those specialty stitch holders, you know they're rather expensive. Here's a better idea. Rummage through your knitting bag and grab one of those loose scraps of yarn you've been holding on to. While the piece is still on the knitting needle, thread the yarn through a large craft needle and transfer all the stitches to the yarn. Tie the yarn ends in a bow (which will be easy to untie when you're ready to pick up those stitches). Ideally, use a strand of yarn that contrasts with the color you're knitting with. It'll make putting the stitches back on the needle a lot easier.

Hold Stitches with a Pickup Stick

❏ Alternatively, scout around your pantry for a chopstick. As long as it's smooth (no splinters for yarn to catch on), long enough, and the same diameter or smaller than the needles you're knitting on, you can just slip your stitches onto that.

Pencil In This Tip

❏ No chopsticks? That's okay. Grab an unsharpened pencil and slip your stitches onto that. Again, make sure the pencil's diameter is the same or smaller than that of the needles you're knitting with.

You'd Kil(t) for This Idea

❏ When you need to hold only a few stitches, slip them onto a large safety pin or a kilt pin.

Don't Drop That Stitch

❑ Anyone who knits knows how important it is to keep stitches from falling off the ends of double-pointed needles. You can buy special needle caps for that purpose, but frugal Yankees have found a better way. With a sharp knife, cut an old wine cork in half so that you have two equal rounds. Use an awl or a nail to punch a hole partway into the center of each piece, and the caps are ready to go.

❑ Alternatively, wrap a lightweight rubber band around the back end of each double-pointed needle. Just choose one that's big enough to stop the stitches from sliding off. It's easily removed when no longer needed, and not bulky enough to get in your way in the meantime.

QUILTING AND PATCHWORK

Wax with Seamless Effort

❑ In some patchwork sewing, you need to press your fabric over or around a paper shape guide that eventually gets basted to (and then removed from) the fabric while you're piecing the project together. To save yourself all the basting time, not to mention some thread and effort, use freezer paper for your guide instead. Use the kind that is opaque white on one side and waxed on the other. Cut your guide from the paper, then place it on the fabric waxed side up and fold the seam allowance over the paper. Press the seam allowance with a medium-hot iron. The wax will melt, and the seam allowance will be basted without thread.

Tired of all that laborious basting? Temporarily hold fabric pieces in place with waxed freezer paper instead of stitches.

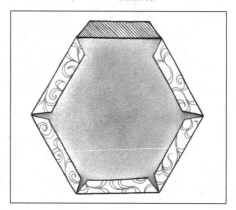

The Can Lid Can Help

❑ Cutting multiple shapes from a template can wear down the template if it's made of cardboard. The shape will change subtly, and the edges will get fuzzy. And

**Recreation,
Sports, and
Hobbies**

that means your pieces won't be consistent. You need to use stronger stuff. Try cutting your template from a plastic coffee can lid or the plastic lid from a take-out food container. If the shape you're cutting is large, cut it from the cover of a lightweight plastic loose-leaf binder.

FINE NEEDLEWORK

Mask the Problem

❏ One of the little distractions of needlepoint or cross-stitch occurs when your yarn or thread gets caught on the unfinished edges of the material. To keep this from happening, fold some good-quality masking tape over the edges. The masking tape won't leave a sticky residue, and it will finish the edges so that the yarn will glide over them.

Day Trips, Weekends, and Vacation Travel

As they say, travel broadens the mind. Do you find that it tends to shrink the wallet, too? Well, not to worry, because half the fun of your next trip will be using some of these ideas to make your travels more enjoyable—and less expensive. We've scrounged around our closets, talked to plenty of experienced (and frugal) travelers, and come up with all sorts of inexpensive ideas for packing, traveling with kids, making quick repairs on the go, providing for fun and comfort on the road, and much more.

So you thought you'd never have a reason to hold on to old Band-Aid tins, film canisters, and eyedrops bottles? You thought shoelaces were good only for keeping your shoes on, or dental floss was mostly a tool for maintaining oral hygiene? Maybe you thought you could actually throw out the cardboard core from that toilet paper roll?

Think again.

PACKING

Jewelry: Get to the Core of Things

❑ It's easy for jewelry to get scratched and tangled if you try to travel with it. Here's a terrific way to keep it safe and cut down on your pile of recyclables at the same time. Wrap your necklaces or bracelets around the cardboard core from a roll of toilet paper. Then use several elastic hair bands to secure the jewelry on the roll.

Wrap and Roll

❑ Looking for a way to pack more necklaces and make room for a few earrings as well? One way is to make a jewelry wrap from an old pillowcase or cloth napkin. Here's how. Cut a 10- by 13-inch rectangle from the fabric and hem any unfinished edges. Lay the fabric on your work surface and fold each short end toward the center, leaving a space of about an inch running down the center. With a sewing machine, stitch five straight lines across the fabric to form eight small pockets. Tuck your jewelry inside the pockets, then loosely roll the fabric into a tube and tie the whole thing with a piece of yarn or ribbon. The pockets will keep the pieces separate and prevent them from scratching each other or tangling.

Let's roll! For a portable jewelry case, hem all sides of a fabric rectangle (A). Fold both ends in toward the center and stitch through the layers to create pockets (B). Insert jewelry, roll up the case, and tie it closed with yarn (C).

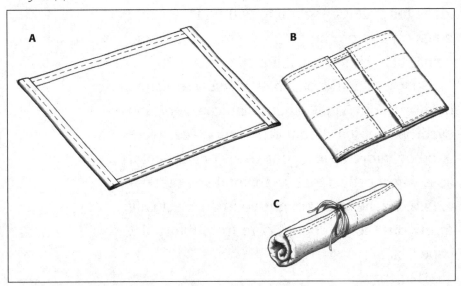

A

B

C

Pack the Organizer You Already Own

❑ When you travel, you need to organize many small items: bobby pins, cotton balls, a sewing kit, even change for highway tolls. You could invest in one of those adorable (and pricey) little travel pouches. Or, if you're smart, you could save the metal container that your plastic bandages came in—the one with the flip top. This sturdy container is perfect for storing almost any small item, including bandages.

Draw an Ace

❑ Looking for a handy way to pack a deck of playing cards for those idle moments on the plane or in the motel? Slip them into a clean travel container designed to hold a bar of soap.

Stop It!

❑ If you've ever been caught in a motel with no sink stopper, you know it's not easy to rinse out your stockings or take out your contact lenses without one. That's why you always pack the cap from a large bleach bottle, right? Turned upside down, the cap will stop up many sink and bathtub drains.

❑ You didn't pack the bleach cap? No problem. In a pinch, plastic wrap or a plastic bag laid over the drain hole also will make a serviceable sink stopper.

Hold the Soap

❑ Looking for a cheap soap holder for your next trip? If you have an empty plastic container that lozenges or candies came in, you have the solution, because it makes a perfect travel soap holder. Pop a couple of soap slivers inside (a full bar probably won't fit), close the lid, and tuck it in a resealable plastic bag just in case it leaks.

Say Good Buy

❑ Many folks, when they know they'll be going on a trip, run out to the drugstore or discount store and stock up on sample sizes of their favorite creams and lotions.

Bad idea: Those sample sizes almost always cost a lot more per ounce than the larger sizes. But if you took pictures on your last trip, you already have an alternative solution for transporting creams and lotions. Find one of those plastic film canisters you have lying around and wash and dry it well. Then fill it with your hand or body lotion, hair gel, or facial cream. Most film canisters won't leak, but store them in a resealable plastic bag just to be sure.

Nip Perfume Problems in the Bud

❏ It's nice to be able to take your perfume along with you when you travel, but most perfume bottles are delicate glass, which means they're breakable. And that could lead to a fragrant disaster. You need a travel container that's small but sturdy. Does that sound like one of those small bottles that airline liquor comes in? Perhaps one saved from your last trip just because it seemed too good to throw away? All you have to do is find it in the back of that bureau drawer, wash it out thoroughly, and fill it with just enough perfume to last through your travels.

Bag It

❏ Packing your shoes so that they don't soil the rest of the clothing in your suitcase can be a problem, especially if you don't want to spend money on store-bought shoe bags. Here's a solution that won't cost you a cent. Next time you're in the grocery store, grab one or two clear plastic bags from the produce section. They're perfect for wrapping your shoes, and they weigh almost nothing.

Try These Stuff Socks

❏ Pack children's shoes and sandals inside old tube socks. They'll fit nicely, and the socks will protect your clothing from getting soiled.

Get That Polished Look

❏ You want to look your best when you travel, and having polished shoes gives you a more, well, polished appearance. But who wants to carry around a tin of shoe polish for touch-ups? Dig around your junk drawer for an old pillbox or aspirin tin. Carefully transfer some shoe polish to the tin and place it in a resealable plastic bag. The tin will carry the perfect amount of polish to meet most travelers' needs.

Bring This into the Buffer Zone

❏ While you're concentrating on shiny shoes, don't forget the buffer. Salvage an old pair of nylon stockings, cut them into a few pieces (any size and shape will do),

---

4 Multipurpose Items No Traveler Should Be Without

We frugal types love it when an item can do double or even triple or quadruple duty. Here are four such items you'll want to take along on your next trip. After all, in each case you get at least two fixes for the price of one.

1. Old toothbrush. Use it on suede shoes or elbow patches to revive the nap and remove stains. Or use it as a travel laundry brush. Clean it up, and it becomes a handy travel nail brush. Finally, once your nails look good, use it to neaten up your eyebrows.

2. Clear nail polish. Sure it gives your fingers a just-manicured shine, but clear nail polish also secures the screws in your eyeglasses. Insert the screw, then apply a tiny drop of the polish. And it stops a run in your stockings. Dab some polish onto both ends of the run.

When the polish dries, it will keep the run from, er, running—at least until you remove the hose.

3. Safety pins. There is no end to the number of problems that safety pins can solve. They'll repair hems, keep motel curtains closed, serve as makeshift clothespins for lightweight items, and repair a waistband after you gorge yourself at the smorgasbord.

4. Duct tape. Keep a stash of the stuff with you at all times. You can use a small piece to hold a hem in a pinch, a larger one to lift lint from your sweater or jacket or to repair a tear in your soft luggage. You probably won't need a whole roll of it, though, so save space by rolling a long strip of the stuff around an old plastic hair curler or a wooden dowel.

Make Yourself a Money Pouch

Top on everyone's mind when traveling is finding a way to keep cash safe. After all, you have souvenirs to buy! But you wouldn't think of spending any of that cold hard cash on a money belt or an around-the-neck money pouch, because you can make your own with any old fabric you have lying around. Terry cloth (an old towel) works well, as does cotton (think old sheets, pillowcases, or tablecloths). You'll also need some Velcro (which you may be able to remove from the closures of an old jacket or purse) and a 2-foot length of scrap ribbon.

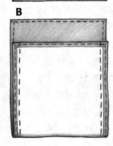

A

B

First, cut the fabric into an 11½- by 5½-inch rectangle. Stitch a hem about a quarter of an inch deep on all the unfinished edges. Lay the fabric right side down on your worktable with the short end toward you (A).

Fold the bottom 5 inches up to form a pocket (B). That should leave an extra inch of fabric at the top; that's your flap.

C

Sew the fabric sides together, forming a pouch, then turn the pouch right side out. Fold the seam allowance of the flap in toward the center, so that it's flush with the sides of the pouch, and stitch a hem to finish off the edges (C).

Now you need a way to hold the pouch closed; that's where the Velcro comes in.

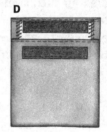

D

Cut the Velcro into two 4-inch strips. Sew one strip on the front of the pouch and the other on the inside of the flap so that you can secure the flap (and your cash) in place (D).

Finally, cut the ribbon so that it's long enough to go around your neck while letting the pouch hang below your chest.

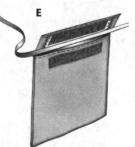

E

Stitch the ribbon to the inside top of the flap (E), and you're finished!

and toss one or two of the scraps into the resealable plastic bag with your shoe polish. The stockings will come in handy for buffing your shoes when you're on the road.

Take Stock(ings)

❏ Organizing your clothing and personal items so that they stay together and are easy to find is one of the great challenges of travel. Well, grab those old panty hose, because they may be the answer to some of your problems. Wash the stockings if they're not already clean, then cut off the legs. Next, cut the legs in half again so that you have two pieces with feet and two tubes. Set the foot pieces aside for another use (you're sure to find one). Take your socks, underwear, or any other relatively small items that don't have sharp edges and stuff them into the tubes. Then loosely knot the open ends. The stockings will keep those items well-organized, and you won't have to open the packages to see what's inside.

Listen to Those Cool Tunes

❏ If you've ever left your favorite cassette in the car on a hot day, you know how fast the sun can wreck a tape. So how do you travel with your favorite music without having to lug it around in a backpack all day? Grab your old insulated lunch bag, the one you used to put your lunch in for work, and place your car tapes in there. The bag will help shield them from the sun's heat, and it makes a terrific, compact carrying case, too.

Sew It Up

❏ Seasoned travelers never leave home without a sewing kit, and seasoned Yankees never buy one. Here's how to make a kit that will suffice for almost any trip. Find an empty aspirin tin and place a needle or two inside. Then, from a piece of scrap cardboard, cut a 1- by ½-inch rectangle. Cut three tiny notches in one of the long edges of the cardboard and then three more directly opposite the first three. Wrap some white thread around the cardboard, anchoring it in one pair of notches. Repeat the wrapping process with some black thread, securing it in the next pair of notches. Then do

10 Uses for a Simple Bandanna

A basic bandanna is so much more than just a scrap of fabric that a cowboy ties around his neck. This inexpensive square of cotton is the traveler's best friend. So if you have an old one tucked in the back of a drawer, pack it along on your next trip. Here are just some of its many uses.

1. Emergency washcloth. When you're caught short, a bandanna does just as well, and it dries fairly quickly.
2. Kitchen aid. In a pinch, if your rental cabin or cottage didn't come equipped with pot holders, a folded bandanna will do.
3. Sweatband. Heading out for a vacation jog? Fold or roll up the bandanna and tie it around your head. Or fold it several times and tie it around your wrist to dab the sweat from your forehead.
4. Terrific picnic napkin.
5. Handkerchief. Forget your tissue? Grab a bandanna instead—just make sure to wash it afterward.
6. Emergency toilet paper. In the middle of nowhere, under dire circumstances, a bandanna can be a woman's best friend.
7. Makeshift bib for a child or for you during a particularly messy meal. (Did somebody mention lobster?)
8. Fancy picnic place mat.
9. Mechanic's glove. Need to check your oil? Don't just grab the dipstick. Place a bandanna over your hand to keep from getting oil all over yourself.
10. Baggage ID. Before you relinquish your identical-to-every-other-suitcase luggage to the baggage handler, tie a bandanna around the handle. When it comes off the baggage carousel, you'll recognize it in an instant.

the same with another color that matches articles of clothing you're packing. Place this homemade spool in the aspirin tin, and you have a mini–sewing kit.

❏ You can do the same thing using an old film canister. The best part is that, in that case, you can fit a thimble inside, too.

Curtail Blowing Curtains

❏ It's a warm summer night, and you leave the motel windows open, just to get a breeze circulating in the room. The breeze is nice, but the curtains keep blowing open, destroying any sense of privacy. You can avoid this problem if you pop a clothespin or two in your suitcase when you pack. On those warm nights when you want a breeze, clip the curtains together with the clothespin. The breeze will waft in, but the curtains will stay closed.

Be a Softy

❑ One of the less pleasant aspects of travel is pulling your suitcases out of the attic and finding that they've acquired a musty odor. One way to freshen them without setting them outside for a week is to throw a fabric softener sheet inside each one for a day or so (or just before you put it back into storage). The suitcase will smell sweet and fresh for your trip.

❑ If you don't use fabric softener sheets, just toss a bar of scented soap into the suitcase.

Lock In Your Return Trip

❑ Now you're back from vacation, but where did you put those house keys? Prevent this problem by making a spare set of all your keys before you set out and using duct tape to affix them to the inside of your car trunk. A good spot is under the carpet on the floor of the trunk.

ORGANIZING THE PAPERWORK

Check It Out

❑ Need help organizing your vacation paraphernalia? If you're one of those folks whose bank sends a new plastic checkbook cover with each box of reordered checks, you're in luck. Don't toss out those extra covers! Use them to store theater tickets, notes, receipts, or cash. Keep them closed with rubber bands.

Register Your Expenditures

❑ Some folks go on vacation and spend with abandon. Others want to know exactly how they spent every cent. If you're one of the latter types, grab that old, unused

check register you couldn't bring yourself to throw away. Here's your chance to use it. It's perfect for logging cash and traveler's checks, as well as any other purchases you make.

Create a (Plastic-Covered) Paper Trail

❏ When you're traveling, you should always have certain information on your person: credit card numbers and their expiration dates, toll-free numbers to call if charge cards are lost or stolen, numbers of traveler's checks, the address and phone number of your hotel (you'd be surprised how many people jump into cabs in strange cities and can't give the cabbie an address). One good way to organize that information is to type or print it on a single sheet of paper. Trim the paper down to a manageable size, then laminate it with that roll of clear contact paper you've squirreled away under the kitchen sink. Tuck the card in your wallet, or hide it under the insole of your shoe, and you'll always have all the emergency information you need.

PERSONAL CARE ON THE ROAD

You Can Handle Those Aching Muscles

❏ If you're not used to walking, that first day of sightseeing can give you pains in places you didn't even know you had muscles! Two of those places are your calves and your quadriceps (tops of your thighs). If you have an old broom (or an old baton) you weren't using anyway, try this. Cut the broom handle down to about 14 inches. (You don't need to cut the baton.) Pop it in your suitcase. After a long day of walking, take a hot shower or bath, then sit down on the floor with your knees bent and feet flat on the floor. Put the handle or baton against your calf and gently roll it back and forth to loosen and soothe the muscles. Then move to a chair and sit with your feet flat on the floor. Gently roll the stick back and forth along the tops of your thighs. Remember, be gentle!

Take Your Feet to the Ball

❏ Your mind may feel refreshed after a day of sight-seeing, but your feet will probably be crying for mercy. One easy way to anticipate the problem and bring comfort to weary feet is to pack along one of those dead tennis balls languishing in your basement. At the end of a long day, sit in a chair and roll the bottom of each foot over the ball several times to ease the tight muscles.

TRAVEL SUBSTITUTIONS

Ditch the Zits

❏ The best treatment for the occasional blemish is a mild astringent. You may have a special product for such purposes in the medicine cabinet at home, but when your skin breaks out on the road, that doesn't do you much good. If you didn't pack the acne medicine, don't worry. Just reach in your toiletries bag and grab the toothpaste. Put a dab on that pimple at bedtime (we admit this is not a treatment for daytime use!), and things will look better by morning.

Make Do without Those Cotton Swabs

❏ Why is it that cotton swabs are so easy to leave behind when you go on a trip? Next time you forget to pack yours, use this handy substitute. Wrap your washcloth (or a baby wipe) over the end of your toothbrush. Use that combination to clean those hard-to-reach spots. But remember, just as you wouldn't insert a cotton swab into your ear canal, don't put your toothbrush in there either. (As if you could, right?)

My Way

My Socks Get Looped

When I was in the navy, living out of a seabag, I had plenty of opportunity to improvise. For instance, I was on a ship with nearly 2,000 other guys who were all wearing the same outfit: bell-bottom jeans and denim shirt. Every item of clothing had the owner's name in it—except our socks. Since all our laundry was done together, I had to figure out a way to get my own socks back. My answer was to tie my socks to my belt loops. I still do that when we go on vacation and we send our laundry out to be washed. (Truth is, I do it at home, too, and I never lose socks.)

–Tom Donnelly
Flushing, New York

Measure Distances to the Nearest Foot

Do you have a tough time translating the scale of miles on your road map when you're in a hurry? Try this trick. Grab a white shoelace from that pair of sneakers you were about to throw away and mark it, using a fine-tipped permanent marker, with the same scale as your road map. Then coil the lace up and keep it, with the map, in the car. Anytime you need to measure your mileage, just lay the shoestring along the route. No more mistakes!

Now If You Could Just Find the Toothbrush

❏ Forgot your toothpaste? If you have access to some salt (saved from lunch, say, in the hotel dining room or a fast-food restaurant), you need not risk offending anyone. A pinch or two of salt makes a serviceable substitute for toothpaste. It doesn't taste great, but it will do the job until you can get to the store.

Tie One On

❏ You're in your motel room getting ready to wash your face. You reach into your toiletries bag for your hair band or scrunchie, and it's not there. Time to run to the local discount store? Not on your life, especially if you have a clean pair of knee-high stockings in your bag. Tie the ends of one of the stockings together loosely and make your own headband. Or make a smaller loop, and you have a scrunchie (one that won't tear your hair the way a rubber band will). And there's no reason you won't be able to use the knee-high afterward.

Squeeze out of a Tight Spot

❏ You shouldn't have, but you did. You brought those brand-new loafers on vacation, but without a shoehorn, there's no chance you'll ever get them on. Or is there? If you can get your hands on a tablespoon (the kind you eat with, not the kind you measure cooking ingredients with), you're in luck. Just use it the same way you would a standard shoehorn.

JUST WHAT YOU NEED

Get Bowled Over

❏ Don't want to buy extra bowls for the summer cottage you rented? Try this cheap idea. Every time you finish a two-liter bottle of soda or water, cut the bottom off, keeping the edges as straight as possible. They make great bowls.

Be Prepared for Meals on Wheels

❏ Save those aluminum fast-food containers with the separate paper or plastic tops. Wash them well and keep them tucked away in your car for your next on-the-road meal. They cost nothing, and unlike paper plates, you can reuse them indefinitely.

No Bag? No Sweat

❏ If you bought so many souvenirs you can't carry them all, grab your lightweight sweatshirt with the drawstring. Tie the arms together and stuff the sweatshirt full of your lightest items. Now pull the drawstring tight so that the waist of the shirt is closed, and use the tied arms as a shoulder strap to carry the whole thing. Okay, so it's not pretty, but it sure is functional!

Pad Along to the Next Stop

❏ If you take a lot of day trips during the course of the year, you know how uncomfortable sitting on hard picnic benches or the ground can get. But if you saved that ratty old closed-cell sleeping pad and stashed it in the attic, you have a solution. Cut a 14-inch (approximately) square from the pad, repair any tears in it with duct tape, and toss the square in your car. Anytime you stop and want to sit down, just place your cushion on the surface first. (This is especially helpful when you're eating at a picnic table that's still damp from a brief shower or morning dew.)

❏ Alternatively, cut the foam seat cushion from an old chair to an appropriate size, then stitch up a cover from a couple of old towels. Or if you're not much of a seamstress, just pop the cushion in a clean trash bag, smooth out any air pockets, and seal the bag shut with duct tape.

Defeat the Dirty Birds

❏ One of the most pleasant parts of a vacation is stopping off at a picnic table for an outdoor lunch or dinner.

Day Trips, Weekends, and Vacation Travel

One of the least pleasant parts is discovering that a flock of birds has found the table first. Keep that in mind next time you're ready to throw away your plastic shower curtain liner. Rather than taking it to the dump, wash it with some hot, soapy water or a solution of household bleach and water. Keep it in the trunk of the car, and anytime you stop for a picnic, use the liner as a tablecloth.

QUICK REPAIRS

Slip On a Sock

❏ Ouch! Your car radiator sure is hot. You don't want to burn your hands on the radiator cap, and you didn't bring along an oven mitt. Got a sock somewhere in your luggage? Slip a thick one (or two) over your hand, and you have an instant glove.

Get Help from the String Section

❏ If the screw pops out of your eyeglasses while you're on the road, it's not a problem—that is, if you practice good dental hygiene. Grab a short piece of dental floss and use it to tie your eyeglasses together. It's not pretty, but it works.

❏ Alternatively, strip the paper from an ordinary twist tie and use the metal wire to hold the pieces of your frames together. Be careful to wrap the ends of the wire around the frames to keep them out of the way until you can make a more long-term repair.

Floss Those Pearly Whites

❏ Just because your string of beads broke doesn't mean your vacation has to end on an ugly note. Carefully collect all the loose beads. Then grab the dental floss (waxed or unwaxed) in your toiletries kit, and with the needle from your emergency sewing kit, restring them. Dental floss is stronger than most string or thread, so it will keep the beads from bursting again.

Give It a Good (Stiff) Belt

❏ Maybe you've seen it: the suitcase that comes around on the carousel, splayed wide open, its contents on display to the world. But don't let the fact that your suit-case doesn't stay closed keep you from using it again. Grab any large old belt from the back of your closet and press it into service. Wrap the belt around the case, punch another hole or two in the belt with an awl if necessary, and use it to keep your suitcase closed. If one belt isn't long enough, grab two that are of similar width. Buckle the two together, and you're in business. (You may want to cover the buckles with duct tape so they won't catch on anything.)

Day Trips, Weekends, and Vacation Travel

Take a Stitch in Time

❑ If you get a tear in your soft-sided luggage while trav-eling, stitch it up with a strand of dental floss. Don't like the looks of your on-the-fly repair? Color the floss with a magic marker or crayon that is the same color as the suitcase.

The Inside Story

Nylon Stockings: Isn't That a Riot?

Riots? Over hosiery? That's right. In 1940, when the first nylon stockings were introduced, they were in such demand that riots actually broke out as women tried to get into the stores selling them.

Before 1940, women could buy only silk stockings, but when World War II began, silk was needed for the manufacture of parachutes, and that left none for stockings.

Enter the DuPont company and its new miracle fiber, nylon—aka polymer 6,6. Touting the stuff as nearly indestructible, DuPont distributed the yarn to hosiery manufacturers. Those early stockings sold out as quickly as they were produced, and that made for a lot of very happy women, who found the stockings long-lived—especially compared to fragile silk. The first year alone, 64 million pairs were sold.

And that's when women were just *wearing* stockings. Few had yet figured out that they were terrific for organizing suitcases, shining shoes, and tying up hair.

FIRST-AID FOR TRAVELERS

Pack Help in a Can

❑ Need a sturdy container for your car's first-aid kit? Why not use a tennis ball can? These cans are generally plastic, and each one comes with a reclosable lid.

Kids Will Love This Treatment

❑ You're pretty sure it's not broken, but you jammed your finger, and it hurts like crazy. How do you keep your finger protected until you can get to the doctor? Eat a frozen ice pop. That's right. And when you're done, rinse off the stick. Lay it against your finger and wrap it (not too tightly) with the fabric tape from your first-aid kit. The stick and tape will keep your finger straight and protected until you can get it checked out. And the ice pop will offer a little comfort in the meantime.

When You Need Just a Drop

❑ You're packing your travel first-aid kit, and when it's time to include the rubbing alcohol, you notice that it comes in a big bottle. Don't run to the store and buy a smaller bottle. Check your bathroom for an old bottle of over-the-counter eyedrops. Pop the dropper off the neck of the bottle by pushing it sideways, empty out the bottle, and give the bottle, top, and dropper a good washing. Next, fill the bottle with rubbing alcohol (you may need a small funnel for that operation). Replace the dropper tip and the lid. The small, plastic bottle won't break, it will fit almost anywhere, and the dropper will allow you to dispense only as much alcohol as you need at any one time.

Take the Sting Away

❑ We know bees make honey and all, but a bee sting can sure ruin your day. The last thing you want to do is make it worse while you're trying to get the stinger out. If you can see the stinger, gently scrape it with the edge of a credit card until it dislodges. Don't grab the stinger with tweezers; you may squeeze more poison into your skin.

Just Add Vinegar

❑ They said there were jellyfish in the water, but you went in anyway, and you got stung. Now what? Don't let the pharmacy sell you something expensive—at least not if you packed a small plastic bottle of vinegar, just in case. Use it to wash the spots where you got stung. The vinegar will take the sting away.

If You Cut Me, Do I Not Haul Out the Duct Tape?

❑ You got a small cut while traveling, and you need to cover it before your clothes start looking as if you just left the scene of a major crime. The problem is, you used up your last plastic bandage protecting that blister on your foot. Not to worry. Make a serviceable bandage from a cotton ball or tissue held in place with a strip of duct tape. It won't be pretty, but it will do the job.

> ## *A Different Twist*
> ### Try the Band-Aid Approach
> Sometimes you need a quick way to hold a couple of lightweight items together on the road—only you forgot the tape. Use the sticky part of a plastic bandage instead. It won't be pretty, but it will do the job.

Don't Be Footsore

❑ If you're concerned about getting blisters on your feet during a day of sight-seeing, you'd be wise to protect the vulnerable spots. Try placing thin strips of duct tape over your heels and other areas where you typically tend to develop blisters. The extra padding may be just enough to get you through that downtown walking tour.

Keep Your Reading at Arm's Length

❑ You hurt your arm in a sudden fall, and you're afraid it may be broken. How do you protect it on the way to the doctor's office? Easy. Grab the magazine you brought along for nighttime reading, fold it in half, and use duct tape to secure it in place over your arm. That should keep the arm stable until you reach the doctor.

First-Aid for Travelers

**Day Trips,
Weekends, and
Vacation Travel**

COPING WITH
THE WEATHER

All the News That's Fit to . . . Dry

❏ Wet shoes? Here's good news for travelers. Even on the road, you have access to a good, cheap fix. No matter where you are, just grab a page or two from the morning newspaper and stuff the paper inside your wet shoes. It will absorb the water, helping the shoes to dry more quickly. Then all you have to do is keep changing the paper as it gets wet.

Hang In There

❏ A sudden downpour is a pain in the neck even when you're at home, but when you're traveling with a limited wardrobe, getting one set of clothes soaked can put a real, um, damper on your plans. In a pinch, you can rig up a makeshift clothesline on which to dry your damp togs without making another trip out into the rain to buy clothesline. Pull the laces out of your shoes, tie them together, and attach each end to something secure, such as a chair arm or cabinet handle. Drape your wet duds over the laces, and you have an instant clothesline.

Bring On the Rain

❏ Sight-seeing in the rain can be one of the underrated pleasures of travel. Crowds are small, the air smells fresh, and noise seems to be lessened when the skies open. But you need to be prepared before you set out, and that's where all those plastic shopping bags you've been accumulating can come in handy. Grab one that you've picked up in the course of your vacation shopping and check it for holes by blowing it up like a balloon. If the bag does have small holes, get another one. Once you find one that's hole-free, tuck inside all the items you want to take with you for the day. Loosely tie the bag closed, then place it inside your day pack, tote, or purse. That way, your tote may get wet, but your belongings will stay dry.

CAR TRAVEL

Trash the Can

❏ During long car trips, you're bound to collect some trash—fast-food and candy wrappers, tissues, miscellaneous garbage. Everyone knows that plastic shopping bags are perfect for stashing the trash (you did know that, right?), but they don't stand up by themselves. A

Day Trips, Weekends, and Vacation Travel

6 Essentials for the Car Trunk

Jack—check; spare tire—check; flashlight—check; kitty litter—huh? Along with all the old standards, here are some items you may not have known belong in your car trunk.

1. Kitty litter. It's a must for any winter traveler in northern climates. If you get stuck in snow on the way to the ski resort, sprinkle the litter around your tires to give them some traction.

2. Vinegar. As long as the outdoor temperature is above freezing, fill a spray bottle with a mixture that's half vinegar and half water and keep it in your trunk. Use it to clean your windows and windshield, your headlights, and your rearview and side mirrors. In a pinch, you can use it to clean a sticky mess from vinyl upholstery. Be sure to remove the bottle when winter comes, though, or you could end up with a fragrant trunk after the solution freezes and leaks all over!

3. Old rags or diapers. Keep them clean, please, and keep them handy in your trunk for cleaning windows, headlights, and mirrors.

4. Sturdy old whisk broom. Use it to clean out your car at rest stops. Just brush the gravel and trash onto a piece of cardboard and toss it out, or brush it right out the door. And in the winter, it's terrific for brushing snow off your car.

5. Old blanket. Even if it's seen better days, don't toss it out. Instead, toss it in your car trunk. Anytime you need to take a look under your car, you won't have to lie down on the dirty pavement. Or use it to cover the backseat when you tote something dirty, or as a ground cover for your next roadside picnic. Or use it as a blanket.

6. Vinyl electrical tape. Use it for everything from taping a broken window closed to making a temporary fan belt.

great solution is to hang on to a coffee can (the bigger the better) after you use the contents. Place a plastic shopping bag inside the can as a liner, and you have a mini–trash can that's easily emptied.

❏ You can also make a good trash can for the car from any old plastic resealable container with a lid that closes tightly—say, a baby wipes container or an old flour or sugar canister. This is especially handy if you put anything, er, fragrant inside, because you can always snap on the lid to contain the smell.

Freshen Up

❏ You ate that tuna sandwich an hour ago, but the aroma still lingers. If you had bought one of those little tree-shaped disposable car fresheners, it might not be a problem. But who wants to spend money when you have a perfectly good solution in your junk drawer? Start with a metal candy tin (the kind that some candies and throat lozenges come in). Open the tin and place just the lid on an old two-by-four or other piece of scrap wood. Hit the lid with a hammer and nail or a hammer and awl to punch a few holes in it. (If you think there's a chance you may cut your hand on the pointy metal, flip the lid over and, while bracing it on a flat surface, tap the points down.) Put a handful of your favorite potpourri or a small bar of sweet-smelling soap in the box. Close the lid and hide the tin under the front seat. The potpourri will freshen the air, and once it loses its strength, you can easily change it.

Don't Brake for Water

❏ When you get into the car for a long car trip, you may be the type who wants to make good time, stopping as little as possible for trifling reasons such as eating and drinking. But it's healthier to keep hydrated during a long trip than to deprive your body of liquids. One way to keep cold water on hand while you drive is to wash out an empty plastic soda or water bottle and fill it with water (leave two to three inches of space at the top) the night before your trip. Replace the lid and put the bottle in the freezer. By morning, the water will be frozen, but it will thaw out as you travel, ensuring that you'll always have a good cold drink right by your side.

AIRPLANE COMFORT

Day Trips, Weekends, and Vacation Travel

A Pillow for Your Head

❏ Maybe you're one of those lucky few who can sleep comfortably sitting up, but for the rest of us, trying to sleep on an airplane can literally be a pain in the neck. Of course, you could buy a neck pillow, but here's a solution that won't cost a thing—and won't take up a lot of space in your carry-on luggage. Tuck some of your soft clothing (socks or underwear) inside a soft cotton T-shirt and knot the ends. You have an instant neck pillow— one you can mold to fit your own personal contours.

Hang 'Em High

❏ Don't know where to hang your lightweight blazer when you board a plane? When you're dressing for your

---

4 Substitutions for the Standard Carry-On

Hey, the airlines never said you had to spend $300 on a Louis Vuitton carry-on bag. Technically, you can use any bag, as long as it measures 9 by 14 by 22 inches (or smaller). So before you panic because you don't have a suitable carry-on bag, scout around your basement, garage, closets, and attic for any of these terrific (and cheap) substitutes.

1. Old bowling bag. Has your spouse given up the bowling habit? Ditch the ball and grab the bag. It'll hold all you need.
2. Used book bag. Okay, the other passengers may laugh at you

when you stroll down the aisle with an old Pink Panther book bag, but if your youngster isn't using it for school anymore, why not?

3. Tool bag. Check your garage for one of those canvas bags with a leather bottom designed for toting tools. If it's clean, it will make a sturdy carry-on bag.
4. Cosmetics tote. You know how, when you make a purchase from a department store cosmetics counter, you get a special gift tote bag? Dig it out of your clothes drawer; it will work just fine as a carry-on.

trip, grab a large paper clip from your desk and stick it in your pocket. Once you are seated on the plane, run one end of the paper clip through the hanging loop inside the blazer. Then open the clip slightly and insert the point directly into the upholstery of the seat in front of you, along a seam. The clip won't damage the upholstery, and your blazer won't get wrinkled or lost.

TRAVEL WITH KIDS

Pack Up Your Kid Bag

❑ Travel with children and grandchildren can be a great joy, but getting everyone dressed and out the door efficiently can be challenging, too. Here's a solution that has worked for some folks. Pick out one entire outfit for each child: top, bottom, socks, underwear, whatever is necessary for the outfit. Place the outfit in a one- or two-gallon resealable plastic bag—the kind that usually holds food. (If you squeeze out all the air, you'll be surprised at how much you can fit in one bag.) When it's time to get dressed, older kids can dress themselves, and anyone can dress the little guys. No longer will you hear, "Where are my socks?" Granted, this method takes

---

4 Toys for Tots—And Adults

When you're on a long car trip, you just have to stop every once in a while to get some exercise. So why limit yourself to walks around the rest area? With a little planning, you can have instant fun anytime, anywhere. For example:

1. If you have an old kite lying around your attic, throw it in your trunk. Anytime you stop where there's a breeze and a little space for running, pull it out. Kites are good fun for kids and adults alike.

2. A Wiffle ball and bat take up almost no room and weigh just about nothing. And no matter how hard you wail on the ball, it won't go very far.

3. A Frisbee will fit under your spare tire.

4. Bring your driver and your putter, as well as some Wiffle golf balls. Practice your technique.

---

more preparation, but it will save time (and aggravation) in the end.

It's a Shoe-In

❏ Long car trips are hard enough on adults, but try being a five-year-old trapped in the backseat of a car for six or seven hours. Here's one family-tested technique for keeping traveling tots happy. First, you'll need some games and toys that you know your child likes. (Some parents recommend special toys that the kids don't get to play with very often.) Next, get your hands on a plastic shoe bag—the kind that hangs flat against a wall or door and has pockets for the shoes. (One that you were just about to throw out will be fine.) Tuck the toys and games inside the pockets—along with small (wrapped) food treats if you like. Hang the bag from the hook above one of the windows in the backseat, making sure your child can get to it easily. The pockets make finding the toys fun, and the bag will keep the hot sun out of the backseat.

Make Room on Board

❏ When you're trying to solve puzzles on a long car trip, the biggest puzzle of all is trying to find a way to write on that flimsy piece of paper lying on your lap. Here's a better way. Next time you're ready to toss out your old plastic or wooden cutting board, save it. Disinfect it with a solution of one part household bleach and three parts water and let it dry. Take it along on your next family outing, and let the kids use it as a lap desk.

❏ And don't let the fact that you've lost all the pieces from that Parcheesi (or Monopoly or Chutes and Ladders) game encourage you to do something ruthless such as tossing out the set. Any old game board will make a lap desk that's portable and sturdy.

TRAVEL WITH PETS

Keep Your Cat Occupied

❏ Looking for a way to relieve your cat's boredom on a long car trip? Okay, so she can't do the *New York Times*

Day Trips, Weekends, and Vacation Travel

crossword puzzle or count Volkswagen Beetles. But relief is at hand, and it won't cost you a dime. You know that foil that came wrapped around your burger at the last rest stop? Don't toss it out. Instead, roll it up into a ball and toss it to your feline. Most cats love to bat around foil balls, so this is a good way to entertain kitty *and* your other passengers.

Use a Litter Ingenuity

❏ If you're planning a car trip and you want or need to bring along your cat, you'll need to provide a litter box. But that doesn't mean you have to haul out the one in your bathroom. Scout around the basement for an old dishpan or even a lid from a heavy-duty (but not too big) cardboard box. Pour the litter in there, add a little baking soda for freshness, and you have a traveling litter box. If you can't stop right away to empty the box, take along some small resealable plastic bags to scoop up the poop and some extra baking soda to freshen the box.

Make a Kitty (or Puppy) Canteen

❏ Dogs and cats that travel in cars need lots of water, especially during the summer, so before you set off on your trip, fill some old, clean plastic soda bottles with water, replace the caps, and keep them in the car with you. Every time you take a drink, pour some water into your pet's bowl so that the animal can do the same.

Scoop the Poop

❏ After Rover does his thing at the rest stop, you'll have to clean up after him (no sneaking away!). That's a good reason to bring along a bunch of clear plastic produce bags from the grocery store. Put your hand inside the bag and grab the poop, then pull the bag inside out around the feces. Tie the bag in a knot and throw the whole thing in the nearest outdoor trash can.

❏ If you can't bear the thought of touching doggy mess, even through a bag, bring along an old, stiff kitchen spatula and use that to pick up the poop.

Celebrations

Any time a group of loved ones gets together—to mark a milestone, to celebrate the season—is a great time to use the materials at hand. This lets you stretch what you have to invite more revelers or accommodate that unexpected guest. And hospitality, after all, is a large part of what celebrations are all about.

Those odds and ends around the house do help stretch the holiday budget. But more important than the money saved are the homemade touches. Valentines with homemade "glitter," napkin rings made from fall leaves, sugar cube "sparklers" for New Year's Eve—they're priceless.

Besides, whether you're making your own luminaria from old tin cans or saving ribbons from a bridal shower for a paper plate "bouquet," you are creating traditions. And this is how families become families, by creating nifty knickknacks and memorable moments—then passing the traditions along from one generation to the next.

Celebrations

NEW YEAR'S

Who Needs Champagne for Sparkle?

❏ Ring in the New Year with ice cream, and at the stroke of midnight, light a spark. Soak sugar cubes in lemon or vanilla extract. Place one on top of each scoop of ice cream (in a dish, not a cone), and at the critical moment, light the cubes with a match. They will sputter and sparkle quite nicely for a few seconds—much like sparklers, but edible.

Let's Make Some Noise!

❏ It's a tradition to make loud noises at the start of the New Year—they say it scares away the bad spirits. The good news is that noise can be cheap. Create your own raucous noisemaker—sturdier than anything you'd find at a party supply store—with an empty soda can. Decorate the outside any way you like, plunk three or four pennies inside, and seal the opening with a couple of two-inch strips of duct tape, crisscrossed. Then shake, rattle, and roll.

VALENTINE'S DAY

Stamp Out Love

❏ To jazz up homemade valentines or store-bought envelopes, make your own rubber stamps. With a pencil or marker, draw the shape you want on a small block of wood, such as a child's building block. (This is easier if you stick to simple shapes.) Then cut pieces of thin rubber bands to fit the shape and glue the pieces to the block with rubber cement. Press your homemade stamp onto an ordinary ink pad and stamp designs to your heart's content.

❏ Alternatively, cut a potato in half and draw a simple outline shape on the flat, freshly cut surface of one half. Cut away the waste around your outline to lift the shape above the surface, and you'll have a simple (though short-lived) stamp for those valentines and other crafts projects.

Say "I Love You" with . . . Cereal

❏ Right in the middle of a valentine-making fest and fresh out of glitter? Try adding six to eight drops of red food coloring to uncooked Cream of Wheat or Cream of Rice. Stir well, spread out the mixture in a thin layer on newspaper to dry, and then apply just like real glitter. It won't sparkle, but it will definitely jazz up those valentines, envelopes, or homemade cookie or candy boxes.

Celebrations

The Inside Story
Esther Turned Glitter into Gold

For hundreds of years, people have given love tokens on St. Valentine's Day as a show of affection, but the earliest precursors of the modern-day valentine were produced in England in the 1840s and 1850s. Artists made or cut out small drawings of beautiful women, flowers, or birds and adorned them with lace, ribbons, and glitter made of ground glass and feathers. They were ornate, to say the least, and they cost anywhere from $5 to $35, a fortune to pay for a printed sentiment even by today's standards.

Perhaps the most famous valentine designer was Esther Howland of Worcester, Massachusetts. She saw the expensive European valentines her father was selling in his stationery store and knew she could make better ones at home. She cut out some pictures, drew others, and glued them all to paper valentines. Then she decorated them with leftover lace and bits of ribbon that she had. Her father agreed to try to sell them. The next year, he was begging her for more.

Eventually, Esther had a booming business. She hired young girls to come into her home and cut and paste the valentines according to her direction. She sold thousands of these every year, including some through shops in Boston and New York City. One year, she cut and pasted together $100,000 worth of valentines—not a bad living from a bunch of scraps.

Celebrations

EASTER

Eggs: What's the Spatter?

❏ For an impressionist egg dye job worthy of Monet, add half a teaspoon of vegetable oil to each color of prepared commercial egg dye. Dip an egg briefly in one color, then lift it out and wipe it completely dry. Dip the same egg in another color, and again wipe it completely dry. The end effect will be spatters of each color, overlaid. Start with the lightest color you'll put on the egg and never use more than three colors, or the egg will end up a motley brown.

Not Fabergé, but What a Display

❏ To display your beautiful colored eggs, haul out an old (and very well washed and dried) goldfish bowl. Layer the eggs gently inside.

❏ Display individual eggs upright by resting each one on a two-liter soda bottle cap. Line them up in a row on

---

My Way

A Dyeing Art

Just before Easter one year, we had some friends over for an egg-decorating free-for-all. Our kitchen table was covered with newspaper and a jumble of rubber bands, twine, magic markers, old candles, and containers of dye. Someone lit a candle and dribbled its wax on an egg, then plunked the egg in the dye next to one wound with rubber bands. Another friend stretched a plastic mesh onion bag tightly around her egg and held it under for the count. One egg went in covered with bits of cellophane tape.

What emerged astonished us all. The candle wax was peeled off to yield a bright polka-dot pattern. The rubber bands gave one egg a watermelon rind texture. The tape had blocked out a confetti pattern, and the mesh bag had left a delicate diamond effect. Each discovery made us secretly pleased that we had never gotten around to cleaning out our catchall drawer.

—**Clare Innes**
Antrim, New Hampshire

Easter Eggs: Color Them Natural

Whether you're bored with the little tablets or caught with no dye in the house and a vat of freshly boiled eggs, these "natural" Easter egg dyes are worth a shot. *Tip:* The colors take longer to sink in than commercial dyes, so let 'em soak for at least 10 minutes.

Pink. Add 1 teaspoon vinegar to 1 cup canned beet juice and soak eggs in the mixture.

Yellow. Dip eggs in ¾ cup hot water mixed with 1 teaspoon turmeric and a splash of vinegar.

Orange-red. Boil ¾ cup water with 1 tablespoon chili powder for 30 seconds. Add 1 teaspoon vinegar. Dip eggs in the solution while it's still hot.

Brown. Start with 1 cup cooled leftover coffee. Add a splash of vinegar, then add the eggs.

Yellow-green. Steam 1 pound asparagus, then save ¾ cup of the cooking water. Add 1 tablespoon vinegar to the water. Dip the eggs in the solution.

Tan. Boil 1 cup water with the brown skins of 3 or 4 onions. Boil the eggs in the water.

the mantel or circling the centerpiece, or set one down at each place setting (above the tip of the knife) at the Easter breakfast table.

Go Hoppin' down the Paper Trail

❑ Want some inexpensive, biodegradable, fairly classy-looking Easter grass for baskets and centerpieces? Try shredding some plain white copy paper in the office paper shredder. (You might throw in a pink or blue flyer or two while you're at it.) If you don't work in a department where document shredding is the norm, ask around in the accounting or legal department, or in the executive suite. They'll most likely be happy to let you shred 5 or 10 sheets, and that's all you'll need for a basket or two.

FATHER'S DAY

Dad Will Love Putting Up with This

❑ If Dad's a big golfer—or just wishes he were—set up a putt-putt course in his honor on Father's Day. Set an

Decoration Day: Flowers for Fallen Soldiers

In the spring of 1866, folks on both sides of the Mason-Dixon line had at least one thing in common: overwhelming grief over the bloodshed and destruction wrought by the Civil War. As the South burst into spring bloom, the women of Columbus, Mississippi, decided to scatter flowers on the graves of the men who had died in the war and agreed that they would repeat that simple action every year to honor the dead.

Two years later, General John Alexander Logan, the head of the large veterans organization called the Grand Army of the Republic (GAR), had a similar inspiration. He asked members to decorate the graves of Union soldiers with flowers every year on May 30. That summer, an act of Congress proclaimed Decoration Day a holiday in the District of Columbia.

Over the succeeding years, Decoration Day—at least in the North—grew well beyond a time for the scattering of flowers. It became a day for veterans to visit schoolhouses and tell tales of the war. It evolved into a day of cookouts and speeches and unrelenting patriotism to honor the Union that had been preserved. In the South, although people didn't spend much time watching parades, in some communities they did still scatter flowers on soldiers' graves.

In 1882, the name of the holiday changed in some communities from Decoration Day to Memorial Day. Later, as the nation became involved in other major conflicts, people began arguing that it was important to honor *all* the American soldiers who had died for their country and its ideals, not just those who had perished in the Civil War. And the holiday has evolved to do just that.

empty tin can on its side at the end of each "hole." Use as many cans as you like and place them all around the house, inside and out. The best spots for them are areas that have smooth surfaces, indoor-outdoor carpeting, or closely cropped grass. Set up broomstick guides, or upend chairs, buckets, or barrels as "obstacles."

For "clubs," use mop handles, baseball bats, croquet mallets, or long-handled rackets (no strings necessary).

Father's Day

The balls can be golf balls, tennis balls, or racquet-balls—whatever will fit in the cans without too much effort. Keep score, tallying one point for each stroke.

Celebrations

FOURTH OF JULY

Combine Fire and Water(melon)

❏ If you plan to serve a watermelon at the conclusion of a Fourth of July party, use it as the centerpiece for the picnic table or a decoration for the buffet. Use a paring knife to dig out three ½-inch-deep rounds in a line down the center of the watermelon, then rest a votive candle in each round. Now you have a candleholder as well as dessert.

Make a Kinder, Gentler Firecracker

❏ To avoid injuries while you keep up with tradition, make English firecrackers—which "explode" into tiny gifts. For each, tie a string about 8 inches long around a gift not more than 1½ inches wide or 5 inches long—say, candy, a figurine, or a balloon. After tying, the string should have 6 inches to spare. Insert the gift into a toilet paper tube, allowing the string to dangle out one end. Then cover the tube with red, white, or blue tissue or crepe paper (you might be able to scrounge this from a shoe box) and twist the ends, candy wrapper style. When you pull the string, out comes the gift.

Try Slip-Sliding Away

❏ For a Fourth of July picnic, make your own "slip 'n' slide" water play area. Lay a clean old plastic sheet, vinyl tablecloth, or shower curtain on a free patch of lawn that your garden hose can reach. Fasten the corners with tent stakes or sharpened sticks driven into the ground. To keep the sticks from injuring revelers, gather up a few tennis balls that have outlived their usefulness; you'll need one for each stick or tent stake. Cut a hole in each tennis ball just big enough to allow you to slip it over the top of a stake. Make sure each stake is capped with a tennis ball, then set the hose nozzle on "spray" and lay it where the water will dribble the length

Celebrations

of the plastic. The youngsters can run, slip, and slide to their hearts' content.

HALLOWEEN

Give Jack a Close Shave

❑ Looking for a way to make your jack-o'-lantern a little more ornate than the one you carved when you were five? To add the neat little nicks and swirls that make a more elaborate Halloween pumpkin, get out the vegetable parer. Use the pointed end to dig little curlicues from the outer layer of pumpkin to make eyebrows, hair, a mustache, freckles, eyeglasses, or earrings.

A Costume Party? Tonight?

You probably won't win any awards with these ready-in-a-hurry costumes, but you *will* be wearing a costume for the party. And after all, isn't that what counts?

Sometimes a costume is just a costume. Wear a lady's full-length slip. (You can always don a turtleneck and tights underneath.) Draw a mustache and goatee with an eyebrow pencil, and see if you can't dig up some wire-framed glasses without lenses. And there you are! A Freudian slip. Either gender can wear this with style.

My favorite costume. Haul out your green turtleneck, green tights, green pants, green socks, and green slippers. Then find a headband and the metal spiral bindings from two old school notebooks. Secure the spirals to the headband top at about 10 o' clock and 2 o'clock, and place the headband on your head. Depending on whether you want to use green eye shadow to dust your entire face or just a circle of mascara on each cheek, you're either a Martian or a bug. Or a Martian bug.

Don't set her off. Dress in a black or red sweat suit. Take two large pieces of red or black poster board and glue them together into a cylinder large enough for you to fit inside. Cut armholes. Tie a six-inch piece of red yarn or twine to a lock of your hair. Carry a pack of matches. Your firecracker or dynamite look is complete.

❏ For a similar effect, scratch lines and swirls with a nut pick.

Whoooo's Got My Lollipop?

❏ If you're going to give out lollipops as treats, make them a bit more festive by tossing a white paper napkin over the top of each to make a "ghost," then fastening it at the "neck" with a twist tie. Kids can use the napkins to wipe off sticky hands and mouths. If you're feeling ambitious and want form without function, draw eyes on the napkin with a black marker or an eyebrow pencil—but don't try to use the napkin for cleanup.

Celebrations

THANKSGIVING

Make a Feast for the Eyes

❏ Make a turkey centerpiece for the Thanksgiving table from a whole pineapple. Lay the pineapple on its side. Then cut a turkey head and tail from old manila file folders. Draw eyes on the head. Cut a beard from a piece of red paper and glue it on. Attach the tail to the flat end of the pineapple with a few pieces of putty. Place the "bird" on a large platter or carving board and surround it with clean fall leaves.

❏ A pineapple "turkey" also works as an hors d'oeuvres tray. Using a vegetable parer, shave long strips of carrot, wind each strip into a roll, and poke it onto the end of a toothpick. Use a nut pick or cake tester to prick 30 to 40 holes in the "body" of the pineapple turkey, then insert your carrot-topped toothpicks to look like feathers. If you like, substitute some cubes of cheese on tooth-picks and/or some green or black olives for some of the carrots.

(En)circle the Napkins

❏ Make quick and easy napkin rings for the Thanks-giving crowd by cutting 2-inch rings from toilet paper tubes, using scissors or an X-Acto knife. Wrap each ring with a scrap of aluminum foil that measures 2½ by 4 inches, taping the overlap and tucking the edges into

Celebrations

the tube. Wash some fresh fall leaves with hot water and dishwashing liquid, then let them dry. Wrap one leaf around each ring and attach it with a stapler or plain white glue such as Elmer's. Insert a napkin in each ring, and you're ready for dinner.

CHRISTMAS TREE ORNAMENTS

Give Your Tree a Different Kind of Cone

❑ Borrow from the Victorians and decorate your tree with ice cream cones. Working with either sugar cones or plain ones, use a sewing needle to poke two tiny facing holes about one-quarter inch from the top edge of each cone. Thread a six- to eight-inch piece of red, green, or white yarn through the holes and tie a knot at each end. Hang the cone with peppermints or gum-

A Snowball Ornament for Tree and Tub

Should you happen to have a box of Ivory Snow around from the last time a baby made an extended visit to your home, consider making a soap snowball ornament. After it comes off the tree, it becomes bubble bath!

Add ¼ cup water to 1 cup Ivory Snow in a medium mixing bowl. Beat with an electric mixer on medium speed. As the mixture starts to froth, sprinkle in another ¼ cup soap. This should make the mixture stiffen. If it doesn't, add more soap, ¼ teaspoon at a time, until it does. If you'd like scented

bubble bath, add a few drops of perfume or cologne now. Then, with dry hands, scoop up a bit of the mixture and roll it into a one-inch ball. The surface should look rough, like snow.

For each ball, partially unbend a metal paper clip to make a hook. Stick the unbent end into the snowball. Allow the balls to dry on waxed paper. If you like, tie a ribbon around each hook.

To turn the decoration into bubble bath, run the faucet in the tub and break the ball open under it, removing the hook and ribbon.

drops inside, or top it off with 6 to 10 cotton balls for "ice cream."

❏ If you'd like to get more involved, squirt some plain white glue on the cotton balls before you put them in the cones. Drop about a teaspoon of candy sprinkles on the glue; shake off any excess. Let the whole thing dry, then place the cotton balls in the cone, sprinkles side up.

Hang by a Thread

❏ When you're faced with a holiday tree that looks pretty bare, look no farther than the sewing basket. Spools of bright thread could provide just the color you need. Unwind a piece of thread about a foot long from each spool, then anchor it in the nick that keeps the thread from unraveling. Tie the spool to the tree by the extended thread.

Jewelry Is a Tree's Best Friend

❏ Got a good collection of clip earrings? Attach one to the end of each tree branch. If you're careful, you can even use current matched sets. If you have marauding cats or rambunctious relatives, stick to the mismatched variety or the strictly costume jewelry. The best part about this use for earrings is that the gaudier they are, the better they'll look on the tree, so you'll get a chance to use some jewelry that might be too flamboyant to wear.

And after We Take Down the Tree, We Can Play Barbie

❏ In a pinch, use dollhouse furniture as ornaments. Tie the pieces on the tree with thin cloth ribbon loops or bows, Victorian style. Or use ornament hooks or partially straightened paper clips.

Garlands: Swingin' on a String

Why draw the line at cranberries and popcorn when you're stringing for holiday garlands? These objects look just as nice when strung together to encircle the Christmas tree or hang in scallops from the mantel. Mix and match any of the following:

1. Largish acorns (Create holes in them with a small drill.)
2. Large or small beads from irreparable costume jewelry
3. Dried rosebuds with holes pierced in the middle with a sewing needle
4. Miniature marshmallows, either white or colored, strung with a sewing needle and a long strand of thread
5. Wrapped Starlite Mints, strung by the wrappers

HOLIDAY WREATHS

Hang Some Green with Beta-Carotene

❏ Want to spruce up an evergreen wreath without tracking down tiny apples or oranges to wire on? Try, um, brussels sprouts. Seriously. Fluff out the leaves a bit, then bore a hole through the bottom of the woody portion with a round (not flat) toothpick or nut pick. Thread florist wire through the hole, then attach it to the greenery. Group the sprouts in clusters of three or four, as you would decorative apples or dried flowers.

Get Attached to That Wreath

❏ Out of florist's wire when you're only halfway through attaching pieces of evergreens to a wreath? Grab some twist ties and use them instead.

Help Evergreens Hold Their Own

❏ To keep the needles in evergreen wreaths and garlands from looking dry and brittle—or popping out all over the arrangement—haul out the hair spray. A few spritzes in strategic places will smooth frazzled strands. Or spray the entire arrangement to give it some sheen.

OTHER CHRISTMAS DECORATIONS

How Many Days until "Here Comes Santa Claus"?

❏ If a small neighborhood friend or a grandchild is marking the days until December 25, help her bide her time with a "Countdown Santa Claus." Use an old 8½-by 11-inch flyer, cutting it down to an 8½-inch square. With the blank side out, form the paper into a cone and staple the end into place. Color the top third of the cone red for Santa's hat, then use plain white glue to secure a cotton ball on top. Draw Santa a nose, eyes, and a mouth with a black marker, then glue 10 to 12 more cotton balls to the bottom third of the cone (on the front) for a beard. Cut one more cotton ball in two and glue one piece above each eye for eyebrows.

Now for the countdown part. Make a paper chain from 24 loops of old wrapping paper, colored magazine pages, or recycled white paper. Glue or tape the chain to the top of Santa's "hat," just below the cotton ball. The child will break one link of the chain each day

Form a square of paper into a cone (A). Cut off the excess paper to make an even base, decorate to look like Santa, and attach the paper chain (B). All that's left is for your favorite child to start counting down.

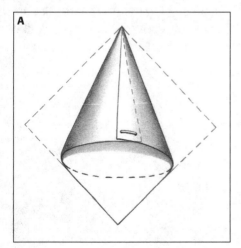

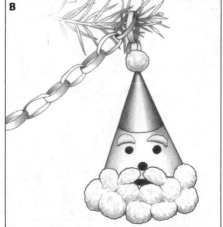

starting December 1. When the last link is cut, it's Christmas Eve.

Whip Up Snow to Go

❏ Have you been eyeing those fancy snow globes in the department stores? And have you been eyeing the price tags, too? Forget them! You can start a glittering storm of your own. Begin with a figurine left over from a Christmas village scene, or a little Santa, snowman, or elf. Make sure it's small enough to fit in a small glass jar, such as a baby food jar. Glue the tiny figurine to the inside of the lid and let the glue dry. Fill the jar with baby oil or light corn syrup, plus ½ teaspoon water. Add 1 tablespoon (or more) glitter or metallic confetti. Spread glue on the inside of the jar lid and screw the lid on securely. Once the glue is dry, shake it up to make it storm.

Roll Out Those Decorations

❏ Here's a Christmas decoration that even a child can make, with a little help from an adult. Raid the recycling bin for 3 cardboard toilet paper cores, then fish out 10 fishhook-style earrings from your box of costume jewelry. (The earrings don't have to match.) Grab the roll of aluminum foil from the kitchen, the cellophane tape from your desk, and the straight pins from your sewing drawer. Use a sharp knife to cut the toilet paper cores into 10 one-inch rings, discarding any leftovers. Tightly wrap each ring in foil, preserving the ring shape. Set the first 4 wrapped rings side by side, so that they look like

Old earrings and cardboard toilet paper cores make a surprisingly attractive holiday decoration (A). Straight pins hold the earrings in place (B).

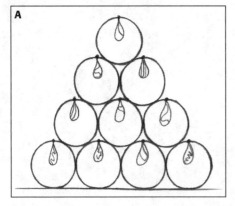

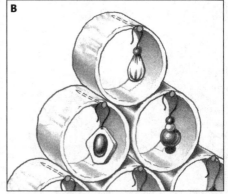

The Inside Story

Ralph the Red-Nosed Reindeer?

As the Christmas season approached in 1939, store managers at Montgomery Ward in Chicago were looking for some kind of clever gift to hand out to shoppers, something to get them in the holiday spirit.

Copywriter Robert May, who wrote ads for the store, got the idea for an illustrated poem. He envisioned a sweet holiday story that parents would want to take home and read to their kids. It could be like "The Night before Christmas."

May wrote the story of one of Santa's helpers. He knew Dasher and Dancer and Prancer and the rest of them, but he wanted a new reindeer. One with a name beginning with R. One with a shiny red nose who is shunned by the rest of Santa's reindeer until he saves Christmas and becomes a hero. May called his story "Rollo the Red-Nosed Reindeer." The Montgomery Ward marketing department loved the story but nixed the name. What kind of a name is Rollo? they asked. May went through a long list of names, but none of them seemed right. Rodney. Ralph. Robert. Roger. May's four-year-old daughter suggested her favorite name: Rudolph.

Montgomery Ward customers liked the story well enough, but it didn't become a classic until 1949, when Johnny Marks set the poem to music and convinced Gene Autry to sing it. Since then, the song has become one of the most-recorded holiday songs of all time, making Rudolph the most famous reindeer of all.

a series of O's. Tape them into that position. Now tape the next 3 rings into place above them, so that they look something like upside-down Olympic rings. Continue the pyramid with 2 more rings in the next row and 1 on top. Press a straight pin into the foil at the top of each ring, but don't push it in all the way; the head of the pin serves as a hanger. Hang one earring from the pin in each circle, and your miniature Christmas tree is complete.

Make a No-Horse Open Sleigh

❑ Make a little sleigh that will hold candy, spray-painted pinecones, or a couple of glass Christmas ornaments. Begin with a box that a bar of soap came in. Cut off one of the large side panels with a single-edge razor blade or X-Acto knife. Wrap the box with Christmas paper or aluminum foil. Then glue two full-size candy canes to the bottom, curved sides pointing up, to serve as "runners." Fill the "sleigh" with any small symbols of the season to complete your decoration.

Take a box from a bar of soap and add wrapping paper and a couple of candy canes. Santa's sleigh awaits!

This Looks Like (It's for) Me

❑ If you're the type that tends to go nuts over those "two-for-one" photo deals or you have a lot of photos that are less than perfect technically, make them into Christmas gift tags. Just cut out a face shot of the person who will receive the gift, poke a hole near the top with a nut pick, and attach it to the gift with a piece of red or green yarn. That way, even those who are too young to read can help distribute the gifts on Christmas morning.

A Different Twist
Fish For Some Flashy Ornaments

Some fishing lures are works of art, while others are at least shiny and bright. Use them to add pizzazz to a tree. Tie them to branches with—what else?—fishing line. Make sure you get the lures high enough that children and animals can't get hooked.

CHRISTMAS STORAGE

Hold the Holiday in a Box

❑ When it comes to storing awkward Christmas decorations and materials, you need a box with gridlike compartments. Discount stores sell boxes made especially for this purpose, but you can accomplish the same thing with an old wine or liquor box salvaged from your last move or from the liquor store. Roll up scraps of Christmas wrapping to

Earl's Favorites

Reel In That Tree

If your Christmas tree lists to one side or you have animals in the house that are bound and determined to knock it over, one of the best ways I know to steady it is with some fishing line. Tie one end of the line to the tree—at the top, the middle, or wherever it seems appropriate. Then unwind a piece of line long enough to reach a sturdy object, such as the fireplace or a window casing. Cut the line and tie it in place. If you're using the window as an anchor, open it a bit, tie the loose end of the fishing line to a rock, and rest the rock between the inside window and the storm window. Then pull the line taut and close the window tight to keep it that way.

For extra security, you can place the tree in a corner or alcove and support it from a couple of different directions.

fit in a couple of sections; stack bows in another. Depending on how much you have, the same box or another can also cradle Christmas candles, stacks of Christmas bulbs (with packing material between bulbs), and gift tags for next year.

Give That Paper a Plain Brown Wrapper

❏ Store fresh rolls of Christmas paper for this year, or those you buy at the end of this season for next year, in old mailing tubes. The tubes will keep the wrapping from getting bent or frayed, and you can easily label the contents.

❏ Alternatively, store several rolls of gift wrap by plunking them in an old kitchen wastebasket. Or use a discarded golf bag to keep them contained. Either is tall enough to be up to the job.

Christmas Storage

Foil the Christmas Light Tangles

No matter how carefully I took down and tied up decorative strings of Christmas lights, they always ended up in a tangled mess come the next year. But not anymore. Now before putting away the lights for the season, I wrap the entire string, as a bundle, in a sheet of aluminum foil. The foil keeps them from getting loose and knotting up, and it also keeps the bulbs from breaking. And since I stick with heavy-duty foil, it's reusable, too.

–Tony Siano
East Meadow, New York

A
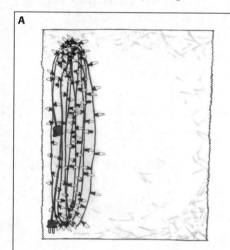

B

Coil the string of lights as you normally would (A), then wrap the whole thing in a sheet of foil (B). No more tangles!

Just Pop That Paper in Here

❑ Not sure why you've been hanging on to that giant Christmas tin that was filled with popcorn a few years back? It makes an eye-catching place to display rolls of Christmas wrap. Just stash the lid under the bottom so that you can use the can for something else after the holidays.

It's a Wrap

❑ In the days when you need Christmas wrap at the ready, you need not have a sprawling mass of half-empty rolls crammed in a brown paper bag. Instead, borrow the umbrella stand and make an artful arrangement of the rolls. Store it on the hearth (unless you have a crackling fire going) or in the foyer. As for tape, scissors, tags, and such, grab an empty clay pot or planter and fill it up. Set those down next to the umbrella stand.

Celebrations

KWANZA

Catch Kwanza Candle Wax

❏ During Kwanza, the celebration that debuts December 26 to commemorate African heritage, special candles are lit on each night of the week. If you want to celebrate but don't have the traditional wooden holder, you can use any stout, cylindrical candles in the appropriate colors, lining them up on the table or mantel. Under each, place the metal disk cut from the end of a can of frozen orange juice. This will catch the wax and protect the table.

Carve Out Your Own Traditions

❏ If you really want to get into the Kwanza spirit, you can carve diamonds and squares on your improvised candles. Use a vegetable peeler to shave the wax.

CELEBRATIONS ALL YEAR LONG

They Took the Shirts off Our Backs for This Party

❏ If you have an old T-shirt handy, you can make a truly original party invitation. Just get the crucial information down to a few words—place, time, occasion—and print it on the shirt with a washable marker in two-inch-high letters. Have the person for whom you're giving the party put on the T-shirt, then snap some close-ups of the person, develop the photos, and mail. This is a particularly great idea for a first birthday, since everyone will get a photo of the baby in the bargain.

❏ The T-shirt approach can be modified for a golden anniversary party. Mark up the backs of a favorite pair

of old T-shirts, put them on the happy couple, pose the two very close together, and photograph them from the back. Now *there's* a priceless invitation.

Sealed with a . . . Stub

❏ You may want to think twice about tossing out those two-inch crayon stubs in your junk drawer. Instead, use them to seal an envelope for an invitation or thank-you card. Peel back the paper from the tip of a wax crayon and melt it with a disposable lighter, carefully letting the wax drip onto the back of the envelope so that it overlaps the flap. If you're relying on the wax to hold the envelope closed, let a little of the wax seep under the flap as well. Firmly press a relatively flat, textured object into the hot wax, then remove it. Try a coin, a piece of junk jewelry, or your signet ring. Practice your technique on a piece of scrap paper before trying it on the real thing, varying the amounts of wax and pressure to develop your touch. Select an object whose impression will leave an interesting signature.

❏ To remove crayon wax from your signet ring, hold the waxy part in the tip of a disposable lighter flame for a second or two, then wipe with a tissue.

We Didn't Fall Far from the Tree

❏ For those grand family reunions that draw folks from all branches of the family, create novel identification tags. First, you'll need to wander in the woods for the free materials. Look for twigs for older members of the family—the first-generation siblings, for example. Then glue each to a different-colored three- by four-inch rectangle cut from an old file folder. Use blue for Great-Aunt Mary, yellow for Grandpa, and so forth. Here's where you get clever. For the younger members of the family, glue small acorns or large acorn tops to three-by four-inch rectangles of file folder material, following the same color coding. That way, everyone descended from Great-Aunt Mary is wearing an acorn tag with a blue background, everyone descended from Grandpa has yellow, and so forth. Of course, you put names on the tags, too, but this approach lets you tell at a glance just where each person fits into the family tree—something that's particularly helpful at a gathering where a lot of descendants have married names.

Have a Pool Party

❏ Looking for a place to keep canned drinks cool for a neighborhood barbecue? Haul out that old plastic wading pool the kids have outgrown. Place it in a shady spot and dump in the ice and canned drinks. Partygoers won't have to go traipsing through your house when they're ready for another soda, and everyone will enjoy helping themselves.

❏ Alternatively, keep those drinks cool in a child's outgrown plastic sled with sides, or in a child's old wagon.

After the Meal, We Can Paddle Some Mosquitoes

❏ At an outdoor gathering, you sometimes need some extra support for paper plates, but you don't want anything breakable. Try Ping-Pong paddles. They can accommodate a smallish paper plate, or a napkin and a beverage. Wash them ahead of time in warm, soapy water.

Butt Nothing—This Idea Works!

❏ If you're not comfortable asking guests to refrain from smoking at your outdoor party, you can at least keep the wind from blowing ashtrays—butts, ashes, and all—across the porch or backyard. How? With an empty milk jug. Cut the top off just below the handle and fill the bottom with sand. Now you have an ashtray that won't go anywhere. And if you mix some baking soda in with the sand, you'll cut down the odor, too.

Make Your Punch Extra Cool

❏ Serving up a big bowl of punch adds a festive touch to any party. If you use conventional ice cubes, though, they can melt too fast and water down the beverage. Here's a better idea. Before your party, start saving one-gallon plastic milk jugs. Starting one inch up from the

Celebrations

base of the first jug, cut off the bottom so that you have a one-inch-deep ice tray. Repeat for all the other jugs you've saved, then wash them well. The day before your party, fill three or four of the trays with water and place them in the freezer. When the water is frozen, pop the ice out of the trays, and you have extra-large ice cubes that will last a lot longer than the small ones.

Say "Walk This Way" with Luminaria

❑ To add extra warmth to wintertime or evening gatherings, start stockpiling one- and two-pound cans. Twenty to 30 are not too many; 3 or 4 are still worth the effort. To make luminaria, partially fill each can with water. Leave enough room at the top so that the water can expand when you place it in the freezer, which is the next step. Remove the cans from the freezer and make patterns in the top two-thirds of each can by pounding 20 to 30 nails into the ice, spacing the nails half an inch to an inch apart. (The ice will help the can to hold its shape and also keep the nails under control.) Let the ice melt, then remove the nails to reveal a pattern through which the candlelight can radiate. Line the driveway or the front porch steps with the cans. Pour an inch of sand into each one, nestle a votive candle inside, and light it. Tell your guests to follow the lights!

Light Up Your Whole Neighborhood

❑ You can also make effective luminaria from all the empty milk jugs you've been hoarding in the basement. For each one, cut off the top of the milk jug and pour about two inches of sand in the bottom. Then firmly anchor a plumber's candle or votive candle in the sand. Line your walkway or the front of your yard with the luminaria, and when night falls, light the candles. The glowing candles showing through the translucent jugs will produce a lovely effect.

All That Glitters . . . Is a Streamer

❑ Need a little extra sparkle for that special party? At last, you've found a worthy use for those scraps of oh-so-expensive foil wrapping paper that simply will not

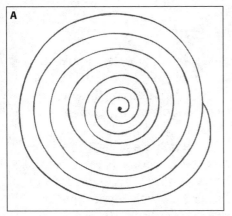

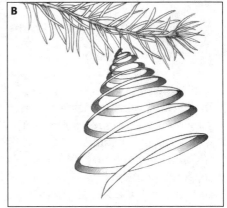

stretch to wrap another gift. Make paper streamers from them, ready to hang on the Christmas tree, from the mantel, or from the ceiling for a party. Here's how. Cut the paper into circles of all different sizes. Draw a continuous spiral on each. Make a small cut in the circle and cut the spiral all the way to the center. To hang, punch a hole in one end of the spiral, then thread string, yarn, or a piece of fishing line long enough to tie or tape the streamer where you want it to go.

You can't get much simpler than this decoration. Start with a circle and cut it into one continuous spiral (A). To hang the new streamer, punch a hole in what used to be the center of the circle (B).

OLD-FASHIONED BIRTHDAY FUN

Plunk Goes the Clothespin

❏ While milk jugs have changed from glass to plastic and clothespins have evolved from pegs to spring-operated, this party game stays the same. It's a great low-budget idea for a child's birthday party, challenging for those ages four and up, and a new twist on hand-eye coordination for kids who play computer games incessantly. It's also a great way to have fun with what's on hand. The idea is to see how many clothespins you can successfully drop into a milk jug.

Clean and dry a one-gallon plastic milk jug. Use a paring knife or X-Acto knife to cut a hole in one side so that you can easily retrieve any clothespins that hit the mark. Pour an inch of sand in the bottom of the jug to keep it steady. Or use gravel, dirt, or pennies. Then draw a shooting line—with masking tape on an indoor floor or with chalk on the sidewalk—about six inches from the milk jug. Each contestant must keep his toes behind that and stand upright while aiming the clothespins at the top of the jug. The one who gets the most clothespins inside the jug wins.

Go Fish!

❏ "Fishing" for treasure never seems to lose its allure for the five and under set, and it's a great way to give out party favors—without putting up more money for store-bought trappings. Collect an assortment of brooms, pool cues, golf clubs, and dry sticks between 18 and 24 inches long. Tie an 8- or 9-foot length of string to each. Use wire cutters to cut off the hooks from a batch of wire coat hangers and tie one hook to the end of each string. Turn a wooden picnic table on its side and set up the treasures so that they're hidden from view behind the overturned table. Instruct each young "fisherman" to stand on the other side with the "fishing rod" and cast the string and hook over the table, where an adult is hidden. The adult will tie a prize on the hook—maybe a small flashlight, candy bar, or memo pad—and the child will pull up the prize. Always let just one tyke take her turn at a time.

❏ If the party has to move indoors, hide the treasures on one side of a bed and let the fishermen work from the floor on the other side.

Who Said You Can't Pin Anything on Him?

❏ No matter how old the birthday honoree is, the "pin the tail on the donkey" concept can make a party more fun. But you don't need a prefab game; you can make your own. Adults and older children might make any number of gentle lampoons based on a "pin the blank on the blank" theme. Just one example: For a lark, pin a mustache on a local politician's campaign poster. Make mustaches from pieces of Post-it Notes, cut in such a way that each piece has a strip of the sticky stuff. Put numbers or names on each, then hand one or more to each contestant.

Each person who takes a turn must submit to having an old scarf tied over his eyes, being spun around three times, and being aimed in the general direction of the poster to slap the Post-it Note mustache into position. Whoever gets closest, of course, wins. But the first time the contestant touches the poster, that's where the mustache goes.

---

3 Invitations That Will Make It through the Mail

For a birthday party. Use a fine-tipped, indelible marker to write the who, when, and where on a deflated balloon. Stick it in an envelope as is. The recipient will inflate the balloon to get the message. (Okay, so the invitee could read the message without blowing up the balloon—but what's the fun in that?)

For a potluck. Send a file card or recipe card listing the party details. If you like, request that each guest use the other side of the card to write down the recipe for the dish he brings.

For a picnic or a party in the park. If you can keep it brief, consider turning a Popsicle stick—or two at the most—into an invitation. Use a dark-colored, fine-tipped marker to fill in the details.

Celebrations

Picture This

❏ Need a big writing surface for a game of Pictionary? How about the picture window in the family room or living room? If you write on it with an ordinary grease pencil, you'll be able to wipe off the marks when you're done and clean the window at the same time. And you'll certainly hold your guests' attention.

WEDDINGS

Here Comes the Beribboned Bride

❏ Save the bows and ribbons from a wedding shower, along with a large paper plate. Then you can make the bride-to-be a "practice bouquet" to carry at the wedding rehearsal. In the center of the paper plate, cut a hole about one inch in diameter. Thread the long strands of ribbon through the hole from the bottom and tape their ends to the face of the plate, so that the loose ends form streamers. Cover up the tape and form a "bouquet" with the stick-on bows, resticking them if necessary with cellophane tape.

AT THE TABLE

And the Napkin Stayed Put with the Spoon

❏ Fresh out of napkin rings? If you have a lot of stray pieces of silver—flea market finds, hand-me-downs, baby spoons—consider giving them new life as innovative napkin holders. All you need is your hands to bend a pliable spoon or fork into a napkin ring–size circle, pointing the business side out. Overlap any excess, and your new ring is ready for a napkin.

Orange You Glad We're Having Sherbet?

❏ If you're the type that goes through a lot of fresh oranges and lemons, start freezing the shells to use later at the type of teas, brunches, and showers given for brides-to-be, mothers-to-be, and those who will retire soon. Citrus shells are perfect for serving sherbet or ice cream, stuffing with softened butter at a brunch, or even to use as "finger bowls" with warm water between courses. To preserve each shell, cut the fruit in half and squeeze out the juice or cut away the sections. Then carefully but firmly press your thumb in the center, turn the shell inside out, and clean off all the pulp and membrane. Turn all the shells right side out, freeze them on a cookie sheet, and then stack and store them in freezer bags. You don't need to defrost them before using, but you may need to shave a piece off the bottom of each so that it will sit level on the plate or table.

Celebrations

Call for a Short-Distance Runner

❏ A table runner can add a fancy touch to the dinner table and protect the wood from scratches at the same time. But that doesn't mean you have to *buy* such a decoration. Grab a colorful scarf that you're tired of wearing and use that to brighten the center of the table.

Freeze Your Floral Assets

❏ Want a centerpiece that's extra special? Grab an old one-quart milk carton (the narrow ones work best). Take those cut flowers that are just past peak and cut the stems down to different lengths, but all short enough that they fit inside the carton. Fill the carton with water and freeze it. Then tear off the carton just before serving time, and you'll have a stunning floral centerpiece.

Make a Glow Fish Bowl

❏ Everyone loves a nice centerpiece for a special dinner party. Cut flowers are wonderful in summer but expensive in winter. And sometimes that same old dried flower arrangement just doesn't cut it. To create an alternative, try scattering some marbles in the bottom of a

> ### *A Different Twist*
> ## Filter Out Party Favors
> Make last-minute party favors by filling coffee filters with candy or other little surprises and tying the filters into sacks. Add a ribbon to each, along with a tag bearing a child's name. Or tie a balloon to each one.

clean goldfish bowl and arranging a few different-size candles inside. Once they are lit, the candles will cast a beautiful glow over the marbles, the bowl, and the room.

❏ If you have only those tiny, foil-wrapped votive candles, put some water in your fishbowl instead of the marbles and float two or three candles inside. They will burn for several hours.

Light a Candle for Creativity

❏ What if you have no votives at all and don't particularly want to go out and buy them? If you're planning ahead, you can make your own from those dinner candles that have burned down to the last couple of inches. Grab a few baby food jars or small condiment jars, soak them in hot water until you can peel off the labels, and drop a candle remnant in the bottom of each jar for a festive touch. The candles should burn for a couple of hours.

Gift Giving

The giver of homemade gifts transcends frugality. Presents contrived from this and that around the home are less expensive, it's true, but they are often more thoughtful, more ingenious, and more personal as well. You have a chance to give a piece of your home—and your heart—to a friend or loved one, safe in the knowledge that she could never find a duplicate at the mall.

Besides, with all the clutter and waste in our lives, homemade gifts are gratifying. They help us use up what we already have on hand or add a few touches to a "found" item and make it useful once more. The ideal present relies more on thought than expense, more on shared memories than a mad scramble for material goods.

In the following pages, you'll find sentimental remembrances, gifts from the kitchen, and, if the young folks are willing, ways to induct another generation into the club of those who can take a little bit of "stuff" and turn it into something.

Gift Giving

FOR MOTHERS AND OTHERS

A Touch of Sugar and Spice Is Nice

❏ For a Mother's Day observance, or to brighten the day (and scent the clothing) of a kindly church friend, neighbor woman, or nursing home patient, make a sachet. Sachets aren't particularly original, but they are practical, they can be made from materials you have on hand, and you can personalize them in a variety of inexpensive ways. To perfume a sachet, open used herbal tea bags and spread the tea on newspaper to dry. For a case that may have some sentimental as well as aesthetic value, use tiny scraps of worn handkerchiefs, lace edges of linens that have outlived their usefulness, or

---

My Way

Soft as a Baby's . . .

I have a lot of friends who have had babies over the past decade, and most of them are older parents who have the big-ticket items covered. But without spending much money, I've been able to give them something I used all the time when my daughters were in that slobbery newborn stage: a collection of soft cotton cloths.

I had a lot of cotton cloths that came with the package when we started renting a house from my mother—cloth handkerchiefs, worn bandannas, cloth napkins, gingham dish towels, waiter's towels. I got in the habit of keeping one in my back pocket to wipe up spills, spit up, runny noses, and all those other things that go with raising kids. Then when I saw suitable cloths at thrift stores and estate sales, I started picking them up. My main requirement was that they be soft and worn, and all cotton. With a warm wash and some chlorine bleach, followed by a second rinse in plain warm water, they're as good as new. If you like, you can also dry them in the sun.

People who had never had a kid would look skeptical when I'd present them with a bundle of these cloths, but within a week of the baby being born, my gift would be in constant use.

–**John A. Hall**
Knoxville, Tennessee

---

scraps from a handmade formal dress. From any of these, cut two pieces of material measuring three by three inches. With the wrong sides together, sew a one-quarter-inch seam on three sides. Turn the pouch right side out, fill it with the dried herbal tea, and stitch it closed.

Tell Her It's Scent(ed) with Love

❏ If herbal tea doesn't strike your fancy as the perfect scent for sachets, you'll find many other options around the house. Try used dryer sheets, cedar shaved from an old wood shingle, shavings from scraps of scented bath soaps, or a cotton ball drenched in vanilla extract.

Hold My Pins, Please

❏ Use a tea or punch cup that has survived the rest of the set to make a novel pincushion that's especially nice for those who use upholstery or embroidery needles. Simply stuff the cup with a sandwich bag filled with sugar or cornstarch. Then secure a piece of pretty cloth, such as a lace handkerchief, to the top with a wide rubber band (the ones that come on asparagus are perfect). Glue ribbon or rickrack over the rubber band, and you're done.

Shell Out for Some Soap

❏ Save those shells next time you have fresh clams or mussels. You can use them to make little shell-shaped soaps that even the most practical-minded recipient will enjoy. You'll also need the remnants of a few bars of inexpensive glycerin soap. Clean and dry the shells, then melt the soap in a clean tin can placed in a pan of simmering water. While the soap is melting, lightly coat the insides of the shells with vegetable oil. As soon as the soap has melted, remove the pan from the heat, pick up the can carefully with a pot holder, and pour the melted soap into the shells. When the soap has rehardened, jiggle each shell around a bit to release a nice little soap shell. For an attractive gift, pack three or four small soaps in a large scallop shell lined with thin (one-sixteenth-inch) shreds of old office letterhead.

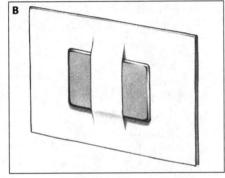

Frame a favorite photo in the front of an old greeting card (A), then cut slits in the back of the card to hold a magnet in place (B). It's a present any mom would love.

Frame That Photo on the Fridge

❏ You can create a truly unique refrigerator decoration for a loved one from an old greeting card and those credit card–size refrigerator magnets that everyone from the pizza delivery guy to the chiropractor gives out. Cut the card down to no more than four by six inches, preserving the fold. Use a razor blade to cut a frame-size opening in the front. Then cut two parallel vertical slashes about an inch apart on the back of the card (without harming the front panel or opening). Glue a favorite photo inside the card so that the edge of the card serves as a frame. Glue the card shut and slip the magnet through the tab in the back. Your photo is ready to hang.

FOR YOUR SWEETHEART

And This Was from Our Trip to Acapulco . . .

❏ Here's a dirt-cheap way to remind a beloved traveling companion of some very special times. Collect a small resealable plastic bag of dirt or sand wherever you and your sweetheart go in your travels. When you've amassed four or five types that look very different from each other, layer them in a glass canning jar. Label the layers on the side hidden from view, and give your companion a terrific souvenir.

If You Break It . . . It's a Paperweight

❏ Next time you accidentally drop a glass or a bottle and it shatters to smithereens, be grateful—you've just created the beginnings of a great gift. Save those shards of broken glass, especially if they're colored, until you have enough to fill a small jar. If some pieces are bigger than one inch square, place them in a paper bag and then, while wearing goggles to protect your eyes, lightly tap the top of the bag with a hammer to break the glass into smaller bits. Layer the pieces in a glass jar to create a gift your loved one can use as a paperweight at the office or a knickknack at home. You might even suggest that the recipient put the jar in a sunny window, where it will catch the light and make rainbows.

Gift Giving

Mementos, Victorian Style

These paper cones, in vogue at the turn of the century, were used to present small gifts or nosegays of dried flowers, or were stuffed with candy and hung on a doorknob or Christmas tree as a surprise. It's a tradition well worth reviving, especially if you just happen to have done a little redecorating recently and ended up with a few odd bits of wallpaper.

MATERIALS
Lightweight cardboard or
    heavy paper
Wallpaper scraps
Ribbon and other trim

DIRECTIONS
1. Cut a five- by eight-inch rectangle from the cardboard or paper.
2. Cut a piece of wallpaper the same size and glue it directly onto the cardboard.
3. Cut another piece of wallpaper to the same size and glue it to the other side of the cardboard.
4. When the glue is completely dry, start at one corner and roll the cardboard into a funnel shape. Staple it to hold the shape. Leave the "point" that results for a background and punch a hole in it about one-half inch from the top. Then insert a loop of ribbon to allow you to hang your masterpiece from a tree or doorknob.
5. Decorate the cornucopia with the remaining ribbon and other trim.

Gift Giving

Surprise Your Hungry Valentine

❏ Sometimes it's tough coming up with a valentine for a man. Here's an idea for making a bouquet the most macho guy (or any woman) can stomach, happily. All you need are six shish kebab skewers from the bottom of the kitchen drawer, a batch of chocolate chip cookie dough, and white or red tissue paper left over from Christmas.

Using your favorite recipe, whip up a batch of chewy chocolate chip cookies. As you drop the batter onto the cookie sheets, make half a dozen cookies that will bake up to be about 2½ inches in diameter. (The remainder of the batch is for you, so you don't have to be fussy about them!) When the six special cookies are just short of fully cooked and still warm, slide the tip of a metal skewer halfway into each. Finish baking, let the cookies

Place each skewered cookie on a diamond of cellophane or tissue paper (A) and wrap it to look like a rose (B). Group all the "roses" together in a newspaper cone (C) and present them to your valentine.

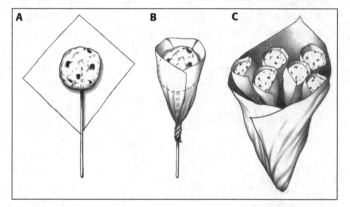

cool on a wire rack, and then wrap the tips of the skewers (where they meet the cookies) with tissue paper to look like roses. Nestle the six long-stemmed cookies in a newspaper cone, or in green tissue paper if you have it, and delight any sweetheart.

FOR THE COOK
OR HOSTESS

Help Them Handle the Hot Stuff

❏ Friends who cook, a bachelor who always has rings on the table left by steaming dishes, the hostess of a potluck or Thanksgiving dinner—these people can use a trivet (or *another* trivet). Make one from a leftover bathroom tile. If you like, use some ceramic paint to decorate the top. A child's handprint or the outline of your favorite cookie cutter is nice and simple, but this is also a great time to let your imagination run wild. To keep the hot tile from touching the table, hot-glue four matching flat buttons on the bottom at the four corners, or glue a scrap of felt to the bottom.

Give Me a Boost

❏ For a friend who frequently has youngsters over to visit—but not frequently enough to warrant her own high chair—craft a homemade booster seat with character. Stack two or three outdated local phone books (or enough to make the pile six to eight inches high) and duct-tape them together. Cut a padded envelope to fit the top of the stack, and duct-tape it to the whole she-bang.

To make a cover, scrounge two scraps of sheet, curtain, or blue jean material that are about three inches wider and three inches longer than the stack of telephone books. With the wrong sides of the material together, stitch a half-inch seam along three edges. Turn the pocket right side out, slip the stack of phone books inside, and hand-stitch the final edge to seal the cover shut. Bingo! A booster seat for junior-size guests.

❏ For friends who host small tykes mostly at holiday gatherings, consider making booster seat covers from pieces of inexpensive vinyl tablecloths in holiday prints. In this case, use duct tape to seal the vinyl in place over the improvised booster seat.

FOR THE KID WHO HAS EVERYTHING

Give an Indoor "Sandbox"

❏ Give this to a neighbor or a grandchild in need of a rainy-day toy that runs on imagination. It's best for ages three to six only, because that's young enough to enjoy pouring and patting, but old enough not to choke on the beans. Beans, you ask? Well, actually, the "sandbox" is

Gift Giving

simply a large Styrofoam cooler or defunct turkey roaster. The "sand" is any past-prime dried beans you have on hand, pinto bean size or larger, plus odds and ends of dried macaroni or other small pasta shells and spirals. Be sure you have enough beans or pasta to cover the bottom of the container to a depth of at least four inches. On top of this base, plop a couple of plastic or metal measuring cups, along with a few well-washed scoops from laundry detergent. It's amazing how long a child can occupy himself with this simple device, and if some of the contents spill, it's no big deal to clean the stuff up.

Pack a Bag Full of Beans

Align the three pieces of fabric with rough edges together (A) and stitch up the unhemmed sides. Turn the bag right side out. Slip the beans between the two longer pieces (B), then stitch the top closed (C). Teddy will be one happy camper (D).

❏ Instead of trying to keep up with the trends in stuffed animals and dolls, focus on making some accessories that will suit small, cuddly toys of any brand or description. A dried bean sleeping bag is a good example. Start by scrounging through scrap fabric and cutting out three 9- by 9-inch pieces of material. Denim is best if the recipient is hard on toys, but otherwise scraps of old

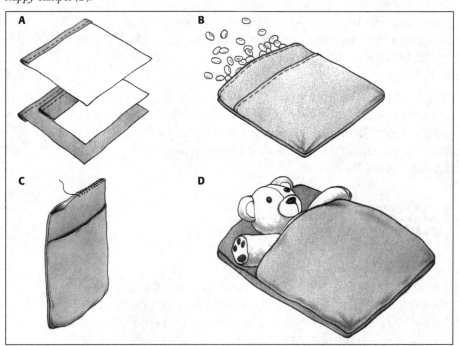

For the Kid Who Has Everything

11 Retro Treasures for the Nintendo Generation

There is a company in California that actually sells a child's junk box, complete with such valuables as a kazoo and Bazooka gum—for cash! But there's no need for you to lay down hard-earned funds for such gizmos. Between the kitchen junk drawer, the attic, and the garage, surely you have 10 or 12 items that will fascinate any child between the ages of six and eight, and maybe as young as four. Add a few trade show treasures and stuff you no longer use—a solar calculator, a stopwatch, a penlight, old jewelry—and stow them all in an old cigar box or shoe box. Label it "My Stuff—Keep Out," and some lucky kid has a starter treasure trove. Here are some suggestions to get you going.

1. The beginnings of a ball of aluminum foil or rubber bands
2. An old golf ball with part of the cover worn off
3. The metal elbow joint, cleaned up, from an old sink
4. Colorful or exotic canceled stamps
5. An unusual coin
6. An oversize nut and bolt or a giant link of a chain
7. Poker chips
8. A largish seashell
9. A rubber stamp from an old job, old address, or old business
10. A horseshoe
11. An oversize marble

sheets or similar materials are fine. Turn down a 2-inch hem on one end of one piece of fabric, then turn down a ½-inch hem on each of the other two pieces. Layer the three pieces on top of each other so that the piece with the 2-inch hem is in the middle and the wrong sides of the other two pieces of material are facing out. By hand or machine, stitch all three pieces together along the unhemmed edges, creating a ½-inch seam. Turn the bag so that the right sides of all the pieces are showing. Slip about a cup of dried lentils, split peas, or navy beans between one outside piece of material and the center piece. Stitch or hot-glue those two pieces of material together at the top, leaving the opening between the bean-filled section and the third piece of material. Voilà! A sleeping bag for a small animal or doll to slip into.

Gift Giving

Dolly Needs a Place to Lay Her Head, Too

❑ Pull together a beanbag "pillow" by folding a four- by six-inch piece of scrap fabric in half widthwise, with the wrong sides together. Stitch the scraps together on three sides with a one-quarter-inch seam, then turn the material right side out. Fill with one-quarter cup of dried lentils and two or three cotton balls. Stitch the last edge closed.

String Them Along

❑ You can make beads for kids ages six and up to string, and all you need are . . . the squishy insides of cantaloupe and honeydew melons? Yes, indeed. Just scrape the guts into a strainer with a tiny mesh, then rinse with cold water and work with your hands until the seeds are separate from the pulp. Discard the pulp and spread the seeds on old newspaper. Leave them overnight or until they're completely dry. Then place them in a small container, such as a single-serving yogurt cup, and add a few drops of food coloring. Swish the container around until the seeds take on the coloring, then place them on fresh newspaper to dry once more. Kids can use needle and thread (with a knot tied at the end) to puncture the centers and string these "beads" into bracelets or necklaces. If you're really into melon and have plenty of seeds available, make several batches in different colors.

Fit It in a Kit

❑ Use dried cantaloupe seeds to create a jewelry-making "kit," with several colors of seeds in separate baby food jars, a piece of felt holding a couple of nee-

---

Pass It On

Somewhere in This Trash There's a Playground

All sorts of American packaged goods companies have started promotions whereby schools can earn things such as computers or playground equipment by collecting and turning in a certain brand of cereal box tops or soup labels. Grocery stores, too, frequently donate money or equipment to local schools on a scale established by how many store receipts they can amass.

If you don't already save such trash tidbits to benefit your child, your grandchild, or a youngster of your acquaintance, call your local elementary school and find out who is collecting what and how you can get with the program.

For the Kid Who Has Everything

Give Teddy a Beanbag Chair

You can make a beanbag chair for a beloved stuffed animal by starting with an empty mesh bag (A), say from a five-pound bag of onions. Measure the onion bag, then cut a piece of old sheet so it's the same width as the mesh plus an additional 1¼ inches. The length should be twice that of the mesh, plus an additional 1¼ inches to allow for a seam on each end. (Your objective is to make an outer bag that will slip over the mesh.)

A   **B**

Fold the fabric in half (B) so it will fit over the mesh. Now stitch a ⅝-inch seam on each of the long sides. Place the mesh bag inside the fabric pouch (C).

C

Grasp about four inches of the closed bottom, where the fold is, and secure the

D

bunched fabric tightly with several heavy rubber bands (D).

Turn the bags mesh side out, with the rubber bands inside. The mesh bag will make the outside look like the same durable upholstery used for beanbag chairs. The fabric, of course, will keep the stuffing from falling out. Fill with about 8 inches' worth of dried pinto beans or Styrofoam packing peanuts (E).

E

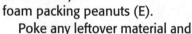

Poke any leftover material and the mesh bag toward the inside, then hand-stitch the opening closed (F). The seam will become the underside of the beanbag chair.

F

My World in Motion

A mobile makes a great gift for anyone with the room to hang it—from office dweller to high school student—and can easily be created by recycling materials you're sure to have on hand. Just select two 12- to 36-inch crossbars and connect them to form an X. Then choose objects that are meaningful or attractive to the person who will receive your moving sculpture, and tie them onto the crossbars with varying lengths of string. Strive for balance, attaching equal numbers of objects with about the same combined weight on facing halves of the crossbars. Do not hang these homemade gizmos over a baby's crib, because baby could choke on any pieces that come off.

You'll need different materials for each part of the mobile. Here are some possibilities; choose one from each category.

CROSSBARS

1. Two plastic rulers with little openings, placed in an X shape and hot-glued together at the cross.
2. Two fairly flat sticks, each about 2 feet long, scrounged from the backyard or the woods.

    Notch the sticks or drill small holes in them to provide places for tying on objects. Then tie them together in the middle with twine or a piece of burlap.
3. Two metal coat hangers, crossed and secured in the middle with twine or duct tape.

STRINGS FOR HANGING

1. Fishing line
2. Waxed dental floss
3. Heavy twine

OBJECTS TO DANGLE

1. Fishing lures
2. Shells
3. Cutouts of a favorite movie idol or sports star glued to pieces of file folder cut to the appropriate sizes and shapes
4. Paper airplanes or balsa gliders
5. Cookie cutters
6. Dollhouse furniture
7. Unshelled nuts and twigs

For the Kid Who Has Everything

dles, and several spools of heavy thread. Print out an instruction card and assemble the kit in a small tin or Christmas card box, with appropriate stickers decorating the outside of the box. "Kits" are popular items at retail stores, so kids tend to understand and respond to them. And parents like them, too, because they save the grown-ups the work of hunting up the needed items to turn the pieces of your gift into a finished craft.

FOR THE PRACTICAL PERSON

Did Someone Mention a Stuffed Shirt?

❏ You know that retiree, the one who has everything or who always says, "Don't spend any money on me"? Or your dad, who scoffs at any gift you can't actually go out and *do* something with—and who already has all the ties and golf balls he can use? Put something practical in his hands for Christmas or Father's Day—a clever barricade against the drafts from window ledges and doors, made from a sleeve from a man's discarded shirt. First, cut the sleeve off the shirt at the shoulder and stitch the cut end shut. Then, working from the cuff end, stuff the sleeve with a mixture that's approximately one-third sand, one-third dried beans, and one-third packing peanuts. Stitch the cuff shut. To add a touch of humor, fill a mismatched work glove with cotton balls, old cloth scraps, old panty hose, or dried beans and hot-glue it to the shirt cuff. Finally, contemplate the recipient's tastes before parting with this "draft sleeve." You may want to glue a telling object to the glove—a trowel, for example, or a fork. Your shivering friend will be delighted.

Keep One More Trick up Your Sleeve

❏ What if the shirt sleeve is not long enough, even with the glove attached, to cover the base of the recipient's door or window? Lengthen it with part of the other sleeve. Or stuff both sleeves and add a glove to each. Then, allowing the gloves to overlap in the middle, glue

them together at the overlap. You could even glue them together in a handshake.

FOR THE ATHLETE OR SPORTS FAN

Make an Odor-Eater in Two Shakes

❏ Save those plastic shaker bottles from parmesan cheese to make a shaker for an athlete in your gift exchange. Inside, mix six parts cornstarch and one part

A Frame for Every Fanatic

Through the miracle of glue guns, you can update old or used picture frames and give them as gifts on a number of special occasions—photos are nice but not required. And you may even be able to clean out the junk drawer at the same time. Just glue the appropriate items in place, wrap, and watch your friend smile when she opens the package.

RECIPIENT	OBJECT	WHERE TO GLUE
Gamester	Dominoes, mah jongg tiles, or poker chips	In a line across top and bottom, or diagonally across two or four corners
Golfer	Golf tees	Lengthwise across top and bottom, or diagonally across two corners
Fishing enthusiast	Fishing lures	Centered at top or in bottom right corner
Parent-to-be	Pacifiers, booties	In diagonally opposite corners
Young child	Legos, Tinkertoys, or Lincoln Logs	Around the entire rim, or diagonally across two or four corners
Dog lover	Small, hard dog biscuits coated with varnish or clear nail polish	Around the rim or in diagonally opposite corners

ground cloves. The recipient can use the mixture to sprinkle in her shoes to kill foot odor and smell faintly exotic. Spiff up the outside of the shaker by gluing on pictures of the recipient's favorite athlete, then laminate the whole thing with clear contact paper.

Gift Giving

Bowl Them Over

❏ Give the same concoction to a bowler to use in place of rosin. In this case, make a label for the outside from a bowling score sheet, preferably one that shows a high score with your pin fanatic's name above it.

FOR THE BIRDER

Feed the Flock

❏ Give a bird-watching buddy a feeder that finches will really go for, made from netting that you don't use any longer. Finches favor tiny thistle seeds. You can make them—and your friend—happy by creating a net bag that will hold thistle seeds just as readily as a store-bought version. Only this one uses a cast-off nylon net bag in which you once encased fine washables. Cut the netting into a 3- by 12-inch strip. Fold it in half to make a 3- by 6-inch bag, stitch up three sides, and turn the bag inside out. Fill the bag with thistle seed, thread a 30-inch string through the material around the rim of the opening, and tie the opening shut. (An old shoelace also will work, if it's long enough, or tie together two shoelaces, say from a discarded pair of high-top tennis shoes.) Use the remainder of the string to hang the bag from a branch. Finches are light enough to land on the bag and swing while they eat.

Small Servings Are Good, Too

❏ If you don't have a net bag, scrounge around your cupboards for a couple of packets of kitchen sponges—the kind that come encased in fine nylon mesh. Carefully cut the mesh off two packages so you have two rectangles, then make a small bag by machine-sewing the pieces together on three sides.

FOR NINE-TO-FIVERS

Win Friends and Influence Co-Workers

Gift Giving

❏ Everyone flocks to the person with the food. If knowing that will aid and abet the career of someone you know, give that person a refillable "goody box." Dig

Stress Management That Comes in a Tube

In Australia, Aborigines play soothing music on "rain sticks," turning them over and over to make sounds like falling rain. Use odds and ends from around the house to create this not-so-natural knockoff for anyone who needs relief from stress at home or work (in other words, anyone you know).

MATERIALS

3-foot mailing tube
Roll of duct tape
Two hundred 1½-inch nails
Roll of masking tape
Brown paste shoe polish
½ cup dried beans
½ cup uncooked rice

DIRECTIONS

1. Completely cover one end of the tube with strips of duct tape.
2. Hammer the nails completely into the mailing tube, spacing them fairly evenly up and down the sides.
3. Tear off 2- and 3-inch pieces of masking tape and tape them over the entire outer surface, overlapping them to create a sort of bamboo or teak look.
4. Polish the taped surface with paste polish.
5. Pour the beans and rice into the tube.
6. To prevent the contents from spilling out, securely seal the open end of the tube with duct tape.
7. Present the stick to your stressed-out friend.

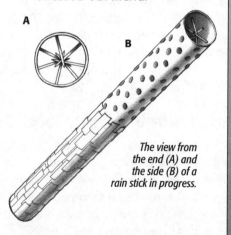

The view from the end (A) and the side (B) of a rain stick in progress.

up a small plastic tackle box, sewing box, or cosmetics box that has compartments. Run it through the dishwasher, or go after it with plenty of very hot, soapy water. Then fill it with chewing gum and small candies.

❏ For really classy treats, try thoroughly cleaning a jewelry box and then using *that* as the office goody box.

Gift Giving

Put a Lid on It

❏ A friend who's recently been promoted to manager or is starting a new job will appreciate a goody box that will help break the ice with co-workers. Take a clean hatbox or a small basket with a lid and stuff it with bagels, fruit, low-fat crackers, pretzels, and other large, bulky (but healthy) food. Even the office health fanatics won't be able to resist such treats. Remember, half of the allure for co-workers is coming to "check out what's in the goody box," so make certain it's a closed container. You need stock it only for the first go-around, and the tradition will be established.

Hey, Buddy, Can You Spare a Drachma?

❏ Need a gift for a fellow travel lover who's deskbound? How about a paperweight to remind him of far-off places? Gather up those odd-looking foreign coins you've collected on your travels and place them in a small glass jar with a reclosable lid (a used jelly jar you were about to throw out would be perfect). Cover the lid with cloth or paper, and you have an attractive paperweight or desk ornament.

FOR A FOUR-LEGGED FRIEND

Mr. Moose's Cat Will Love This

❏ If you'd like to remember a cat on a special occasion or give a congratulatory gift to a friend who's recently adopted a kitten—without spending all outdoors on catnip or kitty toys—forage in your garage or rec room for a Ping-Pong ball. Wrap it in a circle of cellophane

Gift Giving

(make sure it's crackly) from a head of iceberg lettuce and tie it at the top with a stray shoelace. The gift, wrap and all, will inspire pouncing and frolicking—highly amusing to cat and owner. It's an especially good gift if the cat lives in a house with hardwood or linoleum floors.

❑ If you'd like to get really cute, draw mouse whiskers, tiny ears, and a pink nose on the Ping-Pong ball, using washable markers or an eyebrow pencil and pink nail polish.

Show Rover the Ropes

❑ Should you have a two-foot remnant of rope left over from a rope swing or tying the Christmas tree in the trunk, consider bestowing it on a deserving dog. Make sure it's a sturdy piece of rope that's not likely to fray easily, and give it to a pooch who's large or medium and likes to chew or play. The transformation from junk to toy is simple: All you have to do is tie a knot in one end for chewing or one in each end to play tug-of-war.

Give Knots Ready for Prime-Time Players

❑ For a gift fit for a medium or small dog who lives to chew, cut both legs off an expired pair of panty hose, making the snip somewhere around mid-thigh. Drop an old tennis ball into one toe, then put that leg inside the other to double the strength of the hose. Tie a knot three inches above the tennis ball and add more knots at three- to four-inch intervals. The knots will give the puppy something to chew on or to grip in his mouth as he totes the rope proudly—or plays tug-of-war with you.

Pass It On

Stuffed Animals for Pound Puppies

If you have some old stuffed animals that are too yucky for the Salvation Army, consider giving the local pet adoption center, Humane Society, or American Society for the Prevention of Cruelty to Animals (ASPCA) a call to see if they'd like them. Unless the center has a policy against stuffed animals, a real puppy awaiting a home could quickly grow to love a soft, comfy animal—as long as it still has strong seams and is made of sturdy material, such as denim, so that it's chewable but won't explode in a burst of stuffing. Make sure to put the stuffed animal through the wash and dry it in the sun before passing it on.

GIFTS FROM THE KITCHEN

Create a Stir(rer)

Gift Giving

❑ Treat java fans and office co-workers with chocolate coffee stirrers, and get rid of those odd plastic spoons at the same time. Thoroughly wash and dry the spoons. In a microwave oven or the top of a double boiler, melt 1 tablespoon butter with 4 ounces semisweet or milk chocolate. Add ½ teaspoon vanilla extract and 2 table-spoons nondairy creamer. Let the mixture cool to room temperature, then dip spoons in up to their necks. Let them dry resting on a plastic plate or a piece of alu-minum foil or waxed paper. Put them in the refrigerator if necessary. For those who like a lot of chocolate flavor in their brew, dip the spoons two or three times, drying after each dunking. Then tie on plastic wrap, à la Tootsie Pops.

Now you can get rid of an extra coffee mug, too. Fill the mug with sugar and "plant" five or six of the spoons, handle ends down, in the sugar. Then wrap the cup with ribbon and present it to your friends.

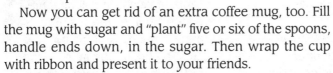

Packin' for Those Who Love Snackin'

All sorts of items will do as containers for food gifts—and some even outdo the traditional versions. Think of these as starting points for your own bursts of creativity.

WHAT GOES OUTSIDE	WHAT GOES INSIDE
Old plastic jewelry or toiletries box with partitions	Mixture of small candies such as red hots or Gummi Bears, raisins, dried cranberries, or chocolate-covered peanuts
A small, clean clay or ceramic pot	Plastic wrap and homemade cheese spreads
Old wineglasses (real glass, not plastic), punch glasses, or beer steins	Homemade jams or jellies

3 Ways to Soup Up the Sauce Jars

You've whipped up something special from your kitchen to give to a friend, and you don't want to spend more on a fancy glass container than you spent on the food itself. And why should you, when you have a cupboard full of old ketchup, salad dressing, spaghetti sauce, mayonnaise, and other jars and bottles? All it takes is a little creative packaging to make your gift look as special as it is. Try any of these options to dress up those old glass containers—or choose several in combination.

1. Create your own label from scraps of old stationery, wallpaper, wrapping paper, or foil. Write or draw on the improvised label, then apply rubber cement on all the edges and press it in place.

2. Add textural interest—but not so much that you can't grip the bottle. Glue dried pumpkin or winter squash seeds in a circle around the bottom and again at the top. Or glue tiny shells (for, say, seafood sauce) around the top. Or dip some string or yarn in glue and wrap it around the bottle on the diagonal, leaving an inch between rings.

3. Try the Olympic treatment. Drape an eight-inch-long, one-half-inch-wide strip of ribbon around the neck of the bottle, crossing the ribbon in front and fastening it at the base with a circular foil seal or any other sticker that's big enough.

Eggs-actly Right for a Delightful Dozen

❑ When every morsel of a homemade confection is a work of art, create a "display case" with an empty egg carton. Dress up the top of the carton by gluing on a pretty piece of wallpaper, gift wrap, or old calendar art, or use a couple of picture postcards. Then line each compartment with shredded coconut or one- by one-quarter-inch shreds of aluminum foil (clean butter wrappers are great). Now you have a resting place for a dozen homemade truffles, pieces of marzipan, petits fours, or chocolate-dipped strawberries.

Leaf a Good Impression

❑ Looking for an attractive way to line a box or basket in which you're presenting a small gift? Perhaps you have a lone linen or cotton napkin that you wouldn't be sorry to see go. You can put some patterns on it and turn it into a glamorous giveaway with the help of Mother Nature. Here's how. Find fresh green leaves in eye-pleasing patterns. Oak or maple leaves are good, and so are ferns. Lay the napkin flat, then set one leaf on it, vein side down. Place a layer of waxed paper on top of the whole thing, then gently pound the entire leaf (under the waxed paper) with a mallet or hammer. It should transfer its pattern in green to the napkin. Continue with more leaves on the same napkin, or let the single one stand on its own. As life goes on, the leaf impression will fade to brown or another fall color, and that will be just as beautiful as the green.

Gift Giving

Wrap Those Gifts to Go

❏ Sending your gift of homemade food by mail or delivery service? Plastic bags make good packing materials for care packages. Crinkle them up as you would newspaper and tuck them around anything that you don't want to get jostled in the mail. Plastic bags are as lightweight as paper, and they won't get ink on your hands—or on your gifts.

GIFTS FROM A GROUP

Sow Far, Sow Good

❏ Looking for a group gift for a friend who is moving across town or even across a couple of states? If the new home is in a growing area similar to where you all live now, collect dried wildflower or annual seeds from each person's garden. For an attractive presentation, thoroughly clean and dry a large Parmesan cheese shaker. Make a paper label telling what's inside and glue it to the shaker with rubber cement. Then pop in the seeds for a gift that will be much appreciated.

Snip It in the Bud

❏ If your friend on the move is more inclined toward indoor gardening, take snips from each person's easy-to-root-in-water houseplants. (Spider plants are good

Gift Giving

candidates for this, as are philodendrons.) Root the delicate snips in water, each in its own juice glass or small vase. Then put each rooted cutting in a sandwich bag with a tablespoon of potting soil over the roots. Take a brick that has six to eight holes—ideally, one from the recipient's old home—and put one cutting in each hole. Hand over the group's greenery in the brick, or rest it in a gift-wrapped shoe box (no lid).

I Am Your Stepping-Stone

❑ A stepping-stone for the front walk or a garden pathway makes a great gift for the elder member of an extended family or a friend who's moving away. There's a benefit for you, too, because you get to use up scraps of "good junk" that are cluttering up your dresser and garage drawers. Here's the plan. Cut the top from a pizza box. Poke six small drainage holes in the bottom with an ice pick or screwdriver, then fill it with wet cement. While the cement is setting, embed objects in the surface. You might choose old keys, coins from foreign travel, pieces of tile, marbles, or tiny toys that are no longer used. Let your imagination run wild, and be sure

---

Personal Magnetism

You know those shower curtain liners that come with the magnets to make them stick to the inside of the tub? Before you dispose of your old liner or reuse it in some other creative way, cut out the magnets. Then glue or hot-glue one of the following objects on one side for a miniremembrance or stocking stuffer anyone would be happy to have hold up the grocery list on the refrigerator.

1. Fishing lure
2. Domino
3. Playing card, either side facing out
4. Sand dollar
5. Aluminum circle from the end of a biscuit can, with a small photo glued on
6. Quarter
7. Gingersnap, with clear nail polish "varnish" to keep it from crumbling
8. Cellophane-wrapped peppermint
9. Laminated cartoon (three by three inches maximum)
10. Campaign button

And Now We Can't Leave Home without It

In the 1950s, department stores began to offer steady customers a line of credit by giving them plastic cards, or "charge plates," with which they could secure their purchases, then pay later in installments. The promotional gimmick was successful—so successful that smaller merchants began to worry that they couldn't compete with the credit systems of these big stores. Almost immediately, people had started spending more money at the chains because they didn't have to pay right away.

Franklin National Bank in Franklin Square, New York, had the answer. It created for bank customers a credit card that could be used in area stores. Bank customers who signed up for the card could charge merchandise that the bank would pay for. Then the customers would pay the bank at the end of the month. The idea took off.

Pretty soon, larger banks were jumping on the bandwagon. Bank of America developed the first bank card to be accepted nationally in all sorts of consumer stores, mailing 60,000 cards—called BankAmericards—to potential customers in 1959.

With this card, customers had the option of paying off the balance in full each month or paying 1.5 percent of the balance in interest after 25 days. This new installment plan quickly became much more popular than taking out loans from the bank. Today the average credit card holder carries four cards and $4,000 in debt. Now that's a lot of Christmas shopping.

to include the younger set when picking the perfect objects to preserve. Let the cement dry, then rip off the box to reveal your creation.

❏ You can also leave imprints in the drying cement, such as the handprints of several grandchildren, leaf impressions, or a message like "With Love from the Cross-Stitch Group" or "Happy Anniversary, Bob and Sue."

Gifts from a Group

For Once, Judge a Book by Its Cover

It's amazing how a cover can turn a few pages into a keepsake album. To make an authentic *scrap*book, take an 8½- by 11-inch piece of cardboard from the back of a writing tablet and cut it in half so that you have two pieces, each 5½ by 8½ inches. Now place an 8½-inch-long strip of duct tape sticky side up on a table. Lay the pieces of cardboard parallel to each other on top of the duct tape, with a gap of about ¼ inch

B

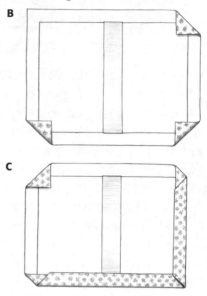

C

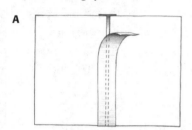

A

between them, so that the duct tape creates a hinge to hold them together. Cut a second piece of duct tape the same length as the first and secure it directly over the first strip and the cardboard, so that no sticky area remains (A).

Now cut a piece of wallpaper or fabric larger than the cardboard. Place the covering wrong side up, place the cardboard on top of the covering, and fold and glue the covering in place, being careful to turn down the corners for a clean edge (B, C). Cover the inside flaps of cardboard with additional wallpaper or fabric (D). Fold several

8½- by 11-inch sheets of paper in half widthwise and staple them to the center of the duct tape (E). Paste keepsakes into place on the pages, and you'll have a gift the recipient is sure to treasure.

D

E

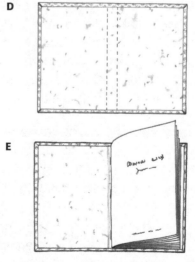

Give It the Old College Cry

❏ If a cohort has a baby on the way, consider banding together with others you know who share an alma mater or sports team allegiance with the mom- or dad-to-be. Have everyone donate old team or school sweatshirts for a quilted baby blanket. Simply cut the fronts and backs into large squares. If some bits are too small to make all the squares the same size, sew several smaller squares together to match the dimensions of the larger ones. Piece the squares together on the machine, allowing three-eighths-inch seams. To finish off your quilt, back it with a flannel receiving blanket or any other scrap material. Placing the wrong sides together, sew the blanket to the pieced-together sweatshirts, allowing a one-half-inch seam on three sides. Then turn the whole thing right side out, fold in the edges on the

Gift Giving

---

9 Keepsakes to Keep Covered

You have your home-made scrapbook. Now what do you put in it? Here are some possibilities.

1. Handwritten and illustrated family jokes and riddles. Put a question on one side of each page, the punch line on the reverse.

2. Recipes collected in honor of a family reunion, class reunion, or holiday.

3. For newlyweds, handwritten advice amassed at a bridal shower.

4. Keepsakes from summer camp, including pressed flowers, certificates of achievement, prize ribbons, badges, photos, and letters from home.

5. Ribbons and awards from a successful school year or sports season.

6. A meaningful set of correspondence—letters your dad wrote during the war, for example, or letters of advice your older sister sent you during a rough patch at college.

7. Memorabilia from a silver or gold wedding anniversary.

8. Your family's genealogy.

9. Ego boosters. Ask everyone in the family, church group, book club, class, team, or club to write down what they like best about each of the other members. Photocopy the results and bind one set for each participant.

---

4 Cool Frames on a Cardboard Budget

It's nicer to give a frame when you give the gift of snapshots or artwork, but some occasions don't call for the gilt-frame treatment. A student who will hang your treasure on a college dorm room bulletin board, for example, probably rates an inexpensive cardboard frame or mat. That's no problem; it's an opportunity—to get rid of those odds and ends that have long since found their way to the back of your desk or kitchen drawers.

Use wood glue or white glue such as Elmer's to attach any of these lightweight decorations to the front of a light cardboard or heavy paper frame to make it unique. Placing the decorations roughly in the middle of the frame's width will lend interest without overwhelming the photo.

Start with a piece of cardboard or heavy paper that's $2\frac{1}{4}$ inches larger in each dimension than what you're framing. For example, to frame a 4- by 6-inch photo, you need a piece that's $6\frac{1}{4}$ by $8\frac{1}{4}$ inches.

Cut a frame from this sheet by marking a border 1 inch in from each edge and cutting out the center section. Mount your photo or artwork inside this handmade frame and decorate it with any of the following:

1. Four pickup sticks, overlapping at the corners
2. Pieces from a defunct picture puzzle, blanketing the surface or clustered in the lower right-hand corner
3. Rickrack, glued down and overlapping or meeting at the corners
4. Eight to 10 small pencil stubs, laid eraser to point across the top and bottom or around the entire edge

unfinished side one-half inch, and hand-stitch those final edges together.

GIFT BOXES, LOOSELY DEFINED

Pack Up the Bulk of It

❏ If the gift you're giving is actually a collection of soft and bulky gifts—linens, sleeping bags, blankets, and the like—plunk them together in a laundry basket. Cover the top, picnic basket style, with one of the items or with a large piece cut from an old sheet, covered with cheery messages in washable marker if you like.

No Boxes? No Problem!

❏ Hard up for a box for a small item? Use the box from a new bar of soap. If you don't want it to rattle, poke some packing peanuts or cotton balls in with the gift. If you want it to rattle even more, fill 'er up with edible peanuts in the shell or dried beans. Wrap the box as you would any gift box, but make sure you're around when this package is opened, so that nothing important gets thrown away by mistake.

Cook Up a Container

❏ When an awkward-to-wrap gift is going to a resident of your home, you have more packaging options because you can always reclaim the "gift box" later. In that case, consider nestling the gift in a large soup pot, putting the lid on, and tying a ribbon around the whole shebang. This is a particularly good idea for basketballs and soccer balls, some hats, and medium-size houseplants (as long as the gift will be opened pronto).

ALTERNATIVES TO WRAPPING PAPER

Of Course, No Guy Will Stop and Look at Your Gift . . .

❏ You can save money on gift wrap and personalize your gift at the same time by using old maps as paper for gifts large and small. Consider state road maps, National Geographic maps, topographical maps, and bus or subway maps.

Butcher That Wrapping Job

❏ If your butcher covers plastic-wrapped purchases with an outer layer of paper and the paper itself never comes in contact with the meat, fish, or poultry, save the paper to use as wrapping paper.

Gift Giving

Be a Poster Girl (or Boy)

❏ To wrap gifts for folks with plenty of hometown pride or an interest in, say, the community theater, call local advertising agencies, theaters, and restaurants and find out who prints their posters. Then contact the printer to ask for cast-off posters, large ads, and color proofs that you could use as wrapping paper. Be sure to specify that you're looking for relatively lightweight paper, not cardboard.

Keep That Gift Fresh and Crispy

❏ You like the foil wrap look but don't want to pay foil wrap prices? Start saving potato chip bags that are foil lined. Just rinse them lightly with warm water, turn them inside out, and wipe them dry with a towel. Cut at the seams to make a sheet of foil wrapping. If you typically buy jumbo-size bags, you can make even a rather large gift shiny and appealing.

A Different Twist

Hold the Ice Cream for Later

For a fun presentation of a small gift, place the present inside an ice cream cone. Then put a scrap of material over the top and fasten it with a thin rubber band. Or top it with a piece of gift wrap and secure the paper with a band of tape, topped with a ribbon.

Go for News You Can Use

❏ Check with your local newspaper to see if the company gives away or sells cheaply the ends of its rolls of newsprint. Many companies do, and it makes great wrapping paper. You (or your kids) can even decorate it with your own designs.

Sew What's Inside?

❏ If you've got the type of sewing machine that does fancy stitches, or even a simple zigzag, you have all you need to turn a plain lunch bag into a snazzy gift bag. Just place the gift inside, fold over the top, and stitch it closed using a heavy-duty needle. This is a great use for those white kraft or patterned fast-food bags that mount up while you're trying to figure out ways to use them. It's also a great way to present "grab bag" prizes at a child's party or for bingo at the local senior center.

Alternatives to Wrapping Paper

Build on This

❏ Old blueprints make great wrapping paper, even for oversize gifts. Inquire at a local architecture or engineering firm about collecting workers' blueprint and computer-aided design "mistakes" and/or interim drafts they no longer need. This is especially good for wrapping gifts for men, when you're looking for something different and want to avoid the hearts-and-flowers look.

Gift Giving

PUTTING IT ALL TOGETHER

Who Needs Ribbon?

❏ Raid your sewing basket for "ribbon" that will make any package pretty—and can be used for other craft

Earl's Favorites

Just Don't Leave It Out by the Curb

I'm not much for getting all fancy when it comes to gifts, and when I'm on the receiving end, I like getting something I can really use. I don't care if it's pretty. I don't care if the wrapping is pretty either. So when a reader told me how she handled hard-to-wrap presents, I decided she was onto something.

Use a very clean trash can, she said, for things from flea markets and for appliances that are too big or bulky to fit in an ordinary gift box. Try a kitchen-size garbage can for a large lamp, a tool for the workshop, or a giant stuffed animal. Use an outdoor trash can for anything that's even bigger or more awkward—a shop vacuum, for example. If you don't have a large bow to top off your gift, twist a large plastic trash bag into a "rope" to tie around the top rim. Then twist a second trash bag into a giant bow.

I think getting a present packed like that would be pretty good. Even if you didn't like what was inside, you could always use the container.

Gift Giving

projects once it's done its decorative duty. Try lengths of rickrack, bias tape, and lace trim. For small packages, such as ring boxes, use several strands of embroidery thread.

Rig Your Gift Bows to Go

❏ You wrap up several gifts in beautiful paper and finish each one with a perfectly coordinated bow. Then you pile them up, load them in the car, and head for the party. When you get there, the paper still looks great, but all the bows are squashed. Next time, place a plastic berry basket upside down over each bow. That way, no matter how the packages shift in transit, the bows will stay perky.

All Taped Out

❏ We've all been there: You're in the middle of a midnight gift-wrapping job when you suddenly discover that you're out of tape. Even if the stores are still open, a few pieces of tape hardly seem worth a special trip. Instead, consider lighting a candle and dripping wax between the layers you'd like to secure.

Give a Whole New Meaning to "Dog Tag"

❏ Store-bought gift tags are expensive, but you can borrow techniques from Japanese origami to make a

---

4 Gift Tags from Stuff You'll Never Miss

Tape these on packages with a sticky-side-out loop of tape. Or poke a small hole in one with a darning needle or the tip of some very sharp scissors, and tie it to a ribbon with a piece of dental floss, embroidery thread, or yarn.

1. Two outdated business cards, glued print side to print side

2. A plain piece of paper affixed to the package with a banana sticker

3. A plain piece of paper affixed to the package with the extra self-stick square that comes in a card of self-stick postage stamps

4. The inside circle cut from a small paper plate

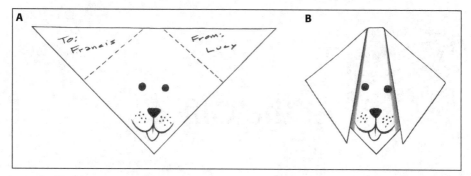

quick tag that the recipient is sure to love. Simply cut the end off a five- by seven-inch file card to leave a five- by five-inch square. Fold this into a triangle, with the point across from the longest side facing you. Fold the remaining two points partway down to form "ears," then draw a face between the ears (don't forget a tongue). "To: Francis" goes on one ear; "From: Lucy" goes on the other. This also works with any single-color or plain white scrap paper, as long as you start with a square.

The face goes in the middle, the names on the outer triangles (A). Fold down the labels to give this dog tag its ears (B).

At the Office

I t's so easy to overlook our frugal ways in the office—what with all the specially designed office supplies around. But there's no need to buy high-priced items just for office use. There are plenty of everyday objects, from cardboard toilet paper cores to laundry baskets, that work every bit as well to organize and furnish office spaces.

You can decorate your office without breaking the bank, too. Think about making an elegant plant stand from the pedestal of a birdbath or a bulletin board from an old picture frame. For equipment maintenance, a few lemon peels and a paper clip or two go a long way.

So put down that office supply catalog and start scrounging around the house. You have everything you need to make your office a model of efficiency and a comfortable, attractive place to work. Here are some ideas to get you started.

KEEPING THINGS CONTAINED

Tools of the Trade

❏ Sometimes it seems that there is never enough room to store all your office supplies. Yet a simple solution is probably sitting in your workshop or basement. Dig up an old tool chest or fishing tackle box—either plastic or metal is fine. Choose a size appropriate for the supplies you use most. Use the larger compartments for storing pens, pencils, markers, scissors, or staplers. Use the smaller compartments for paper clips, erasers, push-pins, and sticky notes. You can store the tool chest out of sight—under the desk or in a closet—or keep it open on top of a desk or bookcase. When you need to work in another location, just close it up and carry it by the handle to take your supplies with you.

At the Office

That's One Small Step for Office Organization

❏ Don't throw away that hanging plastic shoe organizer that you never seem to use. Bring it to the office and hang it over a cubicle wall or on a wall hook. Fill it with pens, pencils, scissors, staplers, staple removers—anything that fits neatly into the pouches. It's not a bad place to stash your gloves, scarf, or rubbers either. To clean the organizer out before using it, find an old hairbrush that fits into the pouches. Tie a clean rag around the brush, spray the rag with a little water, and move it around inside each pouch to pick up the dust and dirt.

> ## A Different Twist
>
> ### Shall We Have a Spot of Twine?
>
> To keep a ball of string knot-free and close at hand, store it in an old teapot that you no longer use. Thread the string through the spout, then cut off a piece whenever you need it.

Wash, Dry, and Hold

❏ Are you drowning in a sea of magazines, newsletters, and newspapers? Keep them neatly arranged in a plastic laundry basket. For short-term storage, just lay them flat. For long-term storage, pack magazines up-

right in a rectangular basket. Use cardboard dividers, which you can cull from the bottom of sturdy cardboard shipping boxes, to separate groups of magazines.

❏ Alternatively, old-style wicker laundry baskets work well for this and are attractive to boot. Spray-paint them to match your office decor.

Keep a Lid on It

❏ Another way to store magazines and newspapers is to stash them in an old trunk. Drag out the big metal trunk that the kids used for college, or use a smaller antique wooden trunk from the attic. Match the size of the trunk to the amount of storage space you need. Close the top to keep the clutter hidden from view.

Contain Those Paper Clips

❏ Paper clips seem to find their way into every crevice in the office. To keep them contained, use a clean, dry plastic soap dish with a cover—the kind used for traveling. Fill the soap dish no more than half-full, to keep the clips from spilling out when you open the cover. Stash the dish in your drawer or office supply cabinet when it's not in use.

❏ Use a soap dish to store other hard-to-contain objects such as pushpins, staples, or coins, too.

Cap-Size It

❏ Rubber bands, buttons, paper clips, pushpins. If that's just *some* of the junk floating around your desk drawer, line the drawer with the caps from aerosol cans. (The tops from spray starch, hair spray, and spray paint all work well.) These caps are the perfect size for spare change, stamps, and all those other odds and ends. All you have to do is lay them in the drawer, open side up. To prevent them from sliding around, you might want to hold them in place with double-sided tape.

A Different Twist

Car Mechanics, Park Your Pencils Here

For the auto buff, an old distributor cap (cleaned, of course) makes a perfect pen and pencil holder—and a great conversation piece.

Pencil In a Great Idea

❏ Pens and pencils seem to vanish quickly in the office. To keep them close at hand, make a pen and pencil holder out of a coffee or beer mug and keep it on your desk. It's best to use a mug that is between 3½ and 6 inches tall. Store the pens and pencils with the points down to avoid staining or pricking your fingers.

At the Office

Build a House of Cards

❏ Business cards never seem to get the attention they deserve. They tend to spill out from wallets and desk drawers, or they get tucked in an awkward stack and bound with a rubber band. Keep track of your collection of business cards by placing them in an old photo album. Use the kind with clear plastic pockets so you can slide the cards in and out. Organize the cards in a way that makes sense to you—by type of business, business name, and so on. The next time you need to track

The Inside Story

So How *Do* They Make Rubber Bands?

Once rubber had been used commercially to create products such as garden hoses, overshoes, and tires, people kept coming up with new ways to use the stuff. One of the best of those ideas was the ordinary rubber band. So how do they make those indispensable office organizers? It's actually a pretty ingenious process.

Long poles are rolled in melted rubber until they are coated. Once the rubber has cooled into a long tube, workers remove it. The tubes are washed, then fed into a cutting machine. The machine can be set for any size—narrower for the kinds of rubber bands that secure newspapers, fatter for the heavy-duty version. The cut bands are scooped into boxes. Before they can be sent out to grateful office workers everywhere, they have to be tested. That's the best factory job in the world—picking up each new rubber band, drawing back one end, and letting it fly. Thwack!

down the phone number of that salesman you met at the trade show last fall, you'll be able to find it quickly.

Train Those Odds and Ends

❏ Who couldn't use a good desktop organizer—something that would keep your favorite pens, notepaper, or markers close at hand? If you buy 3½-inch computer disks in boxes of 10 or more, put those cardboard boxes to use. Separate the top from the bottom of each box

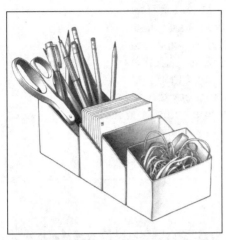

(they should be the same shape and very nearly the same size). Place both pieces on a flat surface, open side up. Hold the pieces together, front to back, so they line up exactly. Staple each pair together. (Use a couple of staples for each pair to ensure that the pieces stay together.) Each piece becomes a separate storage compartment. A "train" of three to five compartments makes a great desktop organizer for sticky notes, pens, notepaper, envelopes, and all sorts of other odds and ends.

Boxes from old computer disks make a great desktop organizer.

Now You Can Really Clean Up

❏ You can make a great desktop organizer from the bottom third of the plastic container that once held dishwashing liquid. Use sharp scissors or an X-Acto knife to cut off the top two-thirds of the container. Discard that piece and use the base to contain paper clips, staples, and other odds and ends. Staple together several of these containers, of varying or consistent sizes, for an even better way to contain all your office paraphernalia.

❏ Alternatively, cut the bottoms off plastic soda bottles and use them in the same way.

Show Off Your Wares

❏ To keep your shallow desk drawers organized, head for the kitchen. Grab an old silverware tray—the kind with rectangular compartments, no more than two inches high—that's no longer needed for its original purpose. The tray should fit neatly into the center, shallow drawer of your desk. The compartments are perfect for storing pens and pencils, scissors, staplers, and other common office items.

Make That One Office to Go

❑ These days, many folks work from more than one office—or from no office at all, because they travel from one client to another. In such a case, it can be a challenge to keep track of all the odds and ends we take for granted in a more traditional office and to make sure the staplers, scissors, and scratch pads are there when you need them. You can't very well remove and take along your old desk drawer. (Well, you *could*, but it might get a bit messy.) What you *can* do is pack up a child's discarded lunch box with all the small office supplies that you want to keep handy in your portable office. Plunk some of the smaller items in old yogurt containers—perhaps a container from a different flavor for each type of supply. Or place them in resealable plastic bags so that you can see the contents at a glance as soon as you open the lunch box.

OTHER WAYS TO ORGANIZE

Band Together

❑ Tired of sorting through a cluster of tangled rubber bands to find just the one you want? Save the cardboard tube from a roll of toilet paper and wrap the rubber bands around it. Put wide rubber bands on one end, thinner ones on the other. Store the tube in your desk drawer. The next time you reach for a rubber band, you'll be able to find the one you want and remove it quickly.

Show Me the Door . . . And I'll Show You Office Supplies

❑ Another way to keep rubber bands accessible is to wrap them around the doorknob on the inside of your

At the Office

office door. That way, you can just reach out and grab one when you need it.

Hang Work Out to Dry

❏ Do your phone messages or "to do" lists get buried under mounds of paper? Here's a solution, using leftover clothesline. String a length of line above office equipment, say your printer or fax machine, and use clothes-

Earl's Favorites

The Indispensable TV Stand

For some reason, people don't like to keep their TV stands around for long. They pack them off to yard sales whenever they change the decorating scheme or buy a new piece of electronic equipment. But a TV stand makes a good rolling utility cart. It fits into tight spaces, moves around easily, and has shelves to store accessories.

I've seen TV stands put to all kinds of uses in offices. You can use one as a telephone stand, for example. Put the phone on top, along with some notepaper and a Rolodex. Put your phone books on the bottom shelves. With a long phone cord, you can move around during the day and take the phone and all of its accessories with you, which saves time walking across the room to look up numbers or grab message paper.

I've also seen TV stands used as printer or fax stands—a great setup for sharing equipment with co-workers. You just unplug and go. No straining your back lifting heavy equipment.

My favorite use comes from an art teacher in a New Hampshire public school. She didn't have a classroom or even office space, so she crammed all her art supplies (some stored in large yogurt containers and shoe boxes) on a TV stand that she rolled from classroom to classroom. The kids jokingly called it "art on a cart," and it worked just fine.

pins to clip lists, files, or phone messages to it. Just collect your office "laundry" when you're ready for it.

SIMPLE CONVENIENCES

Keep That Pencil Where You Need It

❑ Never able to find a pencil when you need one? Look to your bulletin board—for a metal tack, that is. Push it into the top of the pencil's eraser, then drum up an old refrigerator magnet. With wood glue, attach the magnet to the underside of a shelf near the telephone, magnetic side down. Let the pencil dangle from the magnet (point side down), then grab it when that important call comes in.

Flag Down Those Ballpoint Pen Thieves

❑ When you work in an office with a lot of walk-in traffic, it sometimes seems impossible to keep your pens from walking out with your customers. To keep that from happening, tie a bright scrap of ribbon to one end of the pen that you loan out to people signing forms or jotting quick notes. You don't even have to anchor it to the desk. In most cases, the ribbon fluttering from one end will be enough of a reminder to keep someone from accidentally pocketing your pen.

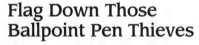

Sealed with a . . . Pastry Brush?

There is nothing less tasty than having to lick a lot of envelopes. Save your appetite for lunch. Dab a wet pastry brush on envelope flaps, and you've licked your mailing problem.

Let Your Mouse Fly through the Month

❑ A mouse pad is a necessity to keep your computer mouse in top working order. But don't go and buy a foam pad. Instead, use a spare calendar. (Most people have plenty hanging around the office.) As long as the calendar is made from a glossy paper, your mouse will glide on it easily. The calendar also makes a handy reference while you work at your computer.

At the Office

Give Your Plants Bottled Water

❏ Don't want to bother with a fancy watering can at the office? Use a clean one- or two-liter plastic soda bottle instead. It has an opening that's wide enough for you to readily add liquid plant food, it's easy to hold on to, and you can target the water so that it lands where you want it (in the plant pot) and not where you don't (on the desktop). Just be sure to label the bottle carefully so that you don't take a sip by mistake.

The Inside Story

Sticky Signs of the Times

On the weekends, chemical engineer Art Fry sang in the church choir. Everything went well during the first service. He could use bookmarks to locate hymns the choir would be singing. But by the second service, the bookmarks had fallen out. He needed a way to stick them in the hymnal without ruining the pages.

In the mid-1970s, Fry spent a year and a half experimenting with light adhesives that would stick but could also be removed easily without leaving a residue the way adhesive tape does. It took some doing, but at last Fry found what he needed. He created book-marks and put a film of light adhesive at one end so that he could peel each one off the stack and attach it where he needed it.

When Fry took his invention to the marketing people at 3M, where he worked, they weren't very impressed. The invention looked like expensive scratch paper to them, and who would buy that?

Despite the salespeople's reservations, Fry convinced them to test-market the product. At first, office managers greeted the little sticky notepads with a fair amount of skepticism. But by the end of the first study, they were begging for more. In the early 1980s, the little yellow pads went from silly to sensational. These days, Post-it Notes are ubiquitous. These sticky notes that do not really stick have become the light glue that holds the business world together.

FILING SYSTEMS

File for Support

❏ Clear up the clutter on your desk by using an old dish-drying rack to store manila or pocket folders. You'll need a rack that is designed with supports to hold dinner plates. A 12- by 15-inch rack about 5 inches high works well. (If the rack is too large, the folders may topple over when they're full.) The supports should be spaced between ¾ and 1 inch apart. You'll want to clean the rack first, of course, then put it on the desktop or on top of a bookcase to keep papers organized and close at hand.

A dish-drying rack can help clean up office chaos.

Make Your Greeting Cards Hang In There

❏ Changing labels on your hanging file folders is easy. Finding enough paper labels to use is hard. Keep an endless supply of paper labels on hand by cutting two- by three-eighths-inch strips from used greeting cards. The thick paper stock will stay securely in place inside the clear plastic tabs. Cut strips from a portion of the card that is plain white or a plain light color (usually the back panel of the card). Just write the words on each strip before you slide the paper into the tab. (If your card stock feels a little light, cut a two- by three-quarters-inch strip and fold it in half lengthwise to add bulk.)

❏ Alternatively, cut strips from old business cards for the same purpose.

Make Absolutely, Positively New Folders

❏ Instead of buying manila folders, save the sturdy letter-size cardboard envelopes that are used by overnight courier services. These rugged holders make perfectly good file folders. After opening and removing the contents of the envelope, cut along the folds of the two short ends, then fold the envelope back so it is in-

side out. Cut a ¾-inch strip off the edge of one long side. Use the other edge as one long tab, or cut out a single tab about 3½ by ⅜ inch. If you need a label, cut up an adhesive mailing label and stick it on the tab.

Let's Stay Together

❏ If you have a computer, you know the problem. Your disks are stored in one place, your papers in another. Sometimes it's hard to find the electronic file to match the paper copy. Here's a simple solution. Use the extra envelopes that come in boxes of greeting cards (a six- by four-inch envelope works well for this). Open the flap on an envelope, then place the envelope inside a slash-cut folder (the kind with a front piece cut on the diagonal for ready access). Make sure the address side of the envelope is facing you and the flap is sticking out of the diagonal cut. Fold the flap back down over the diagonal cut (creasing it in the reverse direction from the way it usually goes) so that the envelope "hangs" inside the folder. Staple the flap to the folder as close to the top edge of the envelope as you can, being careful to staple from the inside out so that the disk will not come in contact with the rougher staple ends. The envelope will create a pocket in which you can store your disk right next to your hard copy.

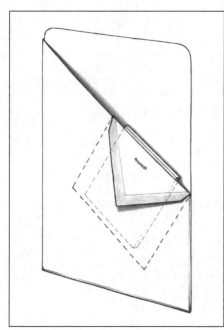

Reverse the crease on a spare envelope and staple the flap to a slash-cut folder. With this improvised pocket, you can hold a floppy disk right next to your hard copy.

Create a Card Holder with a Hidden Advantage

❏ Your kitchen is filled with products that adapt beautifully to office use—such as a recipe box that can have a second life as a Rolodex. Use a recipe box designed for four- by six-inch cards. Write entries on appropriate-size index cards, listing each person's name, address, phone number, and other information. Reverse the tabbed dividers to their blank sides and create your own

Remember the Typewriter?

In 1867, long before the first microchip came along, inventor Christopher Latham Sholes set out on a mission: He would create a machine that would help people write faster than they could in longhand.

His first effort was purported to be portable, but it was so heavy that few people would volunteer to move it. The next year, he created a lighter model that looked a little like its modern counterpart. It had a moving carriage that turned to advance the paper up and down, as well as two rows of keys marked with letters and numbers that would stamp the top sheet of carbon paper so that it marked the bottom sheet of stationery. To describe this wonder, Sholes came up with the term "type-writer." With some practice, he found that he could fulfill his goal of typing faster than he could write.

This was a revolution. Of course, modern typewriters that could show you the lines you were typing as you worked were years down the road—as were typewriter ribbons, truly portable machines, and correction fluid. Still, Sholes was able to sell his invention to F. Remington and Sons, which cranked out the first commercially sold typewriter in 1873. It cost $125.

Shortly thereafter, Mark Twain became the first author to type a book manuscript. In fact, he typed *The Adventures of Tom Sawyer* on his Remington—quite a feat when you consider that Twain did most of his writing in bed.

lettering scheme (A–E, F–K, and so on). Recipe boxes have another advantage: You can close their tops to hide the cards from view, making for a neater-looking desk.

Clip and Save

❏ Small, seldom-used office supplies sometimes tend to get buried in large storage areas. To prevent this from happening, place such items in big, resealable plastic

bags and clothespin them to hangers in your storage closet. This storage method works well for extra office supplies that are small (and therefore easy to miss in bigger storage areas) and aren't too heavy. Things such as tape, light bulbs, and mailing labels are good candidates for such treatment.

COMPUTERS

We Always Knew Kids Were Handy around Computers

❏ Work-at-home parents do have certain advantages, and one of them is that they have easy access to some ideal files for floppy disks. Where? In the little ones' closets. The shoe boxes from tiny sneakers and sandals are the perfect size for storing 3½-inch computer disks.

In Brief, Place Your Laptop Here

❏ Just purchased a laptop computer but didn't want to spend the extra money on a carrying case? If you're a frugal Yankee, you probably have an old briefcase lying around. Make sure the laptop fits inside with some room to spare. Then cut stiff foam from an old seat cushion to take up the remaining space and to cushion the computer. Make sure it's a snug fit so that the computer doesn't slide around when the briefcase is standing upright.

Laptop Computers: Carry On

❏ If you need a carrying case for your laptop computer but there's no money left in the computer budget, use an old diaper bag instead. It's soft, reasonably strong, and padded—and who would steal a diaper bag?

Insulate the Problem

❏ People who spend a lot of time on computers often complain of sore wrists and forearms. When this soreness becomes severe enough, it's called carpal tunnel syndrome. You can buy fancy wrist rests or pads to keep your wrists from bending too much while you're working on the computer—or you can get the same benefit by slicing open some leftover foam pipe insulation. Wrap the insulation around each wrist (it should be long enough to keep your wrist immobile) and hold it in place with a rubber band or piece of string. You want your hand, wrist, and arm in a straight line when you are at the keyboard.

At the Office

Compute with the Old Bean

❏ If you're working on your computer a lot and find that using the mouse gives you a pain in the wrist, here's something that'll give you a lift. Fill an old, orphaned sock with dried peas or beans. Tie off the end, and you have an ergonomic wrist rest. Place it at the bottom end of the mouse pad to support your wrist while you use the mouse. Make a longer version, or use two small

Hidden Treasures

Get Wired

I hit the jackpot one day when I was using the Internet. I was playing around with my favorite search engine and entered the words "free" and "items." Up came a list of thousands of Web sites that offered free items for the taking. After about 15 minutes of browsing, I found several sites that offered great office supplies such as phone cards, calendars, mouse pads, coffee mugs, pens, you name it. I even got some free jelly beans that way—another office staple!

To get the goods, I had to fill out a form with basic company information and some personal data—nothing too confidential. (This information is likely to be used for future mailings from the company, so if you don't like junk mail, think twice.) Then I just sat back and waited for the items to arrive in the mail.

Sometimes you can do especially well if you narrow the search as much as possible when looking for items. For example, when I entered the words "free" and "modem" into my search engine, I found a company that was raffling off a modem. Now, whenever I need office supplies, I check out the Internet first for freebies.

–**Tina Rapp**
Sharon, New Hampshire

Computers

6 Uses for Old CD-ROMs

You now have a drawer full of out-of-date office software, all on CD-ROMs. You can't give away the software, and it seems a shame just to throw the discs away. You're not alone in your dilemma. We've compiled these creative solutions from others in the same position.

1. Throw them as mini-Frisbees, just as they are. Or warm the edge with a butane lighter to create an aerodynamic curl. Keep the flame from touching the edge as you mold it to your desired shape, and let it cool if it becomes hot to the touch.

2. Hang one from a pull chain in the back of a dark closet or in the attic. The CD-ROM is big enough to be hard to miss, even in the dark, and it will reflect even dim light, making it easier to spot than the pull chain alone.

3. Keep one in your desk drawer at work. The reflective surface is great for a last-minute grooming check before an important meeting.

4. Let children use them as play mirrors. CD-ROMs are light, hard to break, and the perfect size for a youngster.

5. Hang one on a string from your garage ceiling to tell you when you've driven your car in far enough. Attach the disc so that it hangs in front of your windshield as you drive into the garage and at a point where you know that the back of the car has passed the garage door. No more guessing whether you're in far enough or whether you're about to hit the wall. And the acrylic won't scratch your car's finish.

6. Nail several to a wooden stake to create a driveway reflector.

ones, in front of your keyboard as well to keep wrist fatigue at bay.

Let Your Computer Wear Hose

❏ A tangle of wires and cords bedevils most computer equipment, but a few lengths of old garden hose can tame that tangle. Slice open some six-inch lengths of garden hose. Wrap the hose around the wires you'd like to tame, then fasten the hose in place using twist ties.

❏ If you don't have any old lengths of garden hose but you do have some extra foam pipe insulation, use it instead.

Cut the Static

❏ To reduce the office static that can cause your computer to fail, mix up your own antistatic spray. Combine ¼ cup liquid fabric softener, ¼ cup ammonia, and 2 cups water. Store the mixture (out of the reach of children) in a carefully labeled plastic spray bottle. During the static electricity "season," spray it on the things that create a spark: the rug, your shoes, or your chair. Just remember not to spray it directly on your equipment! (It could damage sensitive electronic parts.)

At the Office

And Won't the Office Food Thief Be Surprised

❏ You want to keep your disks from overheating as the weather turns warmer. If you're transporting your disks on a hot day, or if your office is unusually hot, put the disks in a precooled soft drink cooler until you're out of the heat. Don't ice them, though—the cooler itself is enough protection.

Unbend a Little

❏ We really do sweat at our keyboard labors. Sweat, skin oil, snacks, makeup, and dust all get under and between the keys. To get rid of that grimy buildup, turn off and unplug your computer, then straighten out a paper clip and slide it between the keys. You'll be amazed at what you can pull up!

SIMPLE FIXES

Straighten That Leaning Tower

❏ Having trouble with a table that rocks from side to side or storage shelves that are developing a definite tilt? You need a shim—and the

---

My Way

Here's an Idea Worth Copying

I use my photocopy machine all the time in my freelance writing business. When the feeder tray on my photocopy machine broke, it just killed me to think of spending a good bit of cash for a new one. A friend of mine gave me this cost-free idea: Use the lid from a big box of legal- or letter-size paper. Fold down the edges on one end and slide it under the paper feeder, just as you would with a plastic feeder. I took her suggestion, and it worked like a charm. In fact, I've been using it for years!

–Ro Logrippo
Burlingame, California

At the Office

perfect material for that is the 3½-inch computer disk you were about to throw out. Disks are solid, compact, and not too thick—all the characteristics you look for in something to jack up (ever so slightly) that not-so-stable piece of office furniture.

Renew Typewriter Ribbons

❏ If your typewriter ribbon is old (but not worn-out), spray some WD-40 on the ribbon. The WD-40 will renew the oil used in the ribbon ink.

Cover Up a Little Longer

❏ Bring your nail polish remover to work and add a few drops to your gunked-up correction fluid. Shake the bottle until the nail polish remover is completely mixed in, and you should be able to use your correction fluid a little longer.

---

11 Uses for a Straightened Paper Clip

You can't beat a paper clip in a pinch. Straighten it, shape it, and—voilà!—you have a handy little office aid: part tool, part Band-Aid. Count the ways that a paper clip can come to the rescue.

1. To extract a staple from a bulletin board or from woodwork.
2. To hook through the hole of a shared key to the office bathroom. Hung on a nail in a discreet spot, the key will be accessible to all employees when needed.
3. To mark a passage in a book (use large paper clips for this).
4. To hang an ornament on an office Christmas tree.

5. To hang from a pushpin on a cubicle wall or bulletin board. With the end extended, it will hold notes, memos, or small calendars.
6. To extend a chain on a light, making it easier to turn the light on and off.
7. To hold papers together that have holes punched in the top.
8. To loop through a belt or buttonhole with a visitor's tag or key.
9. To set the function buttons on a wristwatch.
10. To break open the shrink-wrap on a package.
11. To substitute for a lost pull tab on a zipper.

Get Silly When You Clean
That Typewriter

❑ Remember Silly Putty? Use it to clean your gummed-up typewriter keys. Press a small amount of the putty into the part of the key that hits the paper and watch it lift off grime and dust.

At the Office

Substitute for Stitches

❑ In a pinch, you have several options for quick clothing repairs at the office. Judiciously placed cellophane tape will keep a hemline in place until you get home. Staples are sturdier, but beware of using them on fabric that can develop runs. Attach wayward buttons (those with an extended button fastener) by threading a safety pin through the fastener from the inside of the fabric.

PACKING AND SHIPPING

Pack Things Up
Like Nobody's Business

❑ Use old business cards—the ones with the old job title, the wrong address or phone number, or the out-of-date logo—as address labels. Write addresses on the backs of the cards and tape them to packages.

Fragile! Handle with Egg Cartons

❑ Protect breakable or fragile package contents by padding them with egg cartons. The cartons will act as shock absorbers, minimizing the impact of rough handling as your precious cargo travels to its destination.

The Easter Bunny Leaves
Great Packing Material

❑ Who needs fancy packing peanuts when you have kids? No, that's not to say the kids themselves should be squeezed in among the breakables. But the grass from their Easter baskets is great cushioning for any package, and it can be used again and again.

Staples: Holding It All Together

After the turn of the twentieth century, people held papers together either with paper clips or with straight pins that they'd pilfered from their sewing boxes. The downside of the clips was that they were hardly permanent. And the downside of the pins was that they tended to leave large, rusty holes in the paper.

It wasn't that staples didn't exist at the time, but they didn't bear much resemblance to the current office wonders. They were more like heavy, U-shaped tacks. And although there were such things as large commercial staplers, they were primarily the tools of the publishing industry, which used them to stitch magazines and booklets together.

Then in 1914, the Boston Wire Stitcher Company (which had invented the huge, foot-operated machines used by publishers) decided to take a chance on making a small staple for office use. It seemed like a good idea, except that it used loose staples, which meant that someone had to methodically load the staples one at a time. And even careful loading did not keep the machines from jamming.

The company's big breakthrough came in 1923, when someone realized the staples could be lightly glued together in one long strip. Eureka! After that, it wasn't long before the simple device that held those strips became an indispensable, er, staple of every office.

A Jug of Twine and Thou

❏ Looking for a way to keep all the twine in the mail room organized? Here's an idea that won't cost you a thing, except a bit of your time. Grab a clean, dry plastic milk jug. You can use either a quart- or gallon-size jug for this trick. First, cut a hole in the side of the jug, making the opening just large enough that you can squeeze a ball of twine or yarn through the opening. Turn the jug upside down and place the ball inside, in such a way that the loose end of the twine extends down through the top of the jug. Whenever you need more twine, just pull the end, and out it will come. Hang the jug by the handle on a pegboard, and it will be easily accessible when you need it.

What an Untangled Web We Leave

❏ Another good way to keep a ball of twine from getting tangled is to keep it in a plastic container with a lid, such as a large yogurt or cottage cheese container, or a container that baby wipes came in. Punch a small hole or cut a cross in the center of the lid, just large enough for the twine to fit through without falling back into the container. Then place the twine inside and replace the lid, pulling a length of twine through the hole. Keep the contraption next to that pile of newspapers and magazines for recycling day.

Weigh the Alternatives

❏ How do you find out if a letter weighs more than an ounce, and so will need more than standard postage, without buying a postal scale or taking a trip to the post office? Here's a neat trick you can do right at your desk, and you'll need only a few coins, a ruler, and a pencil. Put a 12-inch ruler on your desk and balance it on a pencil at the 6-inch mark. Place the letter you want to weigh on the 9-inch mark of the ruler. At the 3-inch mark, place a stack of five quarters, which weighs one ounce. The side of the ruler with the quarters on it will stay down if the letter is less than one ounce. (Nine pennies, which also weigh one ounce, will work in a pinch,

At the Office

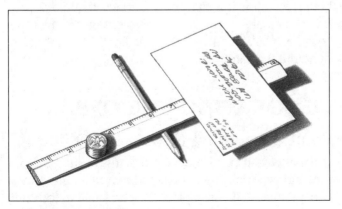

Stamp out postage weight problems! Balance a ruler on a pencil and place your letter and a stack of quarters at equal distances from the pencil. If the letter tips the ruler, you need an extra stamp.

At the Office

but they're a little harder to keep in a stack than five quarters.)

FURNISHINGS

Copy, Roger

❏ Are the piles in your office starting to overwhelm you, but you're reluctant to spend your hard-earned cash on fancy shelves? For quick, sturdy storage, use copier paper boxes. Tip them on their sides (long sides down) and line them up, side by side, to make a row of shelves. They're great for storing colored paper, manila folders, 9- by 12-inch envelopes, magazines, and other letter-size supplies. You can place relatively lightweight items (letterhead, envelopes, paper tablets, and the like) on top of the boxes, too. These containers often fit neatly under a desk, where you can hide them from view but keep items handy.

Get a Little Trashy

❏ Never know what to do with those oversize holiday tins filled with popcorn? They make perfect wastebaskets. Spray-paint them to match your decor, then line them with medium-size garbage bags.

Throw Your Umbrella in Here

❏ Old popcorn tins and metal wastebaskets make fine umbrella stands, too. The container should be at least 18 inches high. To keep it from tipping over with umbrellas in it, line it with a small garbage bag and pour a few inches of sand or gravel on top of (not inside) the bag. This will add ballast. Stick the tips of the umbrellas right into the sand.

DECORATING THE OFFICE

Plant Something New in the Office

❏ It's always nice to keep some plants around the office, and especially nice to show them off in an attractive planter. But nice planters can cost a fortune.

Instead, salvage an old birdbath. The pedestal will make an elegant plant stand. Put a plastic catch pan and plastic planter on top of the pedestal. The diameter of the pan should be about double the diameter of the pedestal top. If you can, match the color of the catch pan and planter to the color of the pedestal for a long, lean line. You'll have an instant classic!

At the Office

"And This Is Suzy Being Adorable Again . . ."

❑ You know the problem. You want to display your photos but can't afford the work space. Instead of cluttering your desktop, stick a pushpin into a cubicle wall or corkboard. Then hang a small binder clip off the pushpin. Attach a photo to the binder clip. You can hang as many photos as you want without wasting a bit of

---

My Way

Kids Love CD-ROM Mobiles

The accounting office where I work gets weekly updates of tax software on CD-ROM. As soon as a new version arrives, the CD-ROM from the week before becomes out-of-date and unusable. We also get lots of promotional software sent to us on CD-ROM. That means we always have plenty of "extra" CD-ROMs floating around the office. Now, it seems just awful to me to throw away something that was useful only a week earlier, so I've made a point of finding new uses for those cast-off discs.

One of my biggest successes in this quest came when I took a pile of CD-ROMs home and made a mobile for each of my three sons. I started out by drilling a small hole in the edge of each disc and stringing thread through it. If you use different-colored thread, this can look really pretty. Then I took the individual CDs and hung them from a wire coat hanger with varying lengths of thread or fishing line. (My youngest son prefers fishing line because then the discs seem suspended in the air.) Finally, I suspended the top of the hanger from some fishing line and attached the entire mobile to the ceiling with a pushpin. All the boys have really enjoyed their CD-ROM mobiles.

—**Jim Sharvin**
Columbus, Ohio

Decorating the Office

desk space—and without damaging the photo with pinholes.

And Now for a Special Bulletin

❏ You can never have enough space for posting memos, photos, calendars, and the like. Although bulletin boards are the perfect solutions, they can be expensive. Instead, rummage around the house for a leftover piece of drywall and an old picture frame, then use them to make a bulletin board. Remove the glass from the frame and set it aside for another use. Cut the drywall to a size that fits comfortably inside the frame (not too snug). Then cut a piece of heavy linen or burlap so that it is about four inches larger (on all sides) than the drywall. Lay the cloth on a flat, clean work surface (a picnic table or workbench works well). Place the drywall on top of the cloth so that the cloth has an equal overhang on all sides. Fold the cloth up and over the drywall and attach it to the back with a staple gun. Pull the cloth tight before you attach each staple to ensure a smooth surface. Fit the cloth-covered drywall inside the frame and hang the frame in a convenient location.

❏ When the drywall has too many holes to take another pushpin, remove it from the picture frame, flip it over, and repeat the process by wrapping cloth around the opposite side. Now you're all set to start over again.

Do You Have a Pierced Bulletin Board?

❏ Looking for a way to add extra interest to an ordinary bulletin board? Finally, you have a use for those 5 or 10 mateless pierced earrings that have been sitting in your jewelry case. You know the ones—you can't wear them, but they're too valuable to toss. Just detach the backs and use them in place of pushpins on that bulletin board. They're especially pretty if you use them to pin up engraved invitations or glamorous photographs.

Stare at Beady Little Things

❏ For those stress-filled times when you need to recharge by staring mindlessly into space, consider making a trinket reminiscent of a lava lamp. Start with a clean glass jar; a baby food jar or one from gourmet mustard is the perfect size. Pour corn syrup or baby oil into the jar, filling it to within one-quarter inch of the top. Then drop in 20 or so beads from old costume jewelry. Apply wood glue or superglue around the rim of the jar, then immediately screw the top back on. When you turn the jar end over end, the beads will slide smoothly and slowly through the oil—fascinating to watch while you try to work through a problem or just reduce your stress.

At the Office

ROOM DIVIDERS

It's Curtains for You

❏ Need some privacy at the office? Let curtains work for you—but not just on the windows. Your old curtains and curtain rods can divide your office space and add a touch of elegance, too. You'll need fairly long curtains (at least four feet) to create a space divider, with a rod high enough for people to walk under. If the space is not too wide, mount a wooden support at each end of the space you want to divide, screwing each support into a wall stud. Then hang your curtain rods or dowels between the supports, and let the curtains act as work space separators.

Old curtains can dress up an office and add a bit of privacy, too. A wooden support at each end (inset) helps hold the curtain rod in place.

Divide and Conquer

❑ If your old curtains aren't long enough, convert old sheets or lightweight bedspreads into office drapes by turning down the hem at the base or foot of the covering and sewing a pocket to put the rope, rod, or dowel through. Hang the curtain dividers at least six feet above the floor so that people can lift a fabric corner and walk into your office without hitting their heads on the rod. It's fine if you have a gap of about a foot between the floor and the bottom of the curtain—it's the space between knees and heads that you most care about.

SOUND BLOCKERS

Turn Down the Volume

❑ Is your office noisy? You can quiet it down without having to change a thing about the way it operates, and without having to look very far for your solution. Soften those sound waves by hanging the quilt that's been sitting in the bottom of your linen closet. Attach wooden rings to it and hang it on the wall from a wooden rod. It'll comfort your ears as well as it comforted your sleep. If you can't bear to part with a handmade quilt, quilted moving pads left over from a previous move work just as well.

Pinups Should Be Beautiful

❑ Leftovers from your last remodeling project may be acoustical paneling in disguise. Bring unused panels of sturdy foam insulation to the office. Staple the fabric of your choice (those spare sheets would work well) tightly around each panel, then attach one or several to the walls of your noisy office (you don't need to cover walls fully to receive sound-deadening benefits). Your beautiful acoustical panels can double as a decorative bulletin board.

Go Fishing for Noise Blockers

❏ Bring out that old fish tank and get it gurgling again as a way of using a pleasant noise to block out annoying ones. The quiet sounds of an aquarium can soothe ears that would otherwise be jangled by the sounds of a busy office.

THE OFFICE KITCHEN

Give Your Lunch Box a Lift

❏ After weeks of carrying your sandwiches to work, your lunch box can start smelling a little tired. To freshen it up, soak a piece of bread in vinegar, put it in the box, close the top, and let it sit overnight.

Who Needs Good China for That Peanut Butter Sandwich?

❏ You hardly want to bring in your fine china for the office kitchen, but using disposable plates and cups isn't kind to the environment. Instead, rescue a few items from the recycling bin. With a thorough cleaning, old wide-mouthed glass jars and one-cup yogurt containers make perfectly serviceable cups, and aluminum pie tins from convenience foods can be used over and over again as plates.

Hang Around after Work

❏ You've just had a great lunchtime party at the office, and everyone even pitched in to help with the dishes. But now you're left with all these wet dish towels and not a drying rack in sight. Break out your office supplies. Twine from the mail room is fine for a quick clothesline, and binder clips and paper clips make good short-term clothespins. Put a piece of waxed paper or scrap cloth between the wet fabric and the clip to prevent rust stains.

At the Office

CONFERENCE ROOMS
Not Just Any Meeting Room

❏ There's no reason meeting rooms have to be bland. Show off your co-workers' artistic talents by putting employee artwork in old picture frames and hanging it on the walls. Or let everyone show off their children's finest drawings this way. It'll make those weekly staff meetings much more interesting for everyone.

Frame It Another Way

❏ White boards, with special markers and erasers, have all but replaced chalkboards as the writing surface of choice for businesses. But you don't have to buy a white board to have a functional, easily erased writing surface. Use that old picture frame instead. Go to the attic, dig up a sturdy frame of an appropriate size (even an 11- by 14-inch frame can provide a reasonable writing surface), and place white paper beneath the glass. The glass needs to be intact and well-seated in the frame. Then write on the glass with an ordinary grease pencil. These pencils are much less expensive than white board markers, and a wipe with a dry cloth will erase them.

THE OFFICE AT HOME
Put That Project to Bed

❏ If your office is really the kitchen or dining room table, the "bedsheet office" is for you. Before you start work, place a spare bedsheet over your work surface. When you need to put your materials away, stack them in the center of the sheet. Tag your files or mark off projects with colored paper so you'll be able to start up quickly again later. Fold the sheet in around the pile and tie the four corners together. Set your "bedsheet office" aside until you're ready to deal with it again.

Peel Kitty off the Computer

❏ Is your cat fascinated by your computer equipment? Cat hair can gum up computers and printers. Luckily,

The Chicks Really Grooved on This Music

I was part of a rock band in high school. We needed a place to practice where we wouldn't disturb people, and since I had a basement bedroom, we decided to use it as our practice space. Concert halls and recording studios use state-of-the-art acoustic paneling to minimize sound reflections, or the bouncing of sound waves off flat surfaces. Every struggling musician quickly learns that egg cartons are the poor man's acoustic paneling. We begged dozens of egg cartons off our families and friends. Once we had enough, we stapled the top flaps of the cartons to the walls, then stapled the bottoms over them, so that all you saw was the egg compartments. We created four- by four-foot squares on three of my bedroom walls. It wasn't a soundproof recording studio, and the walls wouldn't have won any artistic awards, but our efforts definitely lowered the noise level.

–Christopher Laine
Los Angeles, California

cats aren't fond of lemon, so the next time you use a lemon in the kitchen, bring peels into your office and hang them over your equipment. Or cover your equipment when you're not using it and set the lemon peels in a bowl on top. The strong scent should end your feline's fascination and act as a refreshing room deodorizer at the same time.

Kids at Work

❏ If there are young children in your life, don't throw out those old computer keyboards. Children love to imitate adults. The next time you need to occupy a child in the office, bring out that extra keyboard and let your young friend enjoy "working" alongside you. (Old phones work well for playing office, too.)

Serendipity

N eed to fix a pipe in a pinch or figure out exactly where a bicycle tire is leaking? Stymied for a way to store crayons or Matchbox cars? Maybe you'd like to escape those mountains of incoming mail, clean mud off your shoes, or find some inexpensive but effective ways to increase your home's security.

Then again, maybe you're just looking for still more bright ideas for using all that stuff you have on hand—ideas that somehow don't fit into any of the other chapters in this book. If so, then you've come to the right place.

File these tips under "miscellaneous," a potpourri of thoughts for reusing tire inner tubes, pie plates, credit cards, even old blue jeans. If it's hanging around your basement or garage, or squirreled away in the back of a desk or bureau drawer—and if you didn't find it anywhere else in this book—you'll find it here.

ORGANIZATION AND STORAGE

It's a Basket Case

❏ Is incoming mail getting dumped in endless piles all over your house? Worse yet, are you starting to lose track of the pieces that are really important? If so, it's time to get organized. But that doesn't necessarily mean a trip to the department store or office supply store. Those wicker gift baskets that fruit and houseplants come in can have a second life as mail bins. Keep one just inside the front door on a table or bookshelf, and you'll always have a place to toss your mail when you come into the house. Line it with some pretty fabric if you'd like to dress it up a bit.

Serendipity

Wipe Out Little Storage Problems

❏ You need something in which to store three dozen loose crayons or a few Matchbox cars for a trip to the babysitter's. No problem—at least not if you've been saving baby wipe containers. Smaller than most specially made plastic containers but larger than a paperback book, they are perfect for those in-between storage problems.

Look Up and Hook Up

❏ Lucky enough to have a high ceiling in your basement but looking for a way to take advantage of that extra space? You can if you have an old vacuum cleaner hose and some heavy-duty picture wire lying around. Run the picture wire through the

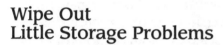

Tape This!

Over the years, I've accumulated a variety of rolls of tape. Some, such as cellophane or masking tape, I use frequently. Others, such as duct or electrical tape, I need less often but still want to keep handy.

The one thing all these rolls have in common is that they all live on a wire I rescued from an old picture frame. I strung the wire through the rolls and hung it from a shelf in my work area. Then I twisted the ends of the wire three or four times around a one-inch screw, which I sank halfway into the top of the shelf.

This system is strong enough to allow me quick access to the tape while it's still hanging on the wire. Or, with a few twists, I can remove a roll from either end of the line.

–Tom Cavalieri
Long Island City, New York

Serendipity

hose and attach it to the floor above with screw eyes. Use the hose to hang clothes to dry, or hang two hoses and suspend spare lumber or molding between them.

Keep the Change (in One Place)

❏ One of life's annoying little duties is amassing the correct change for a child's lunch or milk money, or for the subway or tolls. You can take care of that organizational task and some scraps of litter at the same time. Fold old receipts and chewing gum wrappers over stacks of coins to make little packets of correct change. Then place them in your pocket before leaving the house, or drop them in a change purse or your kid's lunch bag or backpack. No more fumbling!

Don't Switch That Flashlight

❏ Your car dies on the road in the middle of the night. That's why you keep a flashlight in the glove compartment, right? So you'll be prepared for just such an emergency? Well, you *would* have been prepared if the flashlight batteries weren't dead. What happened? Something jammed against the switch and accidentally turned it on. To prevent this minor catastrophe, tape a small piece of duct tape over the switch. That way, you can still

Hidden Treasures

So You Need a Giant Jar . . .

At last, the day arrives when that bumper crop of cucumbers or green tomatoes comes in and you start thinking pickles. Or you decide to round up all the pennies in the house and add to the collection for your grandchild's college education. In either case, you need a jar—a *big* jar. Preferably a glass one, definitely one with a screw-on lid. There are at least six places that might have a couple—and most would probably be happy to let you take those jars off their hands.

1. The local school cafeteria
2. A local family restaurant that does a brisk trade
3. The hospital cafeteria
4. A nearby prison's food service division
5. The cafeteria at the local community college or university
6. A camp or day camp

turn the light on easily after you lift the tape, but nothing will accidentally move the switch in the meantime.

CLEANING SHORTCUTS

Serendipity

Add Humidity, Not Odors

❏ Humidifiers are common appliances these days, especially in dry climates and in the snowbelt during the heating season. Although the moisture they add to the atmosphere improves personal comfort and keeps woodwork from shrinking, these devices also can spread funny smells if the reservoir builds up an off odor. To keep humidifiers fresh, dissolve 1 tablespoon borax in 1 gallon water and pour the solution into the humidifier. Repeat once or twice a year.

Photo Frames: Avoid Sticker Shock

❏ The glass of a photo frame may be the most conspicuous place to put the price sticker, but it's also a spot from which it's particularly hard to remove. Never fear! Scrape off as much of the sticker as you can, then cover any remaining residue with a thick coating of mayonnaise or salad dressing. Wait a few minutes for it to soak in, then wipe off the coating and the residue. Wash the area clean, and your new frame will be ready for your favorite photo.

Make Price Stickers Come Unglued

❏ You can also remove price stickers from glass with nail polish remover, the kind with acetone. Dip a cotton ball in the remover and really soak the sticker. This will dissolve the glue behind it. If the sticker doesn't slide off easily, use a new single-edge razor blade to lift it, being careful not to scratch the glass. To remove the glue residue, apply another drop of nail polish remover to a paper towel and polish the glass in a circular motion. No need to rinse.

Get Your Flowers Sitting Pretty Again

❏ When a narrow-necked glass vase accumulates a residue at its base, it's not easy to get it clean. But you

Serendipity

can do the job with a couple of tablespoons of un-cooked rice. Just pour the rice into the vase, then add water and swirl the water around a bit. The abrasive action of the rice will clean the vase.

STUCK STUFF

Sand Open Those Jars

❏ If the lid on that jar of pickles is too tight, grab hold of it with a piece of used sandpaper, rough side down. It will give you a tighter grip on the problem.

❏ A rubber glove or thick rubber band also works well to open jars.

A Different Twist

Have a Ball

Twist-off bottle caps are a challenge if you don't have strong hands. But old tennis balls can come to the rescue. No, they don't have strong hands, but cut in half, they can be used to give you a better grip on the caps.

Gum on Your Shoe? Chew on This!

❏ When you step in gum, it's usually at the park, the baseball field, or the movie theater—never close to your gum-cleaning supplies. So getting through the trip home, particularly if you're driving, can be tricky. The temporary fix? Find a chewing gum wrapper, flatten it completely, and affix it, foil side out, to any gum you can't scrape off easily with a stick. It will stick to the gum, and it won't stick to the floor.

ODD JOBS

Rattles Are for Babies, Not for Windows

❏ Rattling windows keeping you awake at night? An old book of matches inserted between the window sash and frame will cut the clamor on windy evenings.

Litter That Leak

❏ Has something icky leaked in the bottom of your trash can? Don't reach in just yet. Sprinkle a little kitty litter in the can to absorb the spill (and some of the odor, too), then dump it out.

A Trick to Stop That Trickle

Here's a quick temporary fix for a leaky water pipe that really appeals to folks like me, who save anything that just might come in handy someday. This works best on a small pipe, such as a soft copper one in the basement that gets "dinged" and develops a trickle.

Start with an old bicycle tire inner tube. Cut a piece of tube an inch or so longer than the hole, and make sure the patch is wide enough to wrap all the way around the pipe. Next, kill the water running through the pipe if possible.

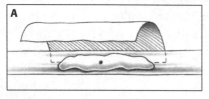

Rough up the problem area of the pipe with a little steel wool or light-grade sandpaper, then spread a thin layer of silicone adhesive (from the hardware store) on both the patch and the pipe. Wait about two minutes to let the glue get tacky, then wrap the patch around the pipe as tightly as possible (A). Start at one end and smooth it down as you go along. Plan for the middle of the patch to cover the hole, with the seam on the other side of the pipe.

Finally, seal the patch in place with duct tape (B). Start taping from the center of the patch and work out to one side, extending the tape beyond the end of the patch. Repeat for the other end of the patch. Once taped, the patch should hold immediately, as long as the pipe isn't under too much pressure.

Kind Sir, Unpin Me

❏ Having a tough time getting that straight pin out of a dry-cleaning tag or price tag? Get out a fine-tooth comb. Slip its teeth around the head of the pin and tug. Out it will come.

The Invention That Held the War Effort Together

The Allies were fighting World War II, and on the battlefields, things were falling apart. Literally. Tents were ripped, boots were wearing out, and equipment no longer held together. Today the solution would be obvious, but in those days duct tape didn't exist. So researchers at Johnson & Johnson invented it. Using medical tape as a starting point, they created a strong, waterproof tape that was more than suitable for emergency repairs.

A few years later, civilians grew to know and love the tape when the postwar housing boom translated into thousands of miles of newly installed heating ducts that needed sealing. In keeping with these peacetime needs, manufacturers changed the tape's color from olive green to silver gray. Consumers responded by discovering an ever-expanding array of uses for the versatile tape, and the rest, as they say, is history.

Lost Items Abhor a Vacuum

❏ Cut down on the anguish when you've dropped a particle-size valuable—an earring back, for example, or a rhinestone from a brooch. Instead of panicking, get out the vacuum cleaner and a pair of old panty hose. Cut the foot off one leg of the nylons, draw that foot tautly over the end of the vacuum hose (no attachments needed), and secure it with a heavy rubber band. Vacuum all around the area where you suspect you dropped the item. The air will suck it to the end of the vacuum hose, and the panty hose will make sure it gets no farther.

For an Instant Adhesive, Lift and Separate (Eggs)

❏ If you're fresh out of glue and need to hold several papers or pieces of lightweight cardboard together, pick up an egg carton and start separating those eggs. Then use the whites in place of glue. It's an old-fashioned technique that still works perfectly today.

SALVAGE JOBS

Make a Screen Saver

❏ Need a temporary fix for a tear in your window screen? Cut a patch from an old pair of panty hose, making the patch slightly larger than the tear. Then sew the panty hose over the hole. It helps to open or remove the screen first and work from both sides. If you can't afford to leave the window open for even a minute, smear some rubber cement over the tear and press the patch into place. The patch will be secure, but it can be peeled away later, and the glue residue can be removed by rubbing it with your finger.

Foil's the Fairest of Them All

❏ When small spots of finish have rubbed off a mirror, it's an expensive proposition to have the mirror resilvered. You may not be able to make it look brand spanking new on your own, but you can eke a bit more life out of the mirror and make it look better until you have the bucks to re-silver. Just tape smooth pieces of aluminum foil on the back of the mirror, so that the shiny side shows through the front, to "patch" the spot.

❏ Alternatively, substitute a flat piece from a disposable aluminum pie tin for the foil.

Teddy Has a Nose for Jelly Beans

❏ When a much-loved stuffed animal loses its eye or nose, don't

Serendipity

Could a Year's Supply Have Saved the *Titanic?*

Manco, maker of Duck Tape (a brand name for a generic product) boasts that it produces 1.37 billion feet of duct tape per year. That is enough to circle the earth 10.4 times, enclose the Washington Monument 136 times, and encase the flight deck of the USS *Nimitz* 15,744 times.

Ironically, duct tape has been superseded in most of today's ductwork by a high-tech aerosol that is sprayed inside heating and cooling systems. Not to worry. We suspect that the average home handyperson will probably stick with duct tape for a long time to come.

Serendipity

exhaust yourself trying to come up with a button that matches or a fancy stitch that will cover the area. Just root around in the candy dish. With the help of a hot-glue gun, you can attach any jelly bean, root beer barrel, or clear red candy as a replacement nose. Hard all-sugar candies, such as Skittles, work well for eyes. Just don't choose anything that has a high fat content, such as chocolate, because it will get rancid.

Tire Leaks: Inflate and Investigate

❏ The time-honored approach to checking for leaks in a bicycle tire is to submerge the tire in a bucket of water and look to see where the air bubbles form. The problem with that method is that you can't see all around the tire, so you don't know exactly where the leak is. But if you have an old aquarium tank sitting in the garage, you're in luck. Inflate the tube, dip it into the half-filled aquarium, and squeeze it. As you look

How Do You Stop a Polar Bear from Charging?

Who doesn't want to cut down on impulse credit card purchases? One somewhat extreme way to limit such splurges is to stash the credit card in a place where you have to wait a relatively long time before you can access it for a purchase. How about freezing it in a block of ice? This doesn't damage the card in the least, and you have to wait a good long while for the card to defrost before you can use it— plenty of time to reconsider that crazy hat or stair-climbing machine. (And, of course, you can't defrost it in the microwave without destroying the card's magnetic strip.)

The best place to freeze it? Try an empty ice cream carton. Wash the carton thoroughly, place the credit card on the bottom with the numbers facing up, and add water until the carton is two-thirds full. (This allows room for the water to expand as it freezes.)

Now you'll have plenty of time to think while taking the freeze off your credit.

through the glass, you will see little bubbles indicating exactly where the trouble is.

A Joy in the Neck

Serendipity

❏ Sure, you've salvaged those old blue jeans by cutting them down to shorts, but what do you do with the rest of each leg? Make a cover for a roll-shaped neck pillow. Sew up one end of the leg and cover any holes in the knee with a decorative patch. Trim the length of the leg to fit the pillow, then stuff the pillow inside. Leave the leg long enough that you can tie off the open end with a ribbon or scrap of denim.

❏ If you don't already have a pillow to fit inside the pant leg, just stuff the leg full of old, clean panty hose or sweat socks.

SECURITY MEASURES

What Burglar Would Take a Marked-Down Item?

❏ You don't need to buy one of those fancy "soup" cans that are actually disguised containers for valuables. Make your own from a can with a replaceable plastic top, such as one that originally held crunchy noodles, potato chips, or icing. Clean the empty can carefully, stash your valuables inside, and place the container in the pantry. How to make sure you don't give it out during the next food drive? Slap on the front a great big "sale" sticker swiped from some other container, or mark "2 for 1" in heavy black marker on the outside. Or dent the side a bit.

Make a Sweet-Smelling Safe

❏ For a new twist on the same theme, store your valuables in an expired push-up deodorant canister. Remove the top from the canister and push down the platform that once held the deodorant. That gives you the storage space you need. Scrub the container clean, dry it, add small valuables, and rest your new "safe" among your toiletries. To keep yourself from trying to

Serendipity

use it every morning, make it a deodorant manufactured for the opposite sex or a brand you no longer use.

Give New Meaning to "Cold Cash"

❏ One good way to hide valuables or small amounts of mad money is in the refrigerator. That's right, the refrigerator. Place your goodies in a spare egg carton or an old yogurt container. (To save confusion, choose a container that's distinctively different from what you

---

Hidden Treasures

The Un–Shopping Center

Back when every New England town had a dump, the caretaker always set aside the "good stuff"— a box of perfectly good canning jars, a sturdy chair in need of refinishing, a snow tire with plenty of tread left on it—for sale to other customers (or for free to his friends). Stringent rules for clean air and water have closed these small local dumps, but traditional Yankee frugality continues.

In Norwich, Vermont, where I live, a transfer station and recycling center replaced the old dump a few years back—but not without a tip of the hat to the old ways. Next to the usual bins for plastic, paper, and cans, the folks at the recycling center set aside a space where townsfolk can leave items that are too good to throw out. And although no money changes hands, leavers and takers both profit.

Over the past few years, I've brought home waxless cross-country skis for my daughter, three different kiddie-size bicycles, old-fashioned steel lawn furniture, an adjustable office chair, a push lawn mower, a printer for my computer, a workbench, and a barbecue grill. During the same period, I've returned two of the three bicycles and the skis (my daughter grew taller), the grill (I got bored with outdoor cooking), some unneeded end tables, several pieces of plastic lawn furniture, and a gas lawn mower. And now that an informal book exchange has been added to the give-and-take, I may become an even more frequent visitor.

Norwich has only a handful of stores in the village proper, but just a few miles away we have a state-of-the-art un–shopping mall. Although the facility is open only to town residents, the idea is free for the taking.

–Lee Michaelides
Norwich, Vermont

---

commonly use.) No thief is likely to check your refrigerator—unless, of course, he's looking for a snack. . . .

Book 'Em

❏ Looking for a crafty place to store your mad money? Or maybe someplace to hide your favorite earrings from a family member who likes to borrow your accessories? Turn an old book into a safe. First, select an old hardcover book that's at least a few inches thick, such as an old dictionary or textbook. Make sure it's one you weren't planning to read again. Open the book past the first few pages, then draw an outline at least one inch in from the edges of the book to form a rectangle. Use an X-Acto knife or a razor blade to cut into the pages. Cut through about a quarter of an inch at a time, remove those cut pieces, and continue cutting, using a previous cut page as a template. Continue cutting until you've almost reached the end of the book, leaving a few pages for camouflage. Now place your valuable contents inside and place the book back on the shelf between other similar books.

Remember that chemistry textbook you were about to throw out? It could make a great hiding place for your treasures.

Hide and Go Peep

❏ If you've lost the cover for the peephole in your front door, all your neighbors can have a peek at you unless you come up with a replacement. Cut a four-inch piece of duct tape and fold it, sticky sides together, *almost* in half. Leave about three-eighths inch of the tacky side exposed. Stick this to the door just above the top of the peep hole, so that the remaining flap covers the hole. That way, you can lift the flap when you want to see who's knocking at your door.

Stick It to Those Burglars

❏ A sliding glass door can be a beautiful window on the world, but if the lock breaks, it can also offer far-too-easy entry to a burglar. To improve security in your home, cut off a broomstick so that it's just long enough to fit in the slider track and prevent the door from opening. You'll be able to remove the broomstick easily when you want to open the door, but prospective thieves will have a harder time.

SEASONAL ISSUES

Resist the Draft

❏ Come winter, you don't have to spend cash on special gadgets to keep the draft from getting in beneath the back door or an outside door leading to a boiler room or mudroom. Got an old tire inner tube lying around? Cut the tube so that it lies flat, then split it open lengthwise to form a thick band of rubber. Nail a length of the inner tube along the inside bottom edge of the drafty door, so that half the tube will sweep the floor as the door closes. Instant weather stripping.

Give Mud the Brush-Off

❏ Looking for a way to cut down on the dirt tracked into your house during mud season? If you're going to retire your wooden-handled, stiff-bristled scrub brush anyway, send it outdoors. Nail it down, bristles up, on the step next to the door. Now you have an effective boot brush ready anytime you need it. Just run your shoes or boots over it before entering the house.

CREATURE COMFORTS

Serendipity

Treat Your Feet

❏ If you have some carpet scraps lying around, you can rejuvenate your old work boots with comfy new liners. Trace the outline of your feet onto the scraps. Then, using a pair of heavy-duty scissors or a carpet knife, cut out the footprints and place them inside your boots or shoes to add new spring to your step.

Much Better Than Rubbing Two Sticks Together

❏ You'll have a nice stock of kindling in the winter if you remember to stockpile the peels from citrus fruits all year long. The average person who puts lemon in tea or makes homemade orange juice will generate a lot of peels. Just cut those peels into half-inch strips with a paring knife or scissors, then leave them out on newspaper to dry in a cool spot with low humidity. Store them in a glass jar or old coffee can with the lid on.

. . . And a Few Items They Might Need

You knew there was a reason you hadn't thrown out all those old tennis balls! Some teachers like to cut a slit a couple of inches wide in each one, then slip them on the bottoms of chair legs to prevent squeaking when the chairs scrape the floor. Other items worth stockpiling for kids' groups include the following, all of which are per- fect for arts and crafts projects.

1. Cottage cheese, yogurt, and sour cream containers
2. Milk jugs
3. Yarn odds and ends
4. Brown paper grocery bags
5. Plastic grocery bags
6. Styrofoam cups and containers
7. Disposable aluminum pie plates
8. Twist ties from bread and garbage bags
9. Two-liter soda bottles

When winter ushers in fireplace weather, grab a handful of peels anytime you need a fire starter.

Bring Your Beach Towel— And a Coat Hanger

❏ Lounging in the hot sun at the beach, you'd love to have a cool beverage at the ready. You've tried insulated drink holders, but it still seems that your soda always ends up tipped over in the sand. Next time, raid your closet for a wire coat hanger before you leave home. Use some pliers to unwind the hanger completely, then bend the wire at a right angle 12 inches from one end. From there, wind the long piece in a coil that will fit fairly snugly around the insulated holder for your favorite glass, sports bottle, or soda can. Leave about an inch between the individual coils. When your coil comes to two inches from the top of the drink container, cut off the end of the hanger with wire cutters. At the beach, plunge the straight bottom wire into the sand for safekeeping, and you have the ultimate beach drink holder.

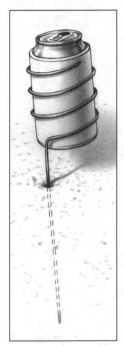

When you're seaside, anchor that soft drink. Encircle it with the wire from an old coat hanger, then stabilize things by poking the end of the wire into the sand.

Walk Softly and Carry a Ski Stick

❏ Walking where there isn't smooth footing, such as on paths in parks, over cobblestones, or even on some sidewalks, can be tricky and tiring. One way to ease the load on your feet and back and steady your gait is to use a walking stick. And if you have some old ski gear languishing in the attic, you're in luck. Before you unload the skis on the Salvation Army, save the poles—they make terrific walking sticks. If the idea of walking around with a brightly colored stick doesn't appeal to you, wrap it in fabric tape of any color you like.

Arthritis Sufferers, Pick Up on This Cue

❏ For those who have a hard time bending at the waist, or those who suffer from back injuries or arthritis, picking up a small item dropped on the floor can be a pain, literally. And even if you're fit as a fiddle, it can still be a challenge to retrieve the occasional stray metal object that falls behind the sofa or refrigerator. To make matters easier, scavenge a pool cue from the playroom. Then take a small magnet from a shower curtain (or use a defunct refrigerator magnet) and glue it to the tip of the pool cue. That way, if you drop a straight pin, needle, earring back, or any other small metallic item, you can just poke the stick in the appropriate spot to re-capture the problem piece.

Serendipity

A Case for a Basket

❏ Anyone could use an extra hand to carry personal belongings—tissues, lipstick, bifocals, newspaper—from sofa to dining room table, kitchen to bedroom, and back again. Someone whose hands are occupied maneuvering a walker has difficulty carrying anything at all. Take care of that inconvenience by raiding the pile of aging sports gear in the corner of the garage. The kind of bicycle basket that attaches to the handlebars with buckles or loops connects just as readily to the front bar of a walker. It also gives the user much more indepen-

The Inside Story

Styrofoam: From Here to Eternity

In 1948, Ray McIntire, a chemist for Dow Chemical, was experimenting with ways to make brittle polystyrene a more flexible electrical insulator. He tried to concoct a new rubberlike polymer by combining styrene with isobutylene, a highly volatile liquid, under pressure.

But to his surprise, instead of a pliable substance, he created a rigid, foamlike material with bubbles in it. At first he wasn't sure what to do with the new material. In fact, according to Mrs. McIntire, all the couple could think to do with it was make Christmas ornaments.

Soon, though, the material's temperature- and moisture-resistant properties were recognized and put to use, and now Styrofoam is used in packaging, construction, and flotation devices.

Not to mention makeshift computer and camera cases.

Serendipity

dence. Just make sure to anchor it carefully so that it doesn't swing when the walker picks up speed.

SUBSTITUTIONS

And Here Is Where I Fell Asleep

❑ Never able to find a bookmark when you want one? Or have a household full of folks who always seem to dog-ear the pages of library books or valuable hard-backs? Make a stack of bookmarks and scatter them around the house. You can afford to if you use the en-velopes from old bills and correspondence. Cut a tri-angle from the bottom corner of each envelope (keep both sides together), about 1½ inches from the point. That's the perfect size to slide over the corner of a page, marking your place without harming the paper.

Shoo, Fly! Or I'll Shoot!

❑ Most insect sprays smell absolutely awful. But if you're not real swift with the flyswatter, you may have to listen to the annoying buzz of a housefly all after-

---

3 Emergency Ice Scrapers for Your Windshield

Ah, that all-too-brisk day when you know winter's really arrived. You head out to the car to drive to work, only to find your windshield covered with ice. And who knows where you left the ice scraper last spring? You don't have to sit in the car with the defroster on for 30 minutes. Just look around the house for one of these perfectly usable substitutes.

1. An expired plastic credit card (or ATM card or library card). If you haven't cleaned out your wallet lately, use an old card to scrape the ice and snow away. Just make sure to wear gloves so you don't freeze your fingers. And don't use a current credit card, because you may damage it with the scraping.

2. A plastic or Teflon-coated spatula from the kitchen. It makes a perfectly serviceable ice scraper.

3. A plastic putty knife from the garage. It'll scrape the ice off your windshield in a jiffy.

---

noon. A better option? Hustle to your vanity table and grab some water-soluble hair spray. Spritz it near the fly, and it'll expire gracefully. The best part is that hair spray dries clear and is water soluble, so should you hit walls instead of the bug, the spray is easily wiped up—as long as the wall is painted or has washable wallpaper. And hair spray lingering in the air smells a heck of a lot better than insect spray.

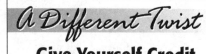

A Different Twist

Give Yourself Credit

Just because you swore off deficit spending, that doesn't mean you can't use that cut-up credit card. The rounded edges are perfect, and gentle, for pushing back your cuticles.

Counterattack Those Keys

❏ Need a quick and inexpensive fob for your key chain? If you've just remodeled your kitchen, don't throw away those samples of countertop laminate you may have collected. Those durable little rectangles are just the right size to make key fobs for cars, boats, snowmobiles, or the neighbor's spare house key. Plus, they're already color-coded for identification and hole-punched for the key chain.

PETS

Rover Doesn't Want a Movable Feast

❏ Does your pet's food dish keep sliding away whenever the animal tries to lap up the food? Take the rubber rings from two or three old canning jars and attach them to the base of the dish. Now your pet won't have to chase his dinner.

You Get a Line, and Kitty Gets a Pole

❏ If you've stopped casting with those bamboo fishing poles "resting" in the attic, your cat can put them to good use. Skipping the hook, just attach a feather or a piece of cellophane to the end of the line, then dangle it from the back of the sofa to the cushion. This will provide hours of batting fun. And when kitty moves on to other pastimes, you can always take up fishing again with no harm done.

Eat Like a (Guinea) Pig–For Free!

As a child, I had a guinea pig who was inordinately fond of lettuce. This was during the days of Cesar Chavez and the farm workers' strike, and iceberg lettuce prices went through the ceiling. But then our neighbors, who had guinea pigs *and* a rabbit, gave us a hot tip: The grocery store on the corner routinely stripped the outer leaves off the heads of lettuce, then threw them away. The store was happy to give us those leaves, which were still crisp and crunchy enough for a guinea pig, and we loved our freebie.

Now my nieces have a guinea pig, and we've struck the same bargain with our grocery store. We just have to wash the stuff really well and avoid getting too many leaves at once. (Guinea pigs won't eat wilted or old produce.)

–Amy Witsil
Raleigh-Durham, North Carolina

Parrots Are Such Babies

❏ Face it, no one wants a used teething ring . . . or do they? A parrot or cockatiel loves nothing better than a teething ring to gnaw on. These birds also get a kick out of discarded baby rattles. The noise amuses them, and they can usually grab such toys with their beaks or claws.

Here's the Long and the Shirt of It

❏ Looking for a quick and inexpensive toy for a hamster? Cut the top and bottom from a clean snack-size tuna fish can. That gives you a metal ring. Now cut the sleeve from a long-sleeved child's shirt. Thread one end of the sleeve through the ring, then fold back the first few inches over the metal to create an opening. Your pet has a shirt sleeve tunnel where she can hide and play to her heart's content.

Index

Underscored page references indicate boxed text. **Boldface** references indicate illustrations. *Italic* references indicate tables.

Baking soda *(continued)*
  uses for *(continued)*
    coffeepot cleaner, 21–22
    denture cleaner, 59
    dishwasher cleaner, 22
    in furniture refinishing, 111
    furniture stain remover, 107
    grease stain remover, 83
    jewelry cleaner, 138
    kitchen cleaner, 19
    laundry cleaner, 79
    lawn mower cleaner, 165
    microwave cleaner, 21
    refrigerator deodorizer, 23–24
    silver polish, 18
    skillet cleaner, 20–21
    smoke stain remover, 115
    sneaker cleaner, 135
    sponge freshener, 26
Ball(s)
  croquet, 220
  foil, as cat toy, 265–66
  golf
    as drawer knobs, 131
    marking, 218
    storing, 215
  homemade, 228–29
  Ping-Pong, as cat toy, 311–12
  tennis *(see* Tennis balls)
Bandage(s), plastic
  for removing ticks, 170
  substitute for, 259
  as tape substitute, 259
Bandanna, uses for, 250
Bangs, trimming, 64
Bank, tennis ball can as, 223
Baseball, 221–22
Basement, storage in, 355
Bat, Wiffle ball, substitute for, 229
Bathrooms
  cleaning, 48–51
  storage in, 52–56
Bay leaves, as pest deterrent, 29
Beads
  melon seeds as, 304
  restringing, 256
Beanbag
  as computer wrist rest, 339–40
  making, 231
Bedrooms
  children's, 129–32
  decorating, 117–19
  guest, 128–29
  organizing accessories in, 119–22
  storage in, 132–33

Beds, raised garden, 184
Bedspreads
  donating, 126
  as room dividers, 350
Bed tray, homemade, 141
Beer, for killing garden pests, 195,
    197
Beer stains, 82
Bee stings, 258–59
Beeswax, for lubricating screws, 154
Belt(s)
  for
    closing suitcase, 256–57
    improving golf swing, 219
  shining buckles on, 140
  substitutes for, 135
Berry basket(s), uses for, 35
  protecting bows, 324
  protecting flower bulbs, 183
  sponge holder, 25
Bicycle basket, as carrier on walker,
    369–70
Biking, 215
Billiards, 229
Binder clips, uses for
  clothespins, 351
  hanging photos, 347–48
Binder sleeve(s)
  as plant markers, 189
  for protecting dovetail saw, 153
Bingo, replacing game pieces in, 230
Birdbath, as plant stand, 346–47
Bird feeder
  deterring squirrels from, 167
  for finches, 309
  homemade, 171
Birthdays, 289–92
Bites, insect, meat tenderizer for, 170
Blackflies, repelling, 168
Blanket(s)
  baby, making, 319–20
  donating, 126
  for sewing table, 235
Bleach
  origins of, 80
  uses for
    cleaning water filter, 209
    floral preservative, 200
    preventing moss growth, 170,
      172
Blisters, foot, preventing, 259
Blocks, building
  cardboard boxes as, 100
  as drawer knobs, 131
Bloodstains, 84–85

Candle(s) *(continued)*
    holder for, 285
    protector for, outdoor, 210
    for fixing squeaky drawers, 122
Candleholder, 209, **209**
Canoe, transporting, on car, 212
Can opener, cleaning, 30
Canopy bed, 123–24, **123**
Car
    care of, 158–61
    deodorizing, 262
    trash containers for, 261–62
Carabiners, substitutes for, 210–12
Cards
    greeting
        as file folder labels, 335
        for refrigerator decorations, 298,
            298
    playing, packing, 245
Carpal tunnel syndrome, wrist pads
    for, 338–39
Carry-on bag, substitute for, 263
Carton(s), milk, uses for
    bowling pins, 231
    conserving flushed water, 51–52
    cutworm collars, 196
    floral centerpiece, 293
    freezer container for fish, 44–45
    rice container, 42
Car trunk, essentials for, 261
Cassettes, protecting, 249
Cat(s)
    bed for, 140–41
    bothering computer equipment,
        352–53
    toy for, 311–12
    traveling with, 265–66
Cattails, decorating with, 98–99
CD-ROMs, old, uses for, 340, 347
Cedar chips, for protection against
    moths, 122
Cement, pouring, 175
Centerpiece
    floral, 293
    goldfish bowl as, 293–94
    turkey, 275
    watermelon as, 273
Chains, jewelry, unknotting, 138–39
Chain saw, filling, with oil, 175
Chair(s)
    beanbag, for stuffed animals, 305,
        305
    preventing squeaking of, 367
    repairing, 107–8
    rocking, origin of, 101

Chalk, for stain removal, 83, 87–88
Chalk markers, substitute for, 238
Changing table
    dry sink as, 129
    as room organizer, 52–53, 129–30
Cheese grater, cleaning, 34
Chicken wire, as plant protector, 197
Chiggers, removing, 170
Children
    games for, 231
    old keyboards for, 353
    sick, 141–42
    traveling with, 264–65
Chipmunks, protecting melons from,
        198, **198**
Chocolate coffee stirrers, 313
Chopstick(s), uses for
    soil tester, 177
    stitch holder, 240
    terrarium tools, 178
Christmas
    decorations for, 279–82
    lights
        for deterring raccoons, 198
        storing, 284, **284**
    storage, 282–85
    tree
        as mulch, 204
        ornaments for, 276–77, 276, 278
        steadying, 283
    wreaths, 278–79
Citrus shells, 292–93
Cleaning products, safety with, 27
Cleats, baseball, cleaning, 221
Clock, alarm, invention of, 118
Closets, freshening and organizing,
        133
Clothesline
    hanging phone messages on,
        332–33
    substitutes for, 260, 351
Clothespins
    containers for, 166–67, 166
    substitutes for, 351
    uses for
        child's birthday party game,
            289–90
        closing curtains, 250–51
        securing strawberry runners,
            186
Clothing
    antique, as wall decoration, 93
    children's, packing, 264–65
    donating, 136
    drying racks for, 74

hanging, on shutters, 132–33
removing lint from, 134
removing pills from, 134–35
repairing, with office supplies, 343
Cloves, as deodorizer, 309
Club soda, uses for
kitchen cleaner, 19
plant nutrient, 194
stain remover, 82
Clutter, storing, 97, 99, 102, 104, 133
Coasters, as floor protectors, 128
Coat hangers. *See* Hanger(s)
Coffee, for furniture scratches, 105
Coffee filters, uses for
deodorizing containers, 23–24
paper plates, 46
party favor holders, 293
Coffee grounds, uses for
compost pile material, 194
storing bait worms, 214
trash can deodorizer, 28
Coffeemaker, as alarm clock, 125
Coffeepot(s)
cleaning, 17, 21–22
as planter, 179
Coffee stains, 81–82
Coffee stirrers, chocolate, 313
Coins
for fitting doors, 150
in paperweight, 311
storing, 76, 119, 356
Cola, for loosening rusted nuts and
bolts, 154
Colander
as grease spatter guard, 30–31
milk jug as, 33
substitute for, 207
Collars, detachable, origin of, 87
Collars, removing dirt rings from,
87–88
Collectibles
displaying, 99–100, 117
dusting, 113
Comb
holder for, 121
for removing pins, 359
Composting, 193–95
Computers, 338–41
keeping cats away from, 352–53
Condiments, holder for, 43
Conditioners, hair, 66–67
Cones
ice cream. *See* Ice cream cone(s),
uses for
paper, making, 299, **299**

Conference rooms, 352
Container(s)
aluminum, for on-the-road meals,
255
baby wipe, uses for
storing toys, 355
twine holder, 345
bandage, as travel pouch, 245
for collecting engine oil, 160
dishwashing liquid, uses for
filling chain saw with oil, 175
storing small office supplies, 330
gardening, 186–87, 187
drainage for, 187
houseplant, 179
lids from, as plant coasters, 180
lozenge, as soap holder, 245
mesh, for protecting flower bulbs,
183
oatmeal, uses for
bed tray, 141, **141**
organizing paintbrushes, 234
storing hamburger patties, 37
wine rack, 14
paint thinner, as workshop
organizer, 146, **146**
for starting plants, 180–81
for storing
bathroom items, 53
car trash, 262
clothespins, 166–67, 166
clutter, 97, 99
detergent, 73
food, 15, 313, 314
rice, 42
soup, 17
utensils, 14
yogurt, uses for
detergent scoop, 75
eyeglass holder, 56
freezer storage, 14–15
hiding valuables, 364–65
making sand castles, 227
in office kitchen, 351
starting plants, 180–81
storing office supplies, 331
twine holder, 345
Cookbooks, holding open, 41
Cookie bouquet, 300, **300**
Cookie cutters, invention of, 31
Cookie dough, container for, 33
Cookie sheets, greasing, 35
Cooking spray, on lawn mower blade,
163
Cooler, storing computer disks in, 341

Draft stopper, making, 307–8, 366
Drainage, after watering plants, 187
Drawer(s), dresser
    as doll bed, 131–32
    freshening, 134
    organizing, 122
    squeaking, 122
    for under-bed storage, 132
Drawer dividers, 14
Drawer knobs, 131
Drawer liners, 16
Dressers, 119–22
Drink holder
    made from hanger, 368, **368**
    shoe as, 127
Drinks
    insulating, 44
    storing, for parties, 287
Driveways, 170–72
Drop cloth, raking leaves onto,
    164–65
Dryer, rejuvenating tennis balls in, 224
Dryer sheets, as trash can
        deodorizers, 28
Drying racks, for laundry, 74
Duct tape. See Tape, duct, uses for
Dumps, finding wood in, 157
Dusters, 27, 113
Dust mask, brassiere for, 159
Dyes, egg, 270, 271

E
Earrings
    organizing, 136–37
    uses for
        bulletin board pins, 348
        Christmas tree ornaments, 277
Earwigs, 195
Easter, 270–71
Egg carton(s), uses for
    confection container, 314
    earring organizer, 137
    hiding valuables, 364–65
    ice cube trays, 46
    packing material, 343
    sound absorber, 353
    starting plants, 181
    storing golf balls, 215
Eggs
    dyed, for Easter, 270–71, 270, 271
    preventing cracking of, 40
    uses for
        facial mask, 62
        fertilizer, 183–84
Eggshells, planting seeds in, 181

Egg whites, as glue substitute, 360–61
Engines, auto, inspecting, 161
Envelope(s)
    sealing, 333
    uses for
        bookmarks, 370
        file folders, 335–36
        funnel, 43
        storing sandpaper, 147
Eraser, as dice, 230
Exercise equipment, from household
        items, 218
Eyebrow brush, 61
Eyeglasses
    holder for, 56
    missing screw from, 256
Eye puffiness, 70

F
Father's Day, 271–73
Faucets, outdoor, winterizing, 204
Feces, dog, cleaning up, 266
Feet
    care of, 68–69
    preventing blisters on, 259
    sore, 253
Fence, picket, as headboard, 124–25
Fertilizer
    eggs as, 183–84
    spreader for, 163–64
Figurines, cleaning, 236
File cards, uses for
    gift tags, 324–25, **325**
    planting seeds, 182
File folder(s)
    for game spinner, 229–30
    labeling and organizing, 335, **335**
    for protecting brass door hardware
        during polishing, 155
    substitute for, 335–36
Filing systems, for office, 335–38
Film canisters, uses for
    holding creams and lotions while
        traveling, 245–46
    organizing
        fishing gear, 213–14
        sewing supplies, 236
    sewing kit, 250
Filters
    coffee (see Coffee filters, uses for)
    oil, removing, 148–49
    water, cleaning, 209
Finches, bird feeder for, 309
Finger, jammed, splint for, 258
Fins, cracked, on prize fish, 214

from group, 315–20
wrapping, 320–25
Gift tags
homemade, 324–25, <u>324</u>, **325**
photographs as, 282
Gift wrap
storing, 283–85
streamers made from, 288–89, **289**
substitutes for, 321–23
Gin, as floral preservative, <u>199</u>
Glass
broken, for making paperweight,
298–99
cleaning, 17–18
as furniture scraper for refinishing
projects, <u>109</u>
Glitter, substitute for, 269
Glove(s)
baseball, reconditioning, <u>221</u>
as dust mitts, 113
as golf club covers, 215
rubber, for opening jars, 358
Glue, substitute for, 360–61
Glycerin, as stain remover, 78, 81, 82
Goggles, ski, preventing fogging of, 225
Gold, cleaning, 138
Golf, 215–19
as Father's Day game, 271–73
practicing, indoors, <u>217</u>
Golf bag
from blue jeans, 217
for storing
gift wrap, 283
lumber, 147
Golf balls. *See* Ball(s), golf
Golf club(s)
covers for, 215
replacing grip on, 216, <u>216</u>
Golf tees
for filling worn screw holes, 154
storing, 216
Grass, Easter
as packing material, 343
substitute for, 271
Grass seed, 163–64
Grass stains, 78
Grater, cheese, cleaning, 34
Grease guard, colander as, 30–31
Grease stains, 83–84, <u>84</u>, 114
Grips, golf club, 216
Guinea pigs, feeding, <u>372</u>
Gum, stuck to
clothes, 77–78
hair, 67–68
shoe, 358

Gutter, uses for
hardware organizer, 144
planter, 185

H
Hair, for deterring deer, 199
Hair band(s). *See* Scrunchie(s) and
hair band(s)
Hairbrush
as foot scrubber, 68
holder for, 121
Hair care, 64–68
Hair spray, uses for
on evergreen wreaths, 278–79
insect spray, 370–71
stain removal, 85, 86
Halloween, 274–75
Hamsters, toy for, 372
Hanger(s)
doubling space on, 133
uses for
croquet wicket, 220
drink holder, 368, **368**
flyswatter, 169
hose hanger, 174
Hardware
brass door, polishing, 155
organizing, 144–46
Headboards, 124–26, 130
Hemlines, temporary repair of, 343
Herbs
alternative uses for, <u>202</u>
in hair rinse, 65–66
preserving, 202
raising, 184
Hiking and backpacking, 210–12
Holes, wall, toothpaste for filling,
118–19
Honey, uses for
facial mask, 60
facial wash, <u>62</u>
hair conditioner, 66
Horseshoes, 219–20
Hose(s)
protecting, 174
rubber, origin of, <u>164</u>
uses for
in auto body sanding, 160
in furniture sanding, 111
in irrigation systems, <u>189</u>
protecting dovetail saw, 153
skate guards, 226
to organize electrical cords, 340
Hose, vacuum cleaner, for basement
storage, 355–56

Houseplants
    displaying, 179–80
    watering, 177, <u>178</u>, 334
Humidifiers, cleaning, 357
Hydrogen peroxide, to treat blood
        stains, 84

I

Ice cream cone(s), uses for
    Christmas tree ornaments, 276–77
    egg salad server, 46
    gift holder, <u>322</u>
Ice cube tray(s)
    egg cartons as, 46
    milk jugs as, 287–88
    uses for
        earring organizer, 136–37
        freezing single servings, 15–16
        hardware organizer, 144–45
        organizing model parts, 233
        preserving herbs, 202
        seed planters, 182
Ice pack, from tennis ball can, 224
Ice scraper, substitute for, <u>370</u>
Ice skates, polishing, 226
Ink stains, 86, 111
Inner tube
    lubricating, 215
    uses for
        golf club grip, 216, <u>216</u>
        patching leaky pipe, <u>359</u>, **359**
        protecting hand tools, 153
        protecting padlocks, 173
        securing sewing machine foot
            pedal, 237
        weather stripping, 366
Insect bites, meat tenderizer for, 170
Invitations, party, 285–86, <u>290</u>, <u>291</u>
Iodine, for furniture scratches, <u>106</u>
Ironing, 88–89
Ironing board, for extra counter
        space, 42
Irrigation systems, for plants, 187–88,
    <u>189</u>

J

Jacket, down, as wine cooler, 44
Jack-o'-lantern, decorating, 274–75
Jar(s)
    baby food, uses for
        candleholders, 294
        hardware containers, 145–46,
            146
        snow globes, 280

    decorating, to hold food gifts,
        <u>314</u>
    large, finding, <u>356</u>
    opening, 358
    uses for
        drying seeds, 203
        holding travel souvenirs, 298
        lava lamp, 348–49
        in office kitchen, 351
        paperweight, 311
Jeans. *See* Blue jeans, uses for
Jellyfish stings, 259
Jewelry
    cleaning, 138–39
    as curtain ties, 94–95
    organizing, 136–38
    packing, 244
Jewelry boxes, uses for
    displaying collections, 99–100
    storing goodies, 311
Joists, storage in, 146–47
Jug(s), milk, uses for
    ashtrays, 287
    bird feeder, <u>171</u>
    birthday party game, 289–90
    closet organizer, 133
    clothespin holder, 166
    colander, 33
    frost protection, 203
    hardware organizer, 144
    ice cube trays, 287–88
    lawn spreader, 163–64
    luminaria, 288
    organizing twine, 344–45
    outdoor game, 226–27
    protecting melons, 198, **198**
    sand spreader, 172
    scarecrow head, 192
    starting plants, 180–81
    toilet brush holder, 51
    toy organizer, 131
    under-sink storage, 17
    watering plants, 187, <u>188</u>
Juice stains, 83, 111–12

K

Ketchup, as
    brass polish, 115
    kitchen cleaner, <u>19</u>
Keyboard, computer
    cleaning, 341
    as toy, 353
Key chain, fob for, 371
Key ring, for carrying hiking
        equipment, 211

Mailing tube(s), for
    making rain stick, <u>310</u>, **310**
    storing gift wrap, 283
Makeup remover, milk as, 62
Mallets, croquet, <u>220</u>, 221
Map(s)
    as gift wrap, 321
    translating scale of miles on, <u>254</u>
    for wall covering, <u>130</u>
Marble, smoke stains on, 115
Margarine
    invention of, <u>32</u>
    for removing sap, 208
Marinades, plastic bags for, 34
Marshmallows, for softening brown
        sugar, 39
Masks, facial, 60, <u>62</u>
Mauls, protecting, 153
Mayonnaise, uses for
    covering water rings, 107
    crayon mark remover, 106
    hair conditioner, 66–67
    sticker remover, 357
    tar remover, 158
Mealybugs, 196
Meat grinder, securing, to counter,
        30
Meat tenderizer, uses for
    soothing insect bites, 170
    stain remover, <u>79</u>, 82, 86–87
Melons
    protecting, 198, **198**
    vertical growing supports for,
        185–86
Memorial Day, origin of, <u>272</u>
Mice
    mothballs for deterring, 204
    protecting melons from, 198, **198**
Microwaves, cleaning, 21
Milk
    for bloodstain removal, 85
    condensed, invention of, <u>36</u>
    laundry stains from, 81–82
    powdered, uses for
        drying seeds, 203
        exfoliant, 57–58
        makeup remover, 62
        poison ivy relief, 71
        sunburn soother, 70
    sour, as
        laundry whitener, <u>79</u>
        silver polish, 18
Milk cartons. *See* Carton(s), milk, uses
        for
Milk jugs. *See* Jug(s), milk, uses for

Mineral deposits, removing, 50, 88,
        115
Minipads, for absorbing hair dye, 67
Mirror(s)
    cleaning, 114–15
    for dresser, 128
    as plant tray, 179–80
    resilvering, 361
Mobiles, making, <u>306</u>, <u>347</u>
Moccasin slippers, resoling, 136
Models, scale, 232–33
Molasses, for trapping moths, 197
Money, hiding, 364–65
Money pouch, making, <u>248</u>
Monofilament, preventing unraveling
        of, 214
Mooring line, marking, 212
Mop, for making scarecrow, 192
Mosquito(es)
    bites, 170
    repelling, 168
Moss, removing, 170, 172
Mothballs
    for deterring mice, 204
    panty hose for holding, 134
Moths
    cedar chips for deterring, 122
    trapping, 196–97
Mouse pad(s)
    calendar as, 333
    as knee pads, 191
Mud
    garden, avoiding, 192
    removing, from shoes, 366–67
Muffin tin(s)
    adding batter to, 36
    for baking potatoes, 37
    as hardware organizer, 144, **144**

N

Nail polish
    clothing stains from, 85
    uses for
        eyeglass repair, temporary, <u>247</u>
        mending prize fish, <u>214</u>
        preventing allergic reactions to
            wristwatch, 139
        restoring putter sight, 218
        shining belt buckles, 140
        stocking run stopper, <u>247</u>
Nail polish remover, uses for
    removing fabric stains, 85
    removing stickers, 357
    thinning correction fluid, 342
Nails, types of, <u>148</u>

Napkin, cloth
    decorating, 314–15
    as jewelry wrap, 244, **244**
Napkin rings
    made from silverware, 292
    for organizing scarves, 140
    Thanksgiving, 275–76
Necklaces, storing, 137–38
Neckties, hanging, 139, <u>139</u>
Needles, rust on, 237
Needlework, 242
Nests, bird, <u>89</u>
Net bags, as bird feeders, 309
Newspapers
    container for, 96–97, 327–28
    uses for
        cleaning windows, 114–15
        gift wrap, 322
        insulating outdoor faucets in
            winter, 204
        stuffing wet shoes, 260
New Year's, 268
Nightstands, 126–27
Noisemakers, 268
Nuts, rusted, loosening, 154

O
Oatmeal, as facial wash, <u>62</u>
Odors, in closed spaces, 134
Office
    decorating, 346–49
    furnishings, 346
    home, 352–53
    kitchen, 351
    organizing, 327–33
Office supplies, free, <u>339</u>
Oil
    baby, for polishing putter, 215
    engine
        changing, 160
        cleaning spills of, 160–61
    filling chain saw with, 175
    olive
        as hair conditioner, 66
        for reconditioning baseball
            glove, <u>221</u>
    stains from, 83
    vegetable, uses for
        foot soak, 68–69
        grease remover, 161
        killing earwigs, 195
        removing paper stuck to
            furniture, 107
        splinter removal, 69
        water ring remover, 107

Oil filter, removing, 148–49
Onion(s)
    for absorbing paint fumes, 158
    storing, 201–2
Onion bag(s), uses for
    beanbag chair for stuffed animal,
        <u>305</u>, **305**
    removing dead bugs from
        windshield, 158–59
    repairing torn badminton net,
        227–28
Ornaments, Christmas tree, 276–77,
    <u>276</u>, <u>278</u>
Oven cleaner, as paint stripper,
    109–10

P
Packing
    of children's clothing, 264–65
    and shipping, 343–46
    for travel, 244–51
Padlocks
    labeling keys for, <u>173</u>
    protecting, from rust, 173
Paint(ing), 156–58
    in hard-to-reach places, 156, 175
    as hobby, 234
    preventing peeling of, 174–75
    protecting surfaces from, 158
    reducing fumes from, 156–58
    straining, <u>159</u>
Paintbrush(es)
    drying, 234
    as duster, 113
    organizing, 234
Paint stripper, oven cleaner as, 109–10
Paint thinner, for removing wax
        buildup, 115
Palette, paint, 234
Panty hose, uses for, <u>159</u>
    dog toy, 312
    dust catcher, 27
    garden hammocks, 185–86
    mothball holder, 134
    potpourri holder, 134
    repairing window screens, 361
    rolling piecrusts, <u>41</u>
    scrubber, 24–25
    securing trash can lids, 167
    shoe buffer, 247, 249
    soap holder, 192
    storing onions, 201–2
    travel organizer, 249
    vacuuming up tiny lost valuables,
        360

Paper
   butcher, as gift wrap, 321
   shredded, as Easter grass, 271
   stuck to furniture, 107
Paper clip(s)
   storing, 328
   uses for, 342
      cleaning keyboard, 341
      clothespins, 351
Paperweight, making, 298–99, 311
Parer, vegetable, for
   carving candle designs, 285
   decorating pumpkin, 274
Parlor, origin of, 95
Parrots, toys for, 372
Parties, 285–91
   invitations for, 285–86, 290, 291
Patchwork, 241–42
Patent leather, cleaning, 135–36
Patterns, sewing, torn, 234–35
Peanuts, packing, for bath pillow, 57
Peephole, covering, 365
Pen and pencil holder, 328, 329
Pencil
   hanger for, 333
   as soil tester, 177
   as stitch holder, 240
Pencil marks, on clothing, 85–86
Pencil shavings, as pincushion
      stuffing, 238
Pens, identifying, 333
Pepper, for plugging car radiator
      leaks, 161
Perfume
   for discouraging skunks, 167–68
   travel container for, 246
Peroxide, hydrogen, for treating blood
      stains, 84
Perspiration stains, 86–87
Pests
   eliminating, 28–29
   garden, 195–99
Pets, traveling with, 265–66
Phone books, for booster seat, 301
Phone messages, keeping track of,
      332–33
Photocopy machine, feeder tray for,
      341
Photographs
   as Christmas gift tags, 282
   displaying, 91–92, **91**, 117
   hanging, in office, 347–48
   as refrigerator decorations, 298,
      298
Piano keys, yellowed, 114

Picket fence, as headboard, 124–25
Picks, protecting, 153
Picnic basket, for storing clutter, 97
Picture frames. *See* Frame(s), picture
Piecrust
   protecting, during baking, 42–43
   rolling, 34, 41
Pillbox, for packing shoe polish,
      246–47
Pillowcase
   for jewelry wrap, 244, **244**
   as laundry bag, 73
Pillows
   bath, 57
   beanbag, 304
   displaying pins on, 117–18
   neck, 263, 363
   sewing, 235
   throw, making, 124
Pills, on fabric, 134–35
Pincushion
   making, 297
   portable, 238
   stuffing for, 238
Ping-Pong paddles, for supporting
      paper plates, 287
Pins
   displaying, on pillows, 117–18
   dropped, picking up, 237–38
   removing, 359
   rust on, 237
   for straightening flower heads, 199
Pipe(s)
   iron, as horseshoe stake, 219
   leaking, repairing, 359, **359**
   measuring diameter of, 150
   painting, 156
   PVC, uses for
      bat substitute, 229
      cutworm collars, 196
      protecting carpenter's level, 152
      watering plants, 186
Pitchfork, for removing roofing
      shingles, 172
Place mats, as shelf liners, 55
Planter
   clay, for cat bed, 140–41
   as clothespin container, 166
Plants
   cuttings from, as gift, 315–16
   frost protection for, 203
   indoor
      displaying, 179–80
      watering, 177, 178, 334
   markers for, 189–90

Runners, for dresser, 119
Rust(ed)
    needles and pins, 237
    nuts and bolts, 154
    padlocks, 173
    stains, 78–79

S

Sachets
    to eliminate moisture in stored
        tents, 208–9
    to freshen closets, 134
    making, 296–97
Safe, book as, 365, **365**
Salad mix, planting, 182
Salt, uses for
    cleaning iron soleplate, 88–89
    deodorizer, 19
    kitchen cleaner, 19
    scouring powder, 48
    skin scrub, 62
    stain remover, 79, 87, 107
    toothpaste substitute, 254
Saltshaker, uses for
    baking soda holder, 59
    seed scatterer, 182
Sandbox, making, 301–2
Sand castles, tools for making, 227
Sanding block, hose for, 160
Sandpaper
    in furniture refinishing, 111
    for opening jars, 358
    storing, 147
Santa Claus decoration, 279–80, **279**
Sap, removing, from tent, 208
Saw
    dovetail, protecting, 153
    flooring, homemade, 150–51, **151**
Sawdust, added to grass seed, 163
Scale models, 232–33
Scarecrow, making, 191–92
Scarves
    as curtain ties, 95
    organizing, 140
    as table runners, 293
Scrapbook, homemade, 318, **318,**
    319
Scratches
    car, 158
    furniture, 105
    watch crystal, 138
Screen(s)
    as colander substitute, 207
    repairing, 361
    as soil sifter, 189

Screw(s)
    lubricating, 154
    for repairing football, 223
Screwdriver, for removing oil filter,
    149
Screw holes, worn, 154
Scrub brush, uses for
    boot brush, 366–67
    cleaning baseball cleats, 221
Scrunchie(s) and hair band(s)
    for
        holding cookbooks open, 41
        organizing socks, 121
        supporting plant stems, 190
    substitute for, 254
Security measures, 363–66
Seed catalogs, origin of, 193
Seeds
    as gift, 315
    grass, 163–64
    melon, as beads, 304, 307
    planting, 180–84
    saving, 203
Seltzer, as stain remover, 82
Sewing, 234–38
Sewing kit, making, 249–50
Shaving brush, for dusting
    collectibles, 113
Shaving cream, for juice stains,
    111–12
Shaving nicks, 71
Sheet(s)
    sizes of, 94
    uses for
        curtains, 93–94
        in home office, 352
        room dividers, 350
        shelf liners, 55–56
        tablecloth, 43
Shells, uses for
    detergent scoop, 74–75
    deterring slugs, 196
    soap molds, 297
Shelves, substitute for, 346
Shim, computer disk as, 341–42
Shingles, roofing
    removing, 172
    removing moss from, 172
Ships, model, 232
Shirt, as apron, 40
Shoe, as drink holder, 127
Shoe bags, as storage containers, 53,
    132, 265, 327
Shoebox, for storing computer disks,
    338

Shoehorn, substitute for, 254
Shoelace(s)
    broken, 221
    uses for
        clothesline, 260
        curtain ties, 96
        translating mileage on map, 254
    whitening, 79
Shoe polish
    for furniture scratches, 106
    packing, 246–47
Shoes
    buffer for, 247, 249
    packing, 246
    wet, 260
Shortening, vegetable, for dry skin, 63
Shorts, boxer, uses for, 159
Shovel
    dibble made from, 188–89
    for removing old roofing, 172
Shower, outdoor, 192
Shower cap, for watering plants, 177, 188
Shower curtain, uses for, 50
    ground cloth under tent, 206
    in raking leaves, 165
    spill catcher, 28
Shower curtain hooks and rings, uses for
    carrying
        golf towel, 217
        hiking equipment, 211
    doubling hanger space, 133
    hardware organizer, 145
    jewelry hanger, 137–38
Shower curtain liner, as tablecloth, 255–56
Shower curtain rod, for hanging laundry, 74, 75
Showerhead, mineral deposits in, 50
Shutter(s), uses for
    clothes hanger, 132–33
    room dividers, 101
    wall decoration, 91
Siding, creating air passages in, 174–75
Silver, polishing, 18–19, 138
Silverware
    as napkin rings, 292
    removing, from garbage disposal, 22
Silverware box, as jewelry organizer, 137
Silverware tray, for storing office supplies, 330–31

Sink(s)
    cleaning, 19, 25
    pedestal, 54
    storage under, 17
Sink stopper, substitutes for, 245
Skating, 226
Skiing, 224–26
Skin care, 59–60, 62–64
Skunks, discouraging, 167–68
Sledgehammers, protecting, 153
Sleeping bag, for doll, 302–3, **302**
Sleeve, shirt, uses for
    draft stopper, 307–8
    hamster toy, 372
Slugs, 195–96
Smoke stains, on marble, 115
Snakes, storing, 153
Sneaker(s)
    cleaning, 135, 222
    for fluffing down items in clothes dryer, 75
Snoring, 140
Snow globes, making, 280
Soap
    shell-shaped, making, 297
    slivers, 59
    uses for
        car deodorizer, 262
        chalk marker substitute, 238
        suitcase freshener, 251
Soap holder
    lozenge container as, 245
    for storing playing cards, 245
Sock(s)
    laundering, 253
    organizing, 121
    static cling hiding, 76
    uses for
        bath mitt, 58–59
        dust mitt, 113
        glove, 256
        golf club covers, 215
        packing shoes, 246
        painting hard-to-reach areas, 156
        pincushion, 238
        protecting carpenter's level, 152
Soft drink stains, 83
Soil, sifting, 189
S.O.S pads, invention of, 20
Sound blockers, office, 350–51
Soups
    absorbing salt from, 40
    containers for, 17
    skimming oil from, 40

Spaghetti, as cake tester, 32
Sparklers, sugar cubes as, 268
Spatter guard, for reviving stale
        bread, 38–39
Spills
    oil, 160–61
    shower curtain for catching, 28
Spinner, game, 229–30
Splinters, 69–70
Sponges
    care of, 25–26
    as knee pads, 190
Sporting equipment
    decorating with, 92
    old, uses for, 213
    rental, buying, 208
Squash, vertical growing supports for,
    185–86
Squirrels, deterring, from bird feeder,
    167
Squirt gun, for eliminating garden
        pests, 195
Stains
    furniture, 106–7
    laundry, 78–88 (see also specific
        stains)
Stakes
    croquet, 220, 221
    horseshoe, 219
    tent, 206
Stamp collecting, origin of, 233
Stamps, rubber, homemade, 268
Staples
    for hemline repair, 343
    invention of, 344
Starch, homemade, 89
Static, spray for reducing, 341
Static cling, on laundry, 76
Steel wool pads
    for cleaning needles and pins,
        237
    invention of, 20
    preventing rust on, 26
Stepping-stone, as gift, 316–17
Stereo equipment, storing, 102–4
Stickball, 222
Stickers, removing, 159–60, 357
Stings
    bee, 258–59
    jellyfish, 259
Stockings. See also Panty hose, uses
        for
    nylon, invention of, 257
Stovepipe, for limiting herb growth,
    184

Strainer, as flour sifter, 30
Strap, nylon carrying, repairing, 210
Strawberries
    growing, in limited space, 184–85
    planting runners from, 186
Streamers, making, 288–89, **289**
String, storing, 327
String cutter, 149
Studs, locating, 155
Stuffed animals
    cleaning, 232
    handkerchiefs for, 142, **142**
    as pet toys, 312
    repairing, 361–62
Styrofoam, invention of, 369
Sugar, brown
    homemade, 42
    softening, 39
Sugar cubes, uses for
    dice, 230
    sparklers, 268
Suitcase(s)
    broken, 256–57
    carry-on, substitute for, 263
    deodorizing, 251
    for guestroom storage, 129
    as ironing board, 88
    rips in soft-sided, 257
Sunburn, 70–71
Sunflower seeds, harvesting, 203
Sweatband(s), 221–22, 223
Sweet rolls, cutting, 35

T
Table(s)
    game board for, 101–2
    setting, 292–94
    trunk as, 104
Tablecloth(s)
    sheet as, 43
    shower curtain liner as, 255–56
    uses for
        bed cover, 124
        booster seat cover, 301
        shelf liners, 55–56
        sink skirt, 54
Table runner, scarf as, 293
Tablespoon, as shoehorn, 254
Tackle box, for storing office supplies,
    327
Tags
    gift
        making, 324–25, 324, **325**
        photographs as, 282
    name, for family reunions, 286–87

Toilet paper core(s), uses for
    (continued)
    napkin rings, 275–76
    packing jewelry, 244
    rubber band holder, 331
Toilet paper holder, as necktie
        hanger, 139
Toilet tank, preventing condensation
        on, 51
Tomatoes, ripening, 37–38
Tomato plants, cones for, <u>183</u>
Tongs, gardening, as terrarium tool,
        177–78
Toolbox, for storing
    bedroom supplies, 133
    office supplies, 327
Tools
    garden, 188–92
        sharpening, <u>192</u>
        storing, 173
    homemade, 150–51
    storing and protecting, 152–53
    substitutes for, 149
Toothbrush
    for cleaning
        bathroom, 48
        can openers, 30
        cheese grater, 34
        jewelry, 138
    origins of, <u>61</u>
    uses for
        cotton swab substitute, 253
        harvesting sunflower seeds,
            203
Toothpaste
    substitute for, 254
    uses for
        blemish treatment, 253
        filling wall holes, 118–19
        in furniture refinishing, 111
        furniture stain remover, 106
        scratch remover, 138
        silver polish, 18, 138
Towel rack
    as magazine holder, 99
    as necktie hanger, <u>139</u>
    quilt rack as, 128
Towels
    for golfers, 217
    guest, 129
    holder for, 52
    for making sweatbands, 221–22
Toys
    containers for, 355
    homemade, 231–32

pet, 311–12, <u>312</u>, 371, 372
    storing, 97, 100, <u>102</u>, 130, 265
    for travel, <u>264</u>
Trash can(s)
    for car, 261–62
    cover for, <u>58</u>
    deodorizing, 28
    keeping raccoons out of, 167
    kitty litter for cleaning, 358
    repairing cracks in, 172–73
    uses for
        bathroom storage, <u>56</u>
        gift holder, <u>323</u>
        root cellar, 200
        storing garden tools, 173
Travel
    airplane, 263–64
    with children, 264–65
    coping with weather during, 260
    first-aid during, 258–59
    organizing paperwork for, 251–52
    packing for, 244–51
    with pets, 265–66
    toys for, <u>264</u>
Tray
    bed, homemade, 141
    for protecting dresser, 119
Treasure box, <u>303</u>
Tree, Christmas
    as mulch, 204
    ornaments for, 276–77, <u>276</u>, <u>278</u>
    steadying, <u>283</u>
Tree needles, as air freshener, <u>51</u>
Trellis
    from baby crib, 186
    as headboard, 125
    ladder as, 98
Trivet, making, 300–301
Trunk
    as coffee table, 104
    storing magazines and
        newspapers in, 328
T-shirt(s), uses for
    carrying laundry, 77
    clothespin holder, 166
    neck pillow, 263
    party invitations, 285–86
    preventing soggy rice, 38
Tub, sunken, <u>169</u>
TV stand, uses for, <u>332</u>
Twine
    as clothesline, 351
    organizing, 344–45
Typewriter, invention of, <u>337</u>
Typewriter keys, cleaning, 343

Typewriter ribbon, renewing, 342
Tyvek house wrap, as tent
    replacement, 206–7

U
Umbrella stand
    for storing Christmas wrap, 284–85
    substitute for, 346
Urine stains, pet, 112–13
Utensils, organizing, 14
Utensil tray, as dresser drawer
    organizer, 122

V
Vacuum cleaner, for finding lost
    valuables, 360
Valentine's Day, 268–69, <u>269</u>
Valuables
    finding lost, 360
    hiding, 363–65
Vanilla extract, uses for
    blackfly repellent, 168
    masking paint fumes, 156–57
    refrigerator deodorizer, 24
Vase(s)
    cleaning, 17, 357–58
    as comb and brush holder, 121
    thermos as, 117
Vegetables
    preserving, 200–202
    slicing, 35
    vertical growing supports for,
        185–86, **185**
Velcro, invention of, <u>211</u>
Veneer blisters, on furniture, 108–9
Vinegar, uses for
    all-purpose cleaner, <u>23</u>
    bathroom cleaner, 48, 49–50
    blackfly repellent, 168
    car cleaner, <u>261</u>
    coffeepot cleaner, 21–22
    dishwasher cleaner, 22–23
    floor cleaner, 26–27
    floral preservative, 200
    glassware cleaner, 18
    hair rinse, 65–66
    insect bait, 197
    laundry cleaner, <u>79</u>, 81, 82, 83
    laundry rinse, 75–76
    lunch box deodorizer, 351
    mineral deposit remover, 50, 88,
        115
    patent leather cleaner, 135
    removing bumper stickers, 159–60
    soothing jellyfish stings, 259

urine stain remover, 112–13
    window cleaner, 114
Vitamin E oil, for skin care, 63

W
Wagon, uses for
    displaying collections, 100
    plant holder, 179
    storing drinks at parties, 287
Walker, adding carrier to, 369–70
Walkways, 170–72
Wall glazing, boxer shorts for, <u>159</u>
Wallpaper
    damaged, 114
    for decorating dressers, 122
    as drawer liners, <u>16</u>
Walls
    decorating, 91–93
    filling holes in, 118–19
Wastebasket
    for storing gift wrap, 283
    substitute for, 346
    as umbrella stand, 346
Watch, skin sensitivity from, 139
Watch crystal, scratched, 138
Water, conserving, from toilet
        flushing, 51–52
Water bottles, for hiking, 212
Water filter, cleaning, 209
Water game, 273–74
Watering can
    as planter, 179
    substitute for, <u>188</u>
Watermelon, as centerpiece, 273
Water rings, 107, 180
Wax
    buildup, on floors, 115
    car, for ice skates, 226
    drips, on furniture, 105–6, <u>105</u>
    uses for
        lubricating screws, 154
        raising window sash, 155–56
        tape substitute, 324
WD-40, uses for
    lubricating skis, 225
    removing crayon marks, 86
    renewing fading typewriter ribbon,
        342
Weather stripping, 366
Weather vane, antiquing, <u>167</u>
Weeds, in walkway, 171
Welsh rarebit, origins of, <u>39</u>
Western sandwich, origins of, <u>45</u>
White boards, substitute for, 352
Wicket, croquet, 220, <u>220</u>

Wig stand, steadying, 56
Windlass, for furniture repairs, 108
Window box, as bathroom organizer, 53
Window cleaner, for cleaning
 pencil marks, 85
 sneakers, 135
Window frames
 as picture frames, 91–92, **91**
 for planting in raised garden bed, 184
 as room dividers, 101
Windowpanes, for covering seed flats, 181–82
Windows
 cleaning, 114–15
 playing Pictionary on, 292
 rattling, 358
Window sash, raising, 155–56
Window treatments, 93–96
Windshield, removing dead bugs from, 158–59
Wine, as hair rinse, 65
Wine cooler, down jacket for, 44
Wine rack, 14
Wine stains, 82, 107

Wire, florist's, substitute for, 278
Wires, electrical, untangling, 340
Witch hazel, for skin care, 60
Wood
 from construction dumps, 157
 cutting, 156
Workshop, organizing, 144–47
Worms
 bait, 214
 in potted plants, 197–98
Wrapping paper
 Christmas, storing, 283–85
 streamers made from, 288–89, **289**
 substitutes for, 321–23
Wreaths, holiday, 278–79
Wrench, for measuring pipe diameter, 150
Wrist rest, for computer use, 339–40

Y
Yarn, preventing tangling of, 240
Yogurt, for cleaning piano keys, 114

Z
Zucchini, uses for, 201